I0810377

Inflation-Proof Your Future

Biographies

Formerly an account executive at Hayden, Stone Inc., in New York City, and now a partner and director of mutual fund sales at Blinder, Robinson, Inc., Westbury, New York, Edward J. Zegarowicz began his investment experience two decades ago when, not long out of college, he began purchasing inexpensive houses, painted and repaired them and rented them out. He soon came to realize that such investment is not in itself an adequate safeguard against inflation.

"I had to hunt out other methods," he says now. "I had to diversify."

Today Mr. Zegarowicz, who is in his forties, owns real estate of many types and has extensive stock holdings. He is also an enthusiastic collector of coins, stamps, and artifacts.

"I live in New York City," says co-author George Sullivan, "and that automatically qualifies me as an expert on the subject of inflation and what to do about it."

It also happens that he is the author of several books on the subject of investment and the problems of consumer finances. These include *The Dollar Squeeze and How to Beat It* and *The Boom in Going Bust*, a study of consumer bankruptcy.

Inflation-Proof Your Future

By EDWARD J. ZEGAROWICZ
and George Sullivan

WALKER AND COMPANY / New York

First published in the United States of America in 1971 by the Walker Publishing Company, Inc.

Published simultaneously in Canada by The Ryerson Press, Toronto.

ISBN: 0-8027-0318-6

Library of Congress Catalog Card Number: 70-123263

Printed in the United States of America.

Book designed by Lena Fong Hor

Contents

1 The Case for Equity Investing   1

Inflation: A Way of Life; Fixed-Dollar Investments;
Equity Investing.

2 Stamps, Coins, Books and Other Collectibles   9

STAMPS: 11

Determining Stamp Values, Charting Value; How to
Buy Stamps; Philatelic Brokers; Selling; Stamp
Catalogs and Guidebooks; Philatelic Periodicals.

COINS: 25

Glossary of Numismatic Terms; Establishing Coin
Values; Coins and Silver; Investing in Uncirculated
Rolls; The Franklin Half Dollar; The Roosevelt
Dime; The Jefferson Nickel; The Lincoln Cent;
Buying and Selling Coins; Proof Sets; Coin Oddities
and Errors; Numismatic "Finds"; Coin Books and
Publications.

RARE BOOKS: 53

Establishing Value; Selling Books; Limited Editions
Club Books; Reference Sources.

MAGAZINES 64

AUTOGRAPHS: 66

How to Invest; Acquiring Autograph Material.

PERIODICALS AND BOOKS 74

OTHER COLLECTIBLES 75

3 Art and Antiques 78

The Learning Process; Buying for Investment.

PRINTS AND OTHER MEDIUMS: 83

The Art Dealers Association of America; Buying at Auctions; Getting Appraisals; Factory Art; Getting Information and Advice.

ANTIQUES: 102

Establishing Value; Where to Buy; Source Material.

4 Growth Stocks 109

What Stocks?; Growth Industries; Pollution Control; Home Sewing; Housing; Crime Prevention; Life Insurance; Computers; Leisure-time Industry; Dollar-Cost Averaging; Stock Maintenance; Getting Information and Advice; Books; Overseas Investing.

5 Growth Funds 138

Types of Funds; Fees; The No-Load Funds; Closed-End Funds; Selecting Funds; Fund Information Sources.

6 The Bond Market — **156**

CORPORATION BONDS — **157**

CONVERTIBLE SECURITIES: — **159**

Convertible Bonds; Selecting Convertible Bonds; Computing Yields; Convertible Preferreds; Warrants; Municipal Bonds; Types of Municipals; Buying a Municipal; Tax Exempt vs. Taxable Income; Tax-Exempt Funds.

7 Government Securities — **176**

TREASURY BILLS: — **176**
Purchasing Treasury Bills.

LIST OF FEDERAL RESERVE ADDRESSES: — **178**

Redeeming Bills; Calculating the Rate of Return; Government Securities Fund.

TREASURY NOTES AND BONDS — **186**

8 Inflation-Proof Annuities — **189**

Building Value and Charges; Buying a Policy; Dollar-Cost Averaging; The Variable Annuity vs. the Mutual Fund.

9 Real Estate Investing — **201**

Owning Raw Land; The Real Estate Syndicate; Owning Rental Property; Real Estate Investment Trusts; Land Developers.

1 · The Case for Equity Investing

Let's say you've saved $1,000. After a year in your savings account earning 5 percent, you've got $1,050, at least that's what it says in the balance column of your passbook.

But you don't have $1,050.

In terms of "real" dollars, you don't even have your original $1,000. In 1969 the dollar lost 6.1 percent of its purchasing power, and $1,000 on January 1st that year was worth only $939 on December 31st. Add the bank interest to that figure and you'll see you don't even break even.

That's what this book is all about.

Inflation is eroding the dollar at an average rate of 5 percent a year. When you put your money into a fixed-dollar investment, the type that pays you a stated rate of interest and gives the right of dollar-for-dollar repayment, the money disintegrates. Savings accounts, government savings bonds and annuities were once called "dollar-safe" investments. Not any more. Because of the gradual reduction of the dollar's buying power, the savings account must now be looked upon as a risk-filled proposition. You do get back your dollars as to number, but not as to value.

Inflation: A Way of Life

Inflation, the cause of this travail, is not new. The present inflationary spiral dates back to World War II, which triggered a rise in price levels. It is a fact that prices have advanced every year since 1940 except for the recession years of 1949 and 1955 when there were declines, but they were of a gentle nature. (*See* page 3). Between 1948 and 1965, prices increased at the average rate of 1.6 percent a year, which is not difficult to live with. But the recent rate of 6.1 percent has to be regarded as intolerable.

The 6.1 percent figure refers to the standard measure of inflation, the Consumer Price Index. Formulated by the Bureau of Labor Statistics, it is, to quote the Labor Department, a "statistical measure of changes in prices of goods and services by urban wage earners and clerical workers, including families and single persons." Changes in prices are measured in reference to a base year: 1957-59 = 100.

Actually, the goods and services we buy are affected by inflationary forces to a widely varying degree. In 1969, the steepest price increases were in food, which rose 7.2 percent, and also in what the federal government calls "homeownership," which shot up 10.2 percent. This chart, based on information from the U.S. Bureau of Labor Statistics, shows inflation's uneven impact:

	December 1968	December 1969	Percent Increase	Relative Weight December 1968
Entire Index	123.7	131.3	6.1	100.0
Commodities	117.2	123.6	5.5	64.2
Nondurables	120.7	127.7	5.8	46.9
Durables	108.7	113.6	4.5	17.3
Services	138.1	148.3	7.4	35.8
Selected Items				
Food	121.2	129.9	7.2	22.5
Meats, Poultry, Fish	114.4	127.2	11.2	5.6
Housing	122.3	130.5	6.7	33.0
Rent	116.7	121.0	3.7	5.2
Homeownership	132.0	145.4	10.2	15.1
Apparel	124.3	130.8	5.2	10.8
Transportation	120.2	126.4	5.2	13.4
New Cars	102.7	104.9	2.1	2.3
Used Cars	118.7	123.9	4.4	2.1
Public	144.3	153.0	6.0	1.3
Health and Recreation	132.8	139.6	5.1	19.9
Medical Care	149.1	158.1	6.0	6.3

These statistics paint a grim picture. The Nixon administration, realizing a continuation of the inflationary surge of 1969 could lead

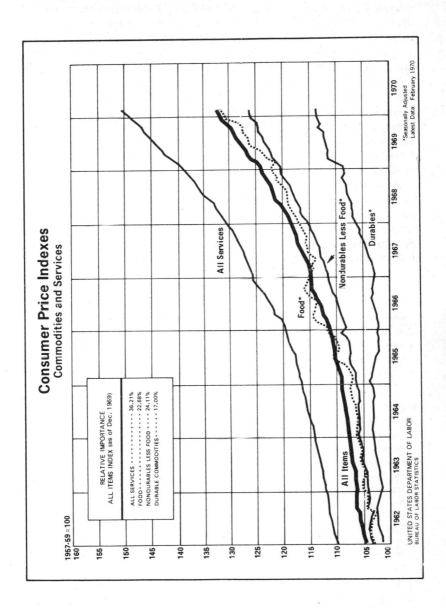

Consumer Price Indexes
Commodities and Services

1957-59 = 100

RELATIVE IMPORTANCE
ALL ITEMS INDEX (as of Dec. 1969)

ALL SERVICES · · · · · · · · · · · 36.21%
FOOD · · · · · · · · · · · · · · · 22.68%
NONDURABLES LESS FOOD · · · · 24.11%
DURABLE COMMODITIES · · · · · · 17.00%

All Services

Food*

Nondurables Less Food*

Durables*

All Items

*Seasonally Adjusted
Latest Data February 1970

UNITED STATES DEPARTMENT OF LABOR
BUREAU OF LABOR STATISTICS

to disaster, tinkered with the nation's economic forces. The Federal Reserve tightened the money supply while the Treasury sought to achieve a budget surplus. This action was intended to slow the country's economic growth. Sales, it was theorized, would then become more difficult to attain; costs would increase; profits would fall and unemployment would rise. As a result, business would be forced to reduce costs and resist labor's demands for higher wages.

Administration officials were confident that their policies would quickly cause a decline in the rate of price increases. Said Treasury Secretary David M. Kennedy: "I would expect—with actions proposed or being taken now to cut spending, along with the extension of the surtax, and present restraints on the side of monetary policy —that this should have not only leveled out inflation but be down the ladder considerably in the price advances." These remarks by Mr. Kennedy appeared in the May 5, 1969, issue of *U.S. News & World Report.* Anyone who shopped in a supermarket or went out to buy a new car in 1970 knows that Mr. Kennedy was very wrong.

By mid-1970, the Nixon administration was ready to admit that the tides of inflation were running stronger than first believed. In a speech to an American Bankers Association Convention, Arthur F. Burns, Chairman of the Federal Reserve Board, declared: "We have been less successful than we would have liked in moderating the advance of prices."

No one in the Nixon administration now looks for a total victory over inflation. Present policies are aimed at reducing the rate of inflation by the end of 1972 to level somewhere below 3.5 percent.

But let's suppose that Arthur Burns, David Kennedy, et al., do prevail, that their manipulations of the economy succeed in holding price increases to a mere 2 percent annually. This is still not an insignificant amount over the long term. A 2 percent a year rise means an increase of 20 percent in ten years, and if prices go up at the rate of 4 percent, they will be 40 percent higher in ten years.

Or let's suppose that there is a severe drop in economic activity. Will that bring the end of high prices? It's not likely. The cost of living index increased rather than decreased in every recession since 1953, although the rate at which prices rose slowed considerably once the recessionary period was established.

What all of this means is that inflation, like air pollution and campus disorder, is something every American must learn to live with. What can you do about it? Plenty. Here are some tips:

• Budget. You must budget. Establish monthly allowances for each of your major expenses. Tabulate everything you spend.

• Become an expert in the art of thrift shopping. Always use a shopping list at the supermarket. Watch for "special purchase" sales when buying big-ticket items. Never buy on impulse.

• Avoid credit if it involves paying interest.

• If you do borrow, get the lowest-possible rates; through passbook loans, for example.

• Use your skills to economize. Learn how to tune up the automobile or make repairs on the television set. A wife can teach herself to sew or the art of home barbering.

In general, a person caught in the dollar squeeze has to develop a fresh attitude toward spending. In times of depression people are always heedful about what they spend, but inflation, with its high levels of income, produces a kind of euphoria. Because they are earning more money, probably more money than ever before in their lives, people tend to be reckless in their spending.

A dollar saved today is much more than a dollar earned. A San Diego housewife drives 17 miles across the border to Tijuana to buy vegetables and other foods that sell at bargain prices. She figures her trips save her about $300 a year.

Equally important is the fact that the family is in the 32 percent tax bracket. To realize $300, the husband must earn $417. That's the actual amount the housewife is saving.

If you can learn to budget shop and spend wisely during a period of inflation, it is almost like having a second job. It never fails to reduce the pressure.

Fixed-Dollar Investments

The fact that a savings account is less than attractive in terms of return on investment should not come as news. Millions of Americans reached this conclusion during the late 1960's. When the Treasury Department raised the minimum on new issues of Treasury bills from $1,000 to $10,000 in March 1970, the action was triggered in part by a wish to stanch the outflow of savings from savings and loan associations, mutual savings banks and other thrift institutions. So great was the public's yen to acquire Treasury bills and other similar instruments in preference to the more conventional methods of saving that, according to George Romney, then Secretary of Department of Housing and Urban Development, their action "aggravated the shortage of mortgage funds and contributed to a serious decline in housing production."

Government savings bonds have the same shortcomings as a savings account. On June 1, 1969, interest rates on Series E and H bonds were raised to 5 percent a year—a most unattractive level, as the reaction of the general public seems to indicate. In April 1970, when savings bonds redemptions exceeded sales by $80 million, it marked the 17th consecutive month of net decline.

I have never been in favor of keeping large reserves of cash in savings bonds or in the bank, and the economy's inflationary surge only bolstered this belief. Many specialists in the field of consumer finance advise families to keep about 25 percent of their capital, or else an amount large enough to pay six month's expenses, in a savings institution. I disagree. Keep only enough cash on hand to meet one month's expenses, that is, food, rent, the electric bill, and all the rest.

Anything over and above what you need to operate for a month's period should be at work, and money that is in a savings account at 5 percent interest is not at work; it is asleep.

Put the excess into a mutual fund (a no-load fund; see Chapter 6) or a convertible bond (Chapter 8). Money so invested *is* available to you. Either type of investment can be converted into cash within 72 hours. Why not put the money into common stock? You can, of course, but you may run into a problem. Should you need cash, you may be forced to sell during a time the stock is in a period of decline, and thus have to take a loss. Or should the stock decrease in price—and this is more likely—your broker is likely to advise you to increase your holdings to average down. And you don't have any reserves to draw upon.

If you do prefer to keep a substantial amount of money in the bank, be sure to shop around and get the best "buy." Banks today offer a dazzling array of interest-rate plans, so many, in fact, you're likely to become bewildered when trying to select the right one.

The most important fact to establish is whether the bank offers a grace period on its accounts. Often the period is ten days in length, which means money deposited on or before the tenth day of the month will be credited with interest from the first of the month. Sometimes a bank will allow a three-day period of grace for withdrawals at the end of a quarter. This period-of-grace feature can be an important benefit if you are constantly switching substantial amounts of money in and out of the stock or bond markets and your savings accounts. Some of the other advantages that savings banks proclaim are not so important.

For example, some savings institutions boast that they compound interest on a quarterly basis, while others tell us breathlessly that their interest is compounded daily. It really doesn't make much difference. This table shows:

Nominal Rate of Interest	Compounded Quarterly	Compounded Daily
4.0%	4.06%	4.08%
4.2	4.27	4.28
4.4	4.48	4.49
4.6	4.68	4.70
4.8	4.89	4.92
5.0	5.09	5.13
5.2	5.41	5.45

Suppose you deposited $5,000 in a savings account. At a 5 percent rate of interest compounded quarterly, the principal would earn $254.50 a year. When compounded daily, it would earn $256.-50, a difference of a mere $2. And this is on a deposit of $5,000 over a full year's time!

Savings certificates have become popular in recent years, and these are more advantageous from a standpoint of interest than ordinary passbook accounts. In 1970, a New York City bank offered a six percent savings certificate with interest compounded daily, giving a yield of 6.18 percent a year. They bore a two-year maturity.

If you are the kind of investor who switches in and out of the market, and have substantial amounts of cash available for short periods of time, find out if thirty-day savings certificates are made available by trust companies in your area. These pay a higher rate of interest than savings account deposits and the money is just as available. If at the end of thirty days you have no need for the cash, you simply redeposit it for another thirty days.

Avoid long-term savings certificates, those with maturities of five or ten years or beyond. You're much better off buying convertible bonds. They're more liquid, pay a higher rate of interest and may even appreciate in price.

Most other types of fixed-dollar investments have the same basic drawback as savings accounts or savings bonds. Inflation simply pilfers a few cents of each dollar so invested every year. Some corporation bonds are in this category. Life insurance and fixed annuities, wherein an insurance company guarantees to provide you a regular monthly income, usually upon retirement, are not worthwhile investments during periods of galloping inflation. Within the past few years, however, many insurance companies began offering *variable* annuities. You'll be hearing a great deal about them during the 1970's. They're discussed in Chapter 8 and are worth considering.

Preferred stock may not be a fixed-dollar investment but it comes awfully close. It is very similar to a bond and thus has many of the same failings.

Equity Investing

A basic problem with a savings account and savings bonds and all other fixed-dollar investments is that your status as an investor is that of a creditor. What you are doing when you put money in the bank is granting the bank a loan, and as a lender your rate of income does not change. The other type of investing, the type this book is concerned with, is equity investing. You put your money into real property; you become an owner.

Equity investments cover a very wide range. They include stamps and coins, antiques and art, common stocks and mutual funds, and raw land and rental property. But no matter the type, they are "variable" investments. Both their value and the income they throw off fluctuate in sympathy with the nation's business activity. That's why they are a hedge against inflation.

I'm a stockbroker. Sometimes I push.

But in this book I'm not going to tell you to take your lifetime savings or to cash in all your government bonds and put the money into common stocks or buy a piece of real estate in Maine. You may earn a high return on your investment, but you may not. There is a risk.

What I am going to say is that fixed-dollar investments are not inflation-proofed, and therefore are almost as much of a gamble as a Las Vegas dice table. Equity investments are your protection. This book explains each type in depth.

2 · Stamps, Coins, Books and Other Collectibles

In March 1970, stamp dealers and investors from every corner of the globe converged upon the Waldorf Astoria Hotel in New York City to bid upon the world's most valuable stamp, a tiny, octagon-shaped reddish bit of paper, the British Guiana 1856 one-cent magenta. The bidding started at $100,000 and took less than three minutes to complete. The final bid: $280,000, a philatelic record.

The purchaser was Irving Weinberg, a Wilkes Barre, Pennsylvania, stamp collector, who represented a syndicate of eight businessmen. "Why did your group purchase the stamp?" Mr. Weinberg was asked.

"It's a long-term investment," he replied. "These men want the stamp to protect them against inflation."

A few weeks later it was disclosed that the seller of the British Guiana one-cent was Frederick T. Small, an 83-year-old retired engineer. Interviewed at his home in Fort Lauderdale, Florida, Mr. Small said he had acquired the stamp and other stamp properties in 1940 as a hedge against the recurrence of the inflationary spiral that occurred after World War I in Germany, England and the United States. Mr. Small had paid $42,500 for the stamp.

The British Guiana has served its purpose well. Indeed, there is probably not a better example of how certain collectibles can serve as protection against the ravages of inflation.

But not every item that lends itself to collecting is worthwhile as an investment medium. There are people who collect streetcar transfers, wooden hat blocks, empty hand grenades and cannon shells, old Coca-Cola bottles and the radio-advertised cereal premiums of the 1930's.

Thousands upon thousands of people collect insulators, the heavy glass, vaguely tumbler-shaped devices that once graced the telephone and power lines of the country. Insulator enthusiasts have formed clubs and organizations to exchange duplicates and a great body of literature is available on the subject.

Milk bottles, now almost entirely supplanted by cardboard containers, are the object of interest of a Newport News, Virginia, collectors' group. Their organization is called MOO, short for *M*ilk Bottles *O*nly *O*rganization.

A variety store clerk in Tama, Iowa, saves oil rags. He claims he has 735 of them, all different. A Springfield, Massachusetts, purchasing agent collects paper-wrapped sugar cubes that bear the names of famous restaurants. Barbed wire is collected by hundreds of people, and they have cataloged dozens of types, like the Watkins lazy plate and the Corsican clip. A small length of an unusual variety mounted on a nicely stained rectangle of plywood can bring as much as $20.

But such items have nothing to do with investment. They're strictly for the hobbyist, the accumulator or the hoarder. Collecting for investment requires an altogether different attitude.

First of all, you have to concentrate on a field with stable market conditions, where accurate information is available as to price. Suppose you decide to invest in coins and you're offered an uncirculated roll of 1960 (Philadelphia) Franklin half dollars for $20. Is this a bargain or isn't it? You have to be able to find out immediately. You also want to be able to determine how many coins of issue were minted, and at what rate the value of the issue has appreciated in recent years. This kind of information isn't available to the people who collect trivets or cigar bands.

There also has to be a demand situation for whatever you collect, a dealer or retail outlet where you can readily sell. Most of the items featured in hobbyist's magazines do have value, but finding a buyer for a collection of 19th-century matchsafes or radiator ornaments from the 1920's can be a difficult task.

Last, and this is probably the most important consideration, you should have a keen interest in the field in which you concentrate, aside from the fact you feel it has investment potential. Your motives have to be something more than merely financial. You might choose a field because of previous interest. If your hobby was stamp collecting as a youngster, what you know about stamps is certain to help you as an investor.

Many people form collections that are based on their professions. I know pharmacists who have a yen for old apothecary equipment and publishers who collect rare books. Many photographers collect old cameras and doctors seek medical instruments of the past. Virtually everyone enjoys collecting coins. Antique toys are another favorite.

"The greatest price appreciation will come to the collection assembled with love, and attention to quality and craftsmanship," says Frank P. Knight, publisher of *Collector's Weekly*. "A collector assembling such a collection will come to know his field and will develop a 'feel' for quality.

"Take my own case," says Mr. Knight. "From an investment standpoint I would collect coins, glass—especially brilliant cut glass—or books. There are probably many other collectibles which will appreciate at a greater rate, but I feel I can make reasonably intelligent choices in these three fields.

"Knowledge is not only the key to investment success. It's the key to pleasure in collecting, too."

There are some drawbacks when you put your money into stamps or coins and other such objects. First of all, there's no dividend income and no interest payments. Your profit has to come from price appreciation exclusively. Storing your collection may be an expense, and insuring it is certain to be, although the premiums involved are usually minimal.

Despite these shortcomings, an enormous amount of "smart" money is going into collectibles, principally stamps, coins, books, and autographs. The pages that follow give information and investment advice in these fields.

STAMPS

That the British Guiana 1856 one-cent magenta recently changed hands for $280,000 shouldn't dissuade you from investing in stamps. Big sums of money really aren't necessary. Here are two examples of successful investments of modest size:

• In 1952, San Marino, a small republic in eastern Italy, issued miniature panes of six air-mail stamps. Each stamp of the six cost $2. In 1968, each could be sold for $148.

• In 1965, the Republic of Korea issued a set of five souvenir sheets which bore the portrait of General Douglas MacArthur and pictured the flags of several different nations. The face value of the five sheets was 12 cents. The number printed was not large—about 100,000 sets—and the topical interest great. Within four years the sheets were selling for between $1.25 and $1.50.

If you do your homework, you can ferret out buys like these. Don't plunge. Don't take your savings and make one great splurge. Instead, establish a regular investment program. Some investors buy on a monthly basis.

Once you've discovered a sleeper, buy it in quantity. Plan to hold your purchases about three years, always keeping informed as to market values.

Before explaining how to recognize stamp values, and how to buy and sell, I want to clear up some misconceptions. One of these concerns U.S. commemorative issues. Experts agree that U.S. commemoratives have virtually no investment value. This has been true since 1940, or ever since the Post Office Department began printing commemoratives in colossal quantities, in excess of 140 million per issue.

Nevertheless, tens of thousands, perhaps hundreds of thousands, of people continue to believe it's worthwhile to collect stamps of this type. For proof of this, you only have to visit your local post office shortly after a new commemorative has been issued and notice how people are lining up to buy it.

U.S. commemoratives are good for postage. Period. Henry M. Goodkind, in an article in *Linn's Weekly Stamp News*, told of a New York lawyer who purchased two panes (sheets of stamps as issued by the post office) of every new U.S. stamp as it was issued. Over a 20-year period his investment came to approximately $2,000. One day, believing his investment had doubled in value, he decided to liquidate.

Imagine his dismay when he found that stamp dealers had no interest in his collection. The only offers he received were well below the *face value* of the stamps. In other words, they were not even worth what he had paid for them.

A friend suggested that the lawyer contact corporations who used the mails to a great extent, and ask them to purchase the stamps at face value. He drew a blank. Most corporations, he found, use metered mail so they won't have to be bothered putting stamps on envelopes.

He also found that the escalating first-class mail rate worked to his detriment. "How can I use sheets of 4-cent or 5-cent stamps when the first class rate is 6 cents?" one mailer wanted to know. The post office, incidentally, does not redeem stamps.

"Up to this writing," said the article in *Linn's*," the lawyer still has his stamps. He is waiting and hoping that some miracle will happen so that he can at least recover the amount of his original investment."

In many instances, those who purchase U.S. commemoratives as an investment do so because they are misled by catalog prices. They purchase a stamp at the local post office and then see it listed in Minkus or Scott's for double or triple its face value.

What these investors fail to realize is that catalog prices are merely approximate judgments. Suppose you accumulated 2,500 unused copies of the current 2-cent and 3-cent stamps. Each lists in the catalogs at 3 cents. This would mean the total catalog value of your holdings would be $75. But if you took the 5,000 stamps to a dealer and asked for an estimate, you would find that they were absolutely worthless.

If you have been unwise enough to have already accumulated mint sheets of U.S. issues, your best bet is to start using them for postage. At least you'll get back what you paid for the stamps.

If the quantity is so large that this course isn't practical, you can liquidate through the World Trade Corporation (Drawer 190, Evergreen, Colo. 80439). A direct-mail company, the World Trade Company wants only adequately gummed stamps. They discount 6-cent values by 10 percent and all other values by 15 percent.

Many people also mistakenly believe that any collection of "old" stamps has value. Heterogeneous mixtures of stamps from many different countries, what dealers refer to as "general collections," lack value because they are almost always composed of "packet material," stamps which are purchased in bulk quantities and consist largely of heavily canceled, off-centered, or otherwise low-quality material.

General collections are a bother to the stamp dealer. The stamps have to be removed from the album, then sorted and packed. Some go into glassine envelopes and are sold as sets or topicals. Others are used in making country or topical packets. Seldom do general collections contain anything worthwhile.

You can purchase general collections on the wholesale market. Here are approximate prices:

```
5,000 stamps . . . $ 15.00
10,000 stamps . . .    45.00
25,000 stamps . . .   200.00
50,000 stamps . . .   950.00
```

As you can readily judge, general collecting is for the hobbyist. It has nothing to do with philatelic investment.

Determining Stamp Values

Before you make your first philatelic purchase, you should be an expert on the subject of condition. Has the stamp you plan to buy been heavily cancelled? Is the design poorly centered? Is the stamp gummed? These and other factors must be weighed in appraising the stamp's condition and thereby establishing its value.

Dozens of different terms are used to describe condition. "Mint" and "unused" are two of the most common. They are often used synonymously but they do not mean the same thing.

Mint refers to a stamp that is in virtually the same condition as it was on the day it was printed. It is bright in color, has full gum and is not torn or spoiled. It's wise to limit your investment purchases to mint-condition stamps. The mint market has more stability than any other.

An unused stamp, on the other hand, is merely one that has not been used for postage. It may be slightly torn, missing a perforation or two or without gum.

J. & H. Stolow & Company of New York City, one of the country's leading stamp dealers, has defined four different classifications of condition. They are:

• superb—a perfect item in the finest possible condition.
• very fine (vf)—exceptionally fine and above average; a selected and most attractive item in top condition.
• fine (f)—above average condition; an attractive premium copy.
• very good (vg)—average condition, usually somewhat off center or fairly heavily cancelled, but not damaged in any way.

In addition to these, you will sometimes see stamps described as "fair" or "good." Steer clear of these; they have no investment potential. While such stamps are likely to be quite low in price, they may be creased, punched, stained, off-center, heavily cancelled, torn or otherwise mutilated. Stamp collectors use fair and good items to fill catalog spaces.

Another important factor influencing value is the stamp's country of origin. Countries are like people in that each has a different character, and stamps from countries of dubious character are worth little. Lundy Islands, the Republic of South Moluccas and the Tannu Tuva People's Republic are political jurisdictions of an uncertain nature. Their stamps are merely collectors' curios.

Always make a brief general appraisal of a country's economic condition before you buy its stamps. Is its money sound? Is its government stable? The South American market in stamps is traditionally sluggish because in the case of most countries the answer is "no" to both of these questions.

Stamps from most of the iron curtain countries—East Germany, Bulgaria, Romania, Hungary and Yugoslavia—are likely to be valueless. They are printed purely for the collectors' market, and are often gummed *and* cancelled, the cancellations an obvious part of the printing process.

Some countries that plan, design and sell stamps with a view toward the collectors' market do produce worthwhile issues for investment. These countries include Monaco, San Marino, Liechtenstein and Vatican City. During the late 1960's and early 1970's, issues from Gibralter, the Netherlands, Italy, Germany, Israel, the Ryukyu Islands and the United Nations were also highly prized by investors.

Events of a political nature also exert an influence on stamp prices. The best example of this is what has happened in Southeast Asia in the past decade. Millions of people, Americans in particular, have become a great deal more informed about the Republic of Korea, Vietnam, Cambodia, Laos and Thailand. As a result, stamps of these countries have been steadily increasing in demand.

What else makes a stamp valuable? Its theme or "topic" is an important consideration. In years past, collectors used to concentrate on building sets of stamps. But with the proliferation of stamp-issuing countries, this became an impossible task. Topicals are what are in vogue nowadays.

Sports, madonnas, the late President Kennedy, nudes, space exploration, Martin Luther King and NATO— these are just a few of the topics on which collectors have been concentrating. Stamps that picture or refer to such topics are likely to increase in value at a far greater rate than a stamp of similar face value and vintage that depicts a hero of the country of origin or an unattractive design.

Milton Ozaki, in *How to Play the Stamp Market*, points out that stamp albums can sometimes serve to forecast demand. Speciality albums, those devoted to the issues of a particular country, are becoming more and more popular, and whenever a publisher introduces a new one, the stamps of that country veer upward in value.

In addition, when a popular general album pictures and provides spaces for a particular set of stamps, that set is likely to increase in value at a faster rate than other but non-pictured stamps of the same country. It's simply that the collectors feel challenged to fill the album spaces.

Naturally, the amount printed of any particular issue has a strong influence on value. U.S. commemoratives have virtually no investment value because they are printed in such enormous quantities. Standard catalogs contain information as to amounts printed.

Finally, look for stamps that are attractive purely from the standpoint of color and design. Eye-appeal is always a definite plus.

Charting Value

What will a given stamp be worth in five years or ten years? To answer this question you have to determine the present degree of scarcity of the stamp, relate it to the current value, and then interpret your statistics.

The table following, prepared by George H. Floyd for *The Philatelic Investor*, spells out this methodology in detail. It concerns stamps issued by the Ryukyu Islands, a territory much favored by investors in recent years.

The first column in the chart gives the Scott number. The second column is an approximation of the number of stamps of each issue available to the public.

Mr. Floyd designated No. 17 as the "key stamp." Of all the issues it was the one least available to the public. He then calculated the ratio between the quantity of each stamp and the quantity of the key stamp to determine a figure he termed the "Floyd's worth" of the stamp. For example, the "Floyd's worth" of No. 18 was figured by dividing 299,500 by 9,800. The result, as shown in column three, is 30.6. "This tells you," says Mr. Floyd, "that there were 30.6 times as many No. 18's publicly available as there were No. 17's."

The fifth column lists what it costs to own a "Floyd's worth." The figures in this column are calculated by multiplying the retail price

RYUKYU ISLANDS

Scott Number	Number Available	Floyd's Worth	Retail Price	Cost of a Floyd's Worth
1	200,000	20.4	—	—
2	200,000	20.4	—	—
3	300,000	30.6	—	—
4	240,000	24.5	$ 6.25	$127.50
5	300,000	30.6	—	—
6	300,000	30.6	—	—
7	300,000	30.6	—	—
1a	61,000	6.2	—	—
2a	181,000	18.5	—	—
3a	181,000	18.5	—	—
4a	181,000	18.5	55.00	176.00
5a	31,000	3.2	—	—
6a	181,000	18.5	—	—
7a	46,000	4.7	—	—
8	3,105,000	316.0	—	—
9	1,199,000	122.0	—	—
10	589,000	60.0	—	—
11	479,000	48.9	—	—
12	599,000	61.0	—	—
13	396,300	40.4	—	—
14	499,000	51.0	7.00	357.00
15	499,000	51.0	7.00	357.00
16-1	200,000	20.4	5.00	102.00
16-11	200,000	20.4	1.40	28.56
16-111	40,000	4.1	6.00	24.60
17	9,800	1.0	200.00	200.00
18	299,500	30.6	11.00	336.60
19	3,013,000	308.0	—	—
20	3,141,300	320.0	—	—
21	2,970,200	302.0	—	—
22	191,800	19.6	7.00	137.20
23	1,118,000	114.0	—	—
24	275,800	28.2	—	—
25	230,800	23.5	—	—
26	219,100	22.4	—	—
27	399,000	40.6	3.00	117.00
28	381,600	39.0	—	—
29	498,800	50.8	2.00	101.60
30	299,000	30.5	2.50	76.25
31	4,768,300	485.0	—	—
32	1,197,500	122.0	1.80	91.80

RYUKYU ISLANDS

Scott Number	Number Available	Floyd's Worth	Retail Price	Cost of a Floyd's Worth
33	499,900	51.0	—	—
34	199,000	20.3	2.00	40.60
35	198,900	20.3	1.85	37.57
36	455,900	46.5	—	—
37	159,400	16.3	1.50	24.45
38	197,700	20.2	—	—
39	199,000	20.3	3.00	60.90
40	599,000	61.0	.75	45.75
41	597,800	61.0	.30	18.30
42	1,195,600	122.0	.12	14.64
43	1,625,400	166.0	.14	23.24

by the "Floyd's worth." In the case of No. 18, it is $11 multiplied by 30.6—$336.60.

When the calculations are completed, the chart is most revealing. The lowest figures in column five are the biggest bargains, the stamps with the greatest investment potential. In the chart above, No. 42 was revealed as the best buy of all.

In building models similar to this, you do not have to calculate the "cost of a Floyd's worth" for every stamp issued. Once you know the quantity and retail price for the key stamp, you can then perform the calculations for any of the others.

Mr. Floyd cautions against relying on his chart or similar ones to the exclusion of all other dates. The model is based on the assumption that the value of a stamp depends entirely upon the quantity available. While this is an overriding factor, value is also related to other considerations, such as the stamp's condition, whether it is a popular topical, etc. Such charts are extremely valuable, but as Mr. Floyd states, "Use them in a general way, not a literal sense."

How to Buy Stamps

Your best source of supply is likely to be a local stamp dealer. He is almost certain to be informed and experienced in buying and selling stamps and his knowledge can't help but be of benefit to you.

There are no standard prices for stamps. Most dealers charge a percentage over cost that serves to reimburse them for their expenses—rent, salaries, advertising, and so on—and also represents a fair profit. Since prices vary from dealer to dealer, it's to your advantage to have a working relationship with several of them. In other words, shop around.

In recent years many department stores have added stamp outlets. If you comparison shop, you're likely to find that the department store charges prices that are slightly higher than the man who operates his own shop.

If you want to buy and sell through dealers outside your own community, it's a good idea to select from among the members of the American Stamp Dealers Association (147 West 42nd St., New York, N. Y. 10036). The organization will provide you with a list of its members.

Once you begin making purchases, you are likely to find that prices often behave in a mercurial fashion. For example, you may buy a few blocks of a certain issue at a price you feel to be quite reasonable. But if you increase the size of your order, buying a complete pane, you may find yourself paying a greater price per stamp. This is because the pane bears other items of value, such as plate numbers or date markings.

Sometimes the size of your purchase can influence price, but not in the way you might expect. A really sizeable purchase, one that depletes the dealer's stock, is likely to make him suspicious. He charges you a premium as a result. Experienced investors tread lightly.

Dealers themselves buy from wholesalers and you may feel that it's to your advantage to buy from a wholesale source. But unless the quantities you want are of dealer-size, that is, extremely large, no legitimate wholesaler will sell to you. You may occasionally purchase minute quantities from a person who says he is a wholesaler, but be assured you will be paying retail prices.

If you scan stamp advertisements, you will see many of them are placed by approval dealers. They will send you an assortment of stamps and you purchase only the ones you wish, only those that meet your "approval." The advantage of this system is that it allows you to deal with suppliers who can be thousands of miles from your home, yet you have a chance to carefully inspect what you're buying beforehand.

The disadvantage is cost. Approval dealers are burdened by heavy expenses. Besides the considerable advertising costs they incur, they must pay postage, a clerical staff to process orders, and

the losses involved when material is lost in the mails or not returned. And, of course, they have to pay a wholesaler for the goods
they're selling.

All of these costs add up to sky-high prices. It is generally believed that material from approval dealers is marked up at least 200
percent. Dealing on an approval basis is fine if you're a collector,
but as an investor you should seek other sources of supply.

The classified advertising that appears in philatelic trade publications may present you with opportunities to buy stamps at reasonable prices. There are instances of investors establishing friendships
with collectors in foreign countries through such advertising, and
then relying on these contacts to fill their stamp needs. But, at best,
the classified columns are an erratic source of supply, and of much
more benefit to the collector than the investor.

Auction sales are another source, but these can be a hazardous
method of acquisition for the unwary. Auctions are advertised in
virtually all of the stamp publications. A long listing of material to
be auctioned is presented in the ad, or you are asked to write for
a catalog. In either case, you are invited to submit bids on the items
that interest you. A "minimum bid" or "reserve price" is established for each item.

Some of the listed items may appear to be bargain-priced, and
indeed may be, but it's unwise to participate in auction sales unless
you have a clear idea of what you're buying and the condition of
the material. The one or two lines of descriptive information that
appear in the ad or catalog are of little value. Like classified advertisements and approval dealers, auctions are for collectors.

When ordering a large quantity of a new issue, it's likely to be
worth your while to deal directly with the issuing government.
Transactions are usually conducted by means of International
Postal Money Order. But bear in mind that dealing in newly issued
stamps is more risky than buying and selling issues that have been
allowed to mature.

Arbitrage is common in philatelic investment. By comparing the
U.S. catalog prices with those published in catalogs in the stamp's
country of origin, it's often possible to find a "sleeper."

Minkus or Scott may list a certain German stamp as 42 cents. But
Michel Briefmarkenkatalog Europa, published in Germany and the
more authoritative source for price information on German stamps,
may list the stamp at 90 cents. This indicates there is a scarcity, but
one not yet made manifest in the United States. It is very likely that
such a stamp would prove to be an attractive investment.

Philatelic Brokers

The last two or three years have seen the advent of the stamp broker, an investment specialist who functions for his clients in much the same way a stock broker buys and sells for those interested in dealing in securities.

The largest and best known of the country's philatelic brokers is Milton K. Ozaki (Drawer A, Evergreen, Colo. 80439). He keeps informed of the stamp market by studying trade publications and by means of buying expeditions to foreign countries, and is personally acquainted with dealers in every part of the world.

Relying on his bank of knowledge, Ozaki makes purchases for his clients, some of whom agree to buy monthly folios for amounts as small as $10. Such clients can discontinue their plans at any time. Others make a lump-sum purchase. A trial folio costs between $10 and $100.

Mr. Ozaki says that his prices are "approximately 10 percent above wholesale" but "substantially below" retail. He buys approximately $500,000 in stamps each month for clients.

A client can sell his holdings through Ozaki, too. He handles liquidations on a fee basis.

Jeffrey L. Needleman (2367 East 18th St., Brooklyn, N. Y. 11229) is another broker who provides stamps for investment. Clients can invest any amount, but the minimum is $20. In return the client receives a "balanced portfolio" of stamps with, according to Mr. Needleman, "the highest investment potential." Most of his current selections are from Western Europe, Asia and the British Commonwealth.

The stamps are mint and in excellent condition, but brand-new issues are almost never included in the folios. "Their printings are too large, and stocks will be ample for years," Mr. Needleman declares. "Any sensible investment program must concentrate on the older scarcer issues, where the initial stocks have been dissipated by sales throughout the years, and which dealers are eager to buy."

A client who is not satisfied with a folio can return it within fifteen days and receive a full refund. Mr. Needleman recommends that clients hold folios at least three years. "By then," he says, "most of the stamps should have gone through several strong price rises, and profits should be excellent."

Mr. Needleman also notifies clients when he believes a folio has reached peak value, and he handles the sale of folios when clients wish to liquidate. His customers receive a monthly bulletin, *Going Up*, and a record of their holdings is maintained to facilitate certification in the case of capital gains.

A Baltimore, Maryland, broker gives advice and sells stamps to investors who prefer to build complete collections of stamps of individual countries, an arrangement that combines the potential financial gains (a complete mint Liechtenstein collection, which could have been assembled in 1964 for $285, sold for $1300 two years later) with the pleasures of stamp collecting.

The client chooses the country in which he wishes to specialize —Austria, Belgium, France, Germany, Italy, Liechtenstein, Luxembourg, Monaco, San Marino, Switzerland or Vatican City. With his first selection of stamps, the client receives a "hingeless" album for mounting stamps sent him.

The first monthly payment must be at least $40 and subsequent purchases must be in the amount of at least $20. For more information write Dr. Keith D. Garlid, 1310 Bolton St., Baltimore, Md. 21217.

Selling

There are four different markets you can utilize when you feel it's time to liquidate your holdings. The highest prices are to be gained by selling directly to collectors, but this means that you will have to operate on a dealerlike basis by advertising your properties and processing the responses. In other words, there are expenses involved if you follow this route, and they can be considerable.

If the quantities you are selling are not large—between five and ten items of any single set—you can sell to a retailer, a dealer. Large quantities, however, you will have to sell wholesale. The prices you will realize on the wholesale market are likely to be only about 40 percent of retail. Bear this in mind when you are making your purchases. The quantity should not be so large that you will have to sell wholesale when liquidating.

The one other method of selling is by means of the auction market. The auction firm takes a commission of ten percent of the sale price. This is bad enough, but the greater disadvantage is that there is no negotiation with the purchaser and you may have to accept a minimum or reserve price if a higher bid is not received.

Stamp Catalogs and Guidebooks

Stamp catalogs contain vital information regarding prices and therefore are invaluable to the philatelic investor. But it must be said at once that the price information listed is enormously subjective, and while each price does represent a good deal of research on the part of the editors, there is no small amount of opinion involved. Proof of this can be seen in the numerous price variations between catalogs.

Collectors and investors use the listed prices as a very general indication of stamp values. Most dealers expect to sell their holdings at "half catalog," which means that when a stamp lists at 50 cents you should be able to buy it for 25 cents. But this doesn't always hold true. The editors of one of the country's leading catalogs state that their prices represent the market value of "a fine specimen when offered by an informed dealer to an informed buyer." Any shading of difference in any one of these characteristics can alter the listed price.

Besides information as to value for both used and unused stamps, a catalog also gives:

- a photographic representation of the stamp.
- the catalog number.
- information as to whether the stamp is watermarked, and, if so, a description of the watermark.
- the size of the perforations.
- the color.
- the date of issue and the quantity in distribution.
- information as to the differences that may exist in color or perforations, and whether the variety has been subject to error.

The principal catalog publishers in the United States are Minkus, Scott, Sanabria, and Whitman. Both Minkus and Scott publish several different catalogs.

Minkus (116 West 32nd St., New York, N. Y. 10001) publishes the *Minkus American Stamp Catalog* ($4) and the *Minkus World Wide Stamp Catalog* (two volumes, $19). New Editions are published every year.

Minkus also publishes regional catalogs for *Austria, Switzerland, and Liechtenstein* ($1.50), *British Commonwealth* ($3), *Germany and Colonies* ($2.50), *Italy and Colonies, San Marino and Vatican* ($2), and *Russia, Poland, and Hungary* ($3.50).

Scott Publications (488 Madison Ave., New York, N. Y. 10022) publishes *Scott's Standard Postage Stamp Catalog*, which has served collectors and dealers as an authoritative guide for more than one hundred years. Volume I lists, describes and prices stamps of the United States, British Commonwealth, United Nations, and Latin America. It is priced at $7.50. Volume II catalogs stamps of the nations of Europe, Africa, Asia, and their colonies. It costs $9.50. A combined edition of the two volumes is $15.

Scott's also publishes a *United States Stamp Catalog*, a highly specialized listing of all U. S. stamps, and those of the Confederate States, United Nations, Canal Zone, Danish West Indies, Guam, Hawaii, Philippines, and Puerto Rico as well. It is published annually at $6.

The U.S. Post Office Department has available the guidebook *Postage Stamps of the United States*, an illustrated description of all U.S. postage and special-service stamps issued from July 1, 1847. Order from the Superintendent of Documents, U.S. Government Printing Office, Washington, D. C. 20402. The book costs $1.25.

Lastly, don't fail to purchase a copy of *How to Play the Stamp Market.* It's crammed with practical advice and is well worth the $2 it costs. Order from Grafo-Art Publications (Drawer M, Evergreen, Colo. 80439).

Philatelic Periodicals

The pages of your local daily newspaper are likely to carry stamp news and perhaps a weekly collectors' column. But if you plan to invest in stamps you need information that is much more incisive than a daily newspaper provides. There are several publications you should appraise:

The *Philatelic Investor and Market Report* (Grafo-Art, Drawer M, Evergreen, Colo. 80439) is one that I recommend. An annual subscription of eleven issues is $5. Each issue of the publication profiles a dozen or so stamps "worth watching," rating each as to its investment potential. The classifications range from "a newly awakened sleeper" to "a long shot, strictly for gamblers." Articles concerning different facets of the investment market are also featured.

The Stamp Wholesaler (Box 529, Burlington, Vt. 05401) is filled with advertisements offering stamps at wholesale prices and news stories about recent stamp issues. A subscription to this semi-monthly publication is $5 a year.

Linn's Stamp News (Box 29, Sidney, O. 45365) is the leading collector's newspaper. It's valuable because of the enormous array of display and classified advertising it carries. It's inexpensive; $4 buys 52 issues.

Stamps, The Weekly Magazine of Philately (Lindquist Publications, 153 Waverly Pl., New York, N. Y. 10014) contains general news and comments for collectors. It costs $3.90 a year.

Minkus Stamp Journal (116 West 32nd St., New York, N. Y. 10001) is also a collectors' publication. It features articles and news stories concerning new issues and stamp programs. A quarterly, it costs $2 a year.

Stamp Monthly (Whitman Publishing Company, 1220 Mound Avenue, Racine, Wis. 53404) contains news and commentary for collectors. A year's subscription is $4.50.

Summing Up

If you're planning to put your money into stamps, plan to make investments on a regular basis. Become a specialist in one or two countries. Then follow these tips:

• Buy from a local dealer on a face-to-face (not mail) basis, or from an established broker.

• Deal only in mint stamps.

• Bear in mind that a stamp's value is related to its scarcity, its "topic" and its design appeal. The country that issues the stamp is another vital consideration.

• Generally, hold your purchases at least three years before selling.

• Keep abreast of market conditions by reading two or three stamp periodicals regularly.

COINS

"It's a wise investor who ties up part of his cash in money," proclaims a brochure recently distributed by a Canadian coin dealer. Indeed, it is true, and probably more true today than any time in the recent past.

Great turbulence characterized the numismatic world during the

1960's. In the early part of the decade, coin prices skyrocketed. Many people, whose previous interest in coins had been limited to whether they had the right change to make a telephone call, began speculating in the coin market, buying rolls and even bags of recently minted United States coins in large quantities. There were stories in the financial press of individual coins changing hands for sums of $10,000 and more. And in coin shops across the country, dealers told prospective customers, "You'd better buy now, because in another week or so I'll have to charge you twenty or thirty percent more."

The bubble burst in 1964. Prices hit a peak, then began to dip. The speculators panicked and in their hysteria they flooded the market with their stored up coins. Prices plummeted, hitting the bottom in 1965.

In the years that followed, the market stabilized. Prices began to edge upward again. The key word is "edge." It was an orderly market. The get-rich-quick philosophy of the early 1960's had dissipated.

The numismatic turmoil of the 1960's was enhanced by what happened in the precious metals market. The price of silver, which the Treasury Department had held stable at 92 cents an ounce for years, was permitted to climb to $1.30 an ounce, the reason being to protect the Treasury reserves from depletion. The government halted the production of Silver Certificates and issued Federal Reserve Notes instead.

Silver reserves continued to decline, and by 1964 it was clear that the future of silver-coin production was bound to end. Millions of people became "collectors" and silver coins began to disappear from circulation. The Treasury Department was faced with a grave coin shortage, and in an effort to solve the problem, to keep as many coins as possible in circulation, announced a "date freeze." The 1964 date would appear on most coins minted in 1965. The Treasury knew that coins dated 1965 would be snapped up not only by collectors but by the growing army of speculators.

In the summer of that year the Treasury Department announced what it hoped was its final solution to the coin problem—the Coinage Act of 1965. Under the terms of the Act, half dollars, formerly 90 percent silver, would have but 40 percent silver content, and all dimes and quarters were to be made from copper and nickel, no silver at all. This resulted in the coin "sandwiches" common today, the quarters and dimes with the copper colored stripe around the edge.

What happened in the silver market had a predictable effect upon coins in circulation with silver content. By the end of 1968, half dollars minted before 1965 and silver quarters had all but vanished.

The surging interest in coins and coinage during the 1960's produced a number of very worthwhile developments. Membership in the American Numismatic Association, the leading collector organization, more than doubled, exceeding 25,000. The 1960's spawned a rash of numismatic publications, the best of which remain. *Coin World*, a tabloid newspaper, was launched in 1960. Today it boasts a circulation of more than 200,000. If you have never seen the publication, you'll be surprised by its size—some issues run to well over one hundred pages—and the exhaustive coverage it gives the field. Magazines like *COINage*, were introduced. Colorful and informative, they are of important benefit to the latter-day collector and investor.

The 1960's also triggered nationwide interest in numismatic medals. Usually of a commemorative nature, medals are now being turned out by approximately six private "mints" solely for the collector market. Many other types of coinlike materials—sales tax and gambling tokens, wooden nickels and political buttons—are now valued by hobbyists; they seldom were before.

The turbulence that characterized the 1960's is no longer in evidence. A period of stability characterizes the coin market today. But it is also a period of growth, and conditions for investment approach the ideal.

Glossary of Numismatic Terms

This chapter, articles about coins, collectors' publications and books are likely to use many numismatic terms and phrases that may not be familiar to you. The most common of these are listed below with their definitions:

Commemorative—a coin issued by a federal act to memorialize an event, place or person; commemorative coins are legal tender, but seldom used as such.

Die—the metal device used in stamping the coin design onto metal.

Double struck—a coin that has been struck twice by the die, creating two overlapping impressions.

Face value—the legal worth of a coin in the country of its issue.

Key coins—coins of each series that are of low mintage,

and usually the highest-priced coins of the issue.

Off metal—a coin minted in the "wrong" type of metal.

Off center—a coin not centrally struck on the planchet.

Market value—the price dealers charge for coins offered at retail sale.

Medal—a metallic piece issued as a commemorative, but without face value and not intended to circulate as money.

Obverse—the "head" side of the coin; the side that bears the portrait or most important design feature.

Planchet—the blank disk upon which the die stamps the coin design.

Premium value—the price over and above face value at which the collector can sell a coin.

Before you do any buying, particularly mail-order buying, have a clear understanding of the terms dealers and collectors use to describe coin condition. Eight different descriptive terms are used, ranging from "uncirculated," the very best, to "poor." It must be said that the assigning of grades is a somewhat subjective matter, and in buying, selling and trading coins, there is often more debate over grades and grading than prices. These are the terms:

Uncirculated (Unc.)—a coin that has never been placed in general circulation. All lettering, the date and design show in sharp detail. An absolutely perfect coin, without even the slightest scratches or abrasions, is sometimes described as "Gem Uncirculated" or "FDC" (Fleur de Coin).

Extremely Fine (EF, XF or E Fine)—all lettering and details of design are sharp and clear, except the very highest points of design which show signs of wear.

Very Fine (VF)—lettering and design are still clear, although the coin shows a significant amount of wear.

Fine (F)—much of the lettering and detail show considerable wear, but this is still a desirable coin.

Very Good (VG)—a serious amount of wear, although a coin still valued by collectors. It should be free of any deep gouges or other forms of mutilation.

Good (G)—this is the minimum standard acceptable to collectors. The date and mint mark are legible and the major features of the design discernible.

Fair (F)—a coin that is badly worn, with perhaps part of the lettering and design worn away. Such coins are used by collectors only as space fillers, that is, until a better specimen can be obtained.

Poor—a coin that is bent, corroded, mutilated or with its features of lettering and design almost completely worn away. Undesirable for collectors.

If you read advertisements in numismatic publications, you will also see coins described as being in "proof" condition. This term refers to coins that have been made at the mint especially for collectors. At first glance, they may seem similar in appearance to uncirculated coins of the same type, but a close examination will reveal that they have received special attention. They are outstanding in detail and sharper-edged. And because they are stamped out on polish planchets using polished dies, each proof coin has a mirrorlike surface. Such coins are never found in circulation.

Mint marks are extremely significant in identifying coins and establishing their value. A mint mark is a small letter placed on either side of the coin to denote where the coin was minted. The most common mint marks on United States coins are "S" for San Francisco, and "D" for Denver. Coins without any such letters indicate they were produced at the Philadelphia mint. On gold coins, "CC" represents Carson City, Nev.; "C" means Charlotte, N. C. and "D" indicates Dahlonega, Ga.

All United States coins are produced at the Denver or Philadelphia or San Francisco mints.

Establishing Coin Values

Experts in the field of coin investment use three criteria in forecasting coin values. They are:

- Availability.
- Quality.
- Denomination.

Availability refers directly to mintage, to the number of coins produced of a single issue in a given year. Louis A. Newitt, a coin collector for twenty years and an officer of several coin clubs, recently completed a thorough study of United States coins and their year-to-year values. He carefully charted the rise and fall in market prices for more than 500 different pieces. This was one of Mr. Newitt's conclusions: "Except for a few exceptions, a startling fact was obvious—the scarcer the mintage of the coin, the higher was the rate of increase."

Other specialists agree. Dr. Robert Bilinski, in his sweeping, well-ordered study, *A Guide to Coin Investment*, calls availability "a prime price determiner."

To illustrate, consider the year 1955. The 1955-S was the lowest mintage cent since 1939, and the last coin of its denomination struck at the San Francisco mint. The 1955 nickel was the lowest mintage nickel since 1939, except for the 1950-D. The 1955 dime was the lowest mintage dime of the entire Roosevelt series and the lowest mintage dime of all since 1938. The 1955-D quarter was the lowest mintage quarter since 1940, and the 1955 half dollar was the second lowest mintage of the entire Franklin series.

This chart shows what happened:

Date	Denomination	Mintage	Lowest Advertised Price Per Roll, 1955	Dealer Price 1970	Percent Increase
1955-S	1¢	44,610,000	$ 1.00	13.50	1250%
1955	5¢	8,266,200	4.00	38.00	850%
1955	10¢	12,828,381	6.00	54.00	800%
1955-D	25¢	13,959,000	11.00	125.00	1120%
1955	50¢	2,876,381	11.00	136.00	1130%

Information concerning mintages is easy to obtain. It's available from the Treasury Department and given in all the standard numismatic catalogs, including the Blue Book and the Red Book (see page 52).

High quality is the second most important consideration, and, with coins, the matter of quality refers to condition. The better the condition, the better the investment.

The third factor important in setting value is the coin's denomination. It is a fact of coin history that the smaller the denomination, the higher a coin's potential market value as compared to other coins of the same year. In other words, cents of any given year are likely to show a greater appreciation than nickels of that year, nickels a greater appreciation than dimes, dimes greater than quarters, and quarters greater than halves.

There are some other factors, but they are not nearly as important. Age, for instance. Most people who have only a casual interest in numismatics believe that age is the overriding element in establishing coin value. Well, it's not—not in coins of this century at any rate, and those are really the only ones to consider from an investment standpoint. With these, age isn't nearly as important as either availability or condition.

Another factor is one that can't be forecast. Occasionally a coin will develop a mystique. Collectors enter the market to buy it up and the price soars. The 1955 double-struck Lincoln cent is the best example of this. Sometimes an entire coin series will be caught up in a mystifying wave of popularity.

To sum up, never make a coin purchase without considering the availability of the issue in terms of mintage, and the condition of the coins you're buying as expressed in grade. Last, weigh in the factor of denomination. These are the preeminent components in determining coin values.

Coins and Silver

Beginning in 1969, the Treasury Department removed the restrictions prohibiting the melting of U.S. coins for their silver content. This change in policy had a profound effect on coin values.

Take the case of the Roosevelt dimes. After the Treasury Department's edict, millions of dimes bearing the common dates of 1960 through 1964 were plopped into melting pots and converted to bullion. As a result, a scarcity has developed in coins of those dates despite their relatively recent mintage. Circulated sets of Roosevelt dimes, which sold for approximately $8 per set early in 1969, that is, before the government's change in policy, jumped about 50 percent in price before the year had ended. Other coins with silver content also spiraled in price.

In mid-1970, silver was selling at $1.80 per ounce. But more than few silver specialists looked for rising prices. This chart shows how the value of coins, in terms of silver content only, relates to the market price of silver:

Price of Silver (per ounce)	Value of Silver Content			
	Dime	Quarter	Half	Dollar
$1.30	$ .09	$ .24	$ .47	$ 1.00
1.40	.10	.25	.51	1.01
1.50	.11	.27	.54	1.16
1.60	.12	.29	.58	1.24
1.70	.12	.31	.61	1.31
1.80	.13	.33	.65	1.39
1.90	.14	.34	.69	1.47
2.00	.14	.36	.72	1.55
2.04	.15	.37	.74	1.58

Price of Silver (per ounce)	Dime	Value of Silver Content Quarter	Half	Dollar
2.08	.15	.38	.75	1.61
2.12	.15	.38	.77	1.64
2.16	.16	.39	.78	1.67
2.20	.16	.40	.80	1.70
2.24	.16	.41	.81	1.73
2.28	.16	.41	.82	1.76
2.32	.17	.42	.84	1.79
2.36	.17	.43	.85	1.83
2.40	.17	.43	.87	1.86
2.44	.18	.44	.88	1.89
2.48	.18	.45	.90	1.92
2.52	.18	.46	.91	1.95
2.56	.19	.46	.93	1.98
2.60	.19	.47	.94	2.01
2.64	.19	.48	.95	2.04
2.68	.19	.48	.97	2.07
2.72	.20	.49	.98	2.10
2.76	.20	.50	1.00	2.13
2.80	.20	.51	1.01	2.17
2.84	.21	.51	1.03	2.20
2.88	.21	.52	1.04	2.23
2.92	.21	.53	1.06	2.26
2.96	.21	.54	1.07	2.29
3.00	.22	.54	1.09	2.32
3.04	.22	.55	1.10	2.35
3.08	.22	.56	1.11	2.38
3.12	.23	.56	1.13	2.41
3.16	.23	.57	1.14	2.44
3.20	.23	.58	1.16	2.47
3.24	.23	.59	1.17	2.51
3.28	.24	.59	1.19	2.54
3.32	.24	.60	1.20	2.57
3.36	.24	.61	1.22	2.60
3.40	.25	.61	1.23	2.63
3.44	.25	.62	1.24	2.66
3.48	.25	.63	1.26	2.69
3.52	.25	.64	1.27	2.72
3.56	.26	.64	1.29	2.75
3.60	.26	.65	1.30	2.78
3.70	.27	.67	1.34	2.86
3.80	.27	.69	1.37	2.94
3.90	.28	.70	1.40	2.99
4.00	.29	.72	1.45	3.09

Investing in Uncirculated Rolls

There are exceptions, of course, but most coin investors deal in uncirculated rolls of U.S. coins, putting their money into issues of low mintage that are relatively low in price. As an example, take the case of two different Roosevelt dimes. As of June 1970, an uncirculated roll of the 1947-S was selling at $36, while an uncirculated roll of the 1952-D could be purchased for $20. The former had a mintage of 35 million, and the latter, 122 million. Obviously, the 1947-S was underpriced. It was almost four times as scarce as the other coin, but was selling at only 70 percent more.

Comparisons can also be made between coins of different denominations. Experts agree that there are a great many underpriced issues. And in some cases issues are being sold at prices that are within 25 to 50 percent of face value.

There are a number of advantages to dealing in uncirculated rolls. It is not likely you will have to scramble to find either a buyer or a seller. Another plus is that price information is always easy to obtain, for coin magazines and newspapers (page 52) carry buy-and-sell advertisements. Trading is not quite so simple when dealing in individual coins or foreign issues.

Another advantage is that the spread between the buying and selling prices for uncirculated rolls is a great deal less than for individual coins. Whereas the dealer's markup is approximately 50 percent on single coins, it only is 25 percent and often less on an uncirculated roll.

This chart gives the number of pieces per standard roll and bag lot of U.S. coins, and the face value for each:

Denomination	No. of Coins Per Roll	Face Value Per Roll	No. of Rolls Per Bag	Face Value Per Bag
Cents	50	$ .50	100	$ 50.
Nickels	40	2.00	100	200.
Dimes	50	5.00	100	500.
Quarters	40	10.00	100	1,000.
Halves	20	10.00	100	1,000.

There is always a greater demand for cent and nickel rolls than for rolls of dimes, quarters and halves. New collectors, often youngsters with limited amounts of money to spend, favor the lower priced denominations because they can obtain the greatest quantity for the smallest cash outlay.

No matter the denomination in which you deal, it stands to reason that the closer you keep to face value, the safer your investment. Why not, then, purchase uncirculated rolls of the current year, buying them from a bank at precisely face value or from a dealer at a slight markup, hold them for a few years, and then put them on the market? Because it usually takes several years for a significant price increase to take place.

The performance of the 1957 Philadelphia cent is a case in point. Dealers charged 75 cents for an uncirculated roll in 1957. In 1970, an uncirculated roll could be purchased for $2, so it was not a particularly wise investment.

Values only begin to increase significantly once the initial stocks purchased by roll dealers begin to be exhausted, and they must enter the market to replenish their supplies. Year by year in the ensuing years the prices continue to edge upward until they reach a point where investors begin to get wary. Then the price remains stable for several years. Later the upward trend is likely to be resumed.

There are hundreds of U.S. issues to select from, but experts agree that most have no leverage factor, no investment potential. All of the older U.S. coins are in this category, including silver dollars and Indian head cents.

There are, however, four series of U.S. coins that do offer investment opportunity. They are: Franklin half dollars, Roosevelt dimes, Jefferson nickels and Lincoln cents. Each of these is surveyed in the pages that follow.

The Franklin Half Dollar

The Franklin half dollar. (*Courtesy the American Numismatic Society*)

Designed by John R. Sinnock and struck at the Philadelphia, San Francisco and Denver mints, the Franklin half dollar was first issued in 1948, but before it could attain the normal minimum circulation span of 25 years, its production was discontinued in favor of the Kennedy memorial half dollar. This was in 1964.

In the 16 years that the Franklin half dollar was in circulation, only 35 different coins were produced. What makes the series so appealing as an investment medium is that in ten of the 35 pieces, mintage was less than five million. Franklin is the only non-President to appear on coins of recent times, which adds to the issue's interest.

One coin of the series is of particular note. The upper and lower dies of the 1955 issue came into contact with one another without a planchet in place, damaging the obverse die slightly in the mouth area of the portrait. As a result, what look to be protruding teeth jut from Franklin's mouth. The coin has been nicknamed the "Bugs Bunny half." It sells for several dollars more than an unmarred coin of the same date.

Unfortunately, many of the Franklin half dollars were lightly struck and thus lack in detail. Strongly struck Franklin halves have the greatest investment potential.

Here is a listing of prices being asked in mid-1970 for uncirculated rolls and singles of the Franklin half dollar:

FRANKLIN HALF DOLLARS

Quantity	Year	Uncirculated Single	Uncirculated Roll
3,006,814	1948	$ 8.95	—
4,028,600	1948 D	4.75	—
5,714,000	1949	19.95	390.00
4,120,600	1949 D	18.95	340.00
3,744,000	1949 S	18.95	—
7,793,509	1950	12.75	230.00
8,031,600	1950 D	8.50	150.00
16,859,602	1951	4.75	75.00
9,475,200	1951 D	16.95	350.00
13,696,000	1951 S	8.75	145.00
21,274,073	1952	2.95	48.00
25,395,600	1952 D	2.50	39.00
5,526,000	1952 S	8.75	170.00
2,796,920	1953	9.75	180.00
20,900,400	1953 D	1.75	26.00
4,148,000	1953 S	3.95	70.00
13,421,503	1954	1.95	33.00
25,445,580	1954 D	1.75	25.00
4,993,400	1954 S	2.50	40.00

FRANKLIN HALF DOLLARS

Quantity	Year	Uncirculated Single	Uncirculated Roll
2,876,381	1955	6.95	136.00
4,701,384	1956	3.50	59.00
6,361,952	1957	2.25	39.00
19,966,850	1957 D	1.25	21.00
4,917,652	1958	2.75	40.00
23,962,412	1958 D	1.25	21.00
7,349,291	1959	1.75	29.00
13,053,750	1959 D	1.75	35.00
7,715,602	1960	1.75	26.00
18,215,812	1960 D	1.50	25.00
11,318,244	1961	1.50	26.00
20,276,442	1961 D	1.30	23.00
12,932,019	1962	1.50	25.00
35,473,281	1962 D	1.00	18.00
25,239,645	1963	1.00	16.50
67,069,292	1963 D	1.00	17.00

The Roosevelt Dime

The Roosevelt dime. (*Courtesy the American Numismatic Society*)

The Roosevelt dime is another series of coins that promises to appreciate in value at a greater than average rate. Also designed by John R. Sinnock, the coin bears Roosevelt's portrait on the obverse and the torch of liberty on the reverse. When the coin was first issued in 1946, some citizens took offense at the appearance of engraver Sinnock's initials—J.S.—on the coin's obverse, saying that they were those of Russian premier Joseph Stalin and indicated a Communist plot. Interestingly, when Sinnock designed the Franklin half dollar, he used his middle initial, signing the coin J.R.S., to still the faultfinders.

Here is a listing of prices being asked in mid-1970 for uncirculated rolls and singles:

ROOSEVELT DIMES

Quantity	Year	Uncirculated Single	Uncirculated Roll
255,250,000	1946	$ .40	$ 15.00
61,043,500	1946 D	.50	22.00
27,900,000	1946 S	1.20	39.00
121,520,000	1947	1.30	35.00
46,835,000	1947 D	1.00	39.00
38,840,000	1947 S	.90	36.00
74,950,000	1948	2.00	82.00
52,841,000	1948 D	1.25	39.00
35,520,000	1948 S	1.00	40.00
30,940,000	1949	6.95	280.00
26,034,000	1949 D	2.40	105.00
13,510,000	1949 S	11.95	575.00
50,181,500	1950	1.40	53.00
46,803,000	1950 D	1.40	57.00
20,440,000	1950 S	7.50	330.00
103,937,602	1951	.75	24.00
52,191,800	1951 D	.80	28.00
31,630,000	1951 S	5.50	215.00
99,122,073	1952	.50	20.00
122,100,000	1952 D	.50	20.00
44,419,500	1952 S	1.95	90.00
53,618,920	1953	.55	24.00
136,400,000	1953 D	.30	12.00
39,180,000	1953 S	.55	22.00
114,243,503	1954	.30	10.00
106,397,000	1954 D	.30	10.00
22,860,000	1954 S	.75	27.00
12,828,381	1955	1.35	55.00
13,959,000	1955 D	.80	34.00
18,510,000	1955 S	.65	27.00
108,821,081	1956	.30	12.50
108,015,100	1956 D	.35	15.00
160,160,000	1957	.30	11.00
113,354,330	1957 D	.45	17.00
31,910,000	1958	.60	22.00
136,564,600	1958 D	.35	11.50
85,780,000	1959	.25	9.00
164,919,790	1959 D	.25	9.00
70,390,000	1960	.25	9.00
200,160,400	1960 D	.25	9.00

ROOSEVELT DIMES

Quantity	Year	Uncirculated Single	Uncirculated Roll
96,758,244	1961	.30	9.00
209,146,550	1961 D	.25	9.00
75,668,019	1962	.25	8.50
334,948,380	1962 D	.20	8.50
126,725,645	1963	.20	8.50
421,476,530	1963 D	.20	8.50
933,310,762	1964	.20	8.50
1,357,517,180	1964 D	.20	7.00
1,652,140,570	1965	.20	7.00
1,382,734,540	1966	.20	7.00
2,244,007,320	1967	.20	7.00
424,470,400	1968	.20	7.00
480,748,280	1968 D	.20	7.00

The Jefferson Nickel

The Jefferson nickel. (*Courtesy the American Numismatic Society*)

The Jefferson nickel is a third series of coins that many dealers recommend to the prospective investor. The design for this coin was selected on the basis of open competition, with engraver Felix Schlag submitting the winner design. His initials—F.S.—appear on the coin beginning with the 1966 issue.

The coin was first issued in 1938. Since the coin design has been in circulation for in excess of the 25-year minimum, it is eligible for redesign at any time.

The Jefferson nickel is a good coin in which to invest if your budget is of modest size, for the various issues have been minted in relatively large quantities, except for 1939-D and 1950-D. These mintages were under four million. The Jefferson nickel series consisted of 76 different coins through 1970.

More than a few coin experts have forecast a spiraling in value of the 1942-45 coins, despite the relatively high mintages during those years. The years 1942-45 were wartime years, and during this period, while nickel production went toward the war effort, the Jefferson coin was minted in a special alloy, consisting of 56 percent copper, 35 percent silver and 9 percent manganese. At this ratio, the silver content is worth about triple the face value of the coin, so speculators have been buying the wartime issues and resmelting them.

To distinguish the 1942-45 coins from those of usual composition, the mint mark was enlarged and placed over the dome of Monticello on the reverse. A "P" was used as the Philadelphia mint mark, marking the first time a Philadelphia mark had ever appeared on a U.S. coin. The 1938-D, 1939-D and S, 1950-P and D, 1949-S and 1951-S are other of the more desirable items in this series.

Here are 1970 prices for uncirculated rolls and singles:

JEFFERSON NICKELS

Quantity	Year	Uncirculated Single	Uncirculated Roll
19,515,365	1938	$ 1.50	$—
4,105,000	1938 S	5.50	—
5,376,000	1938 D	5.65	—
120,627,535	1939	1.25	34.00
6,630,000	1939 S	10.50	—
3,514,000	1939 D	37.50	—
176,499,158	1940	.75	20.00
39,690,000	1940 S	.95	—
43,540,000	1940 D	1.00	34.00
203,283,720	1941	.75	21.00
43,445,000	1941 S	1.50	32.00
53,432,000	1941 D	1.00	30.00
49,818,600	1942	1.40	42.00
13,938,000	1942 D	9.00	—
	Wartime Silver Content		
57,900,600	1942 P	—	—
32,900,000	1942 S	4.00	—
271,165,000	1943 P	1.40	—
104,060,000	1943 S	1.40	38.00
15,294,000	1943 D	4.50	125.00
119,150,000	1944 P	2.00	—
21,640,000	1944 S	2.75	85.00
32,309,000	1944 D	2.25	80.00
119,408,100	1945 P	2.95	—

JEFFERSON NICKELS

Quantity	Year	Uncirculated Single	Uncirculated Roll
58,939,000	1945 S	1.30	37.00
37,158,000	1945 D	1.75	45.00

Prewar Nickel Content

Quantity	Year	Uncirculated Single	Uncirculated Roll
161,116,000	1946	.25	8.00
13,560,000	1946 S	.95	30.00
45,292,200	1946 D	.60	19.50
95,000,000	1947	.35	10.00
24,720,000	1947 S	.75	22.50
37,822,000	1947 D	.70	21.50
89,348,000	1948	.40	9.50
11,300,000	1948 S	1.20	30.00
44,734,000	1948 D	1.00	30.00
60,652,000	1949	.60	16.00
9,716,000	1949 S	2.00	18.00
35,238,000	1949 D	1.00	23.50
9,847,386	1950	2.25	60.00
2,630,030	1950 D	11.50	—
26,689,500	1951	.75	22.00
7,776,000	1951 S	3.25	105.00
20,460,000	1951 D	.95	—
64,069,980	1952	.40	11.00
20,572,000	1952 S	.65	.25.00
30,638,000	1952 D	2.00	55.00
46,772,800	1953	.25	6.50
19,210,900	1953 S	.60	20.00
59,878,600	1953 D	.25	9.50
47,917,350	1954	.25	7.50
29,384,000	1954 S	.30	8.00
117,183,060	1954 D	.20	7.00
8,266,200	1955	1.50	37.50
74,464,100	1955 D	.25	5.50
35,397,081	1956	.25	5.00
67,222,040	1956 D	.15	4.50
38,408,000	1957	.20	5.00
136,828,900	1957 D	.15	3.50
17,088,000	1958	.35	11.00
168,249,120	1958 D	.15	3.50
27,248,000	1959	.20	5.00
160,738,240	1959 D	.20	5.00
55,416,000	1960	.15	3.00

JEFFERSON NICKELS

Quantity	Year	Uncirculated Single	Uncirculated Roll
192,582,180	1960 D	.15	3.35
76,668,244	1961	.15	3.00
229,372,760	1961 D	.15	3.00
100,602,019	1962	.15	3.00
280,195,720	1962 D	.15	3.00
178,851,645	1963	.10	2.75
276,829,460	1963 D	.10	2.75
1,028,622,762	1964	.10	2.75
1,787,297,160	1964 D	.10	2.75
136,131,380	1965	.10	2.75
156,208,283	1966	.10	2.75
107,325,800	1967	.10	2.75
91,227,880	1968 D	.10	2.75
103,437,510	1968 D	.10	2.75

The Lincoln Cent

The Lincoln cent. (*Courtesy the American Numismatic Society*)

The humble, commonplace penny is strictly blue chip when it comes to coin investment. Coin expert Louis Newitt, writing in *Coin World*, recently termed the cent "one of the finest investment coins in the United States series." And it is.

The history of the Lincoln cent is garnished with a number of remarkable events that have imparted incredible value to many of the coins in the series. Add to this the fact that in many years low mintages were produced, and you can understand why extreme shortages exist for uncirculated rolls and even uncirculated individual coins in some of the early years of the series. Even for a sprinkling of the more recent years, dealers find it difficult to maintain stock.

The Lincoln cent was first issued in 1909 to commemorate the

100th anniversary of Lincoln's birth. The coin has been produced by the Philadelphia, San Francisco and Denver mints, with the mint marks, in the case of San Francisco and Denver, appearing directly beneath the date.

In 1909 the Philadelphia and San Francisco mints produced a small number of coins that bore the initials "VDB" to honor the coin's designer, Victor D. Brenner. Protests were immediately registered concerning the size of the initials and their prominence—they were positioned near the base on the reverse—and so the mint removed the initials before the year's production was completed. Thus, the first coin of the series became a key coin.

Brenner's initials were restored to the coin after the 1918 issue. This time they were positioned at the bottom of the obverse, but were so minute they were difficult to discern without the aid of a magnifying glass.

In 1914, a mere 1,193,000 cents were produced by the Denver mint. The going purchase price for one in uncirculated condition is $700.

The year 1922 produced the most valued of all Lincoln cents. That year the Denver mint turned out 7,160,000 cents; Philadelphia did not produce any. But collectors were quick to note that a number of cents produced in 1922 bore no mint mark, no "D." What happened was that the die had filled so as to obliterate the "D." In uncirculated condition, the coin sells for about $1,000 today.

Most Americans age 40 or older are familiar with the 1943 Lincoln cent. Copper went to war that year, so the Treasury introduced zinc-coated steel cents. Production lasted only one year. Cents were made of discarded copper-shell casings until 1946, the year that the use of bronze was resumed.

In 1955, the Philadelphia mint produced an abundance of double-struck cents. Estimates of the number range from 20,000 to 50,000. There have been countless other double-struck coins in the nation's numismatic history, but this one has caught the fancy of collectors. In very fine condition, it is listed at $145.

The Lincoln cent was redesigned in 1959 to picture the Lincoln Memorial on the reverse. The obverse remained the same. The new design was the work of Frank Gasparro.

The only key coins to be developed in recent years occurred in 1960. There is a variation in the size of the date for that year, and "Small Date" cents for 1960 (Philadelphia) have won a place in price books. The error is likely to have been caused by a gradual filling of the stamping die. These pieces sell for about $425 in uncirculated condition. They have, quite naturally, disappeared from circulation.

One word of warning concerning the purchase and storage of cents. Copper is subject to corrosion from air pollutants, and when the condition is serious it has an adverse effect upon cent values. In the case of uncirculated cents of gem condition for which you pay a substantial amount, consider vacuum storage, specifically, transparent pouches of three-ply plastic. Information as to package types and costs can be obtained from Frank V. Jannusch, Box 35097, Elmswood Park, Ill. 60635.

Here is a listing of dealer prices as of mid-1970 for uncirculated rolls and singles of Lincoln cents:

LINCOLN CENTS

Quantity	Year	Uncirculated Single	Uncirculated Roll
27,995,000	1909 VDB	$4.00	—
484,000	1909 S VDB	—	—
72,702,618	1909	—	—
1,825,000	1909 S	—	—
146,801,218	1910		—
6,045,000	1910 S	—	—
101,177,787	1911	—	—
4,026,000	1911 S	—	—
12,672,000	1911 D	—	—
68,153,060	1912	—	—
4,431,000	1912 S	—	—
10,411,000	1912 D	—	—
76,532,352	1913	—	—
6,101,000	1913 S	—	—
15,804,000	1913 D	—	—
75,238,432	1914	—	—
4,137,000	1914 S	—	—
1,193,000	1914 D	—	—
29,092,120	1915	—	—
4,833,000	1915 S	—	—
22,050,000	1915 D	—	—
131,833,677	1916	—	—
22,510,000	1916 S	—	—
35,956,000	1916 D	—	—
196,429,785	1917	—	—
32,620,000	1917 S	—	—

LINCOLN CENTS

Quantity	Year	Uncirculated Single	Uncirculated Roll
55,120,000	1917 D	—	—
288,104,634	1918	—	—
34,680,000	1918 S	—	—
47,830,000	1918 D	—	—
392,021,000	1919	—	—
139,760,000	1919 S	—	—
57,154,000	1919 D	—	—
310,165,000	1920	—	—
46,220,000	1920 S	—	—
49,280,000	1920 D	—	—
39,157,000	1921	—	—
15,274,000	1921 S	—	—
	1922	—	—
7,160,000	1922 D	—	—
74,723,000	1923	—	—
8,700,000	1923 S	—	—
75,178,000	1924	—	—
11,696,000	1924 S	—	—
2,520,000	1924 D	—	—
139,949,000	1925	—	—
26,380,000	1925 S	—	—
22,580,000	1925 D	—	—
157,088,000	1926	—	—
4,550,000	1926 S	—	—
28,020,000	1926 D	—	—
144,440,000	1927	—	—
14,276,000	1927 S	—	—
27,170,000	1927 D	—	—
134,116,000	1928	—	—
17,266,000	1928 S	—	—
31,170,000	1928 D	—	—
185,262,000	1929	—	—
50,148,000	1929 S	—	—
41,730,000	1929 D	—	—
157,415,000	1930	—	—
24,286,000	1930 S	4.00	—
40,100,000	1930 D	—	—
19,396,000	1931	—	—
866,000	1931 S	—	—
4,480,000	1931 D	—	—
9,062,000	1932	8.00	—
10,500,000	1932 D	—	—

LINCOLN CENTS

Quantity	Year	Uncirculated Single	Uncirculated Roll
14,360,000	1933	9.50	—
6,200,000	1933 D	—	—
219,080,000	1934	2.50	—
28,446,000	1934 D	2.50	—
245,388,000	1935	1.25	—
38,702,000	1935 S	2.25	—
47,000,000	1935 D	1.25	—
309,637,569	1936	.75	—
29,130,000	1936 S	1.25	—
40,620,000	1936 D	1.00	—
309,179,320	1937	.75	—
34,500,000	1937 S	.65	—
50,430,000	1937 D	.75	25.00
156,696,734	1938	.95	29.00
15,180,000	1938 S	1.75	—
20,010,000	1938 D	1.50	—
316,479,000	1939	.65	21.00
52,070,000	1939 S	.65	22.00
15,160,000	1939 D	2.75	—
586,825,872	1940	.30	12.50
112,940,000	1940 S	.40	13.50
81,390,000	1940 D	.65	19.00
887,039,100	1941	.50	16.00
92,360,000	1941 S	.90	35.00
128,799,000	1941 D	.90	34.50
657,828,600	1942	.30	8.00
85,590,000	1942 S	3.00	109.00
206,698,000	1942 D	.25	8.50

Wartime Steel-Zinc Content

Quantity	Year	Uncirculated Single	Uncirculated Roll
684,628,670	1943	.25	7.75
191,550,000	1943 S	.75	29.00
217,660,000	1943 D	.45	16.00

Copper Cents

Quantity	Year	Uncirculated Single	Uncirculated Roll
1,435,400,000	1944	.20	4.75
282,760,000	1944 S	.25	7.75
430,587,000	1944 D	.20	4.75
1,040,515,000	1945	.25	8.00
181,770,000	1945 S	.30	8.50
226,268,000	1945 D	.25	8.00

LINCOLN CENTS

Quantity	Year	Uncirculated Single	Uncirculated Roll
	Bronze Composition Resumed		
991,655,000	1946	.20	5.25
198,100,000	1946 S	.20	5.25
315,690,000	1946 D	.20	5.00
190,555,000	1947	.40	15.75
99,000,000	1947 S	.45	25.00
194,750,000	1947 D	.20	6.00
317,570,000	1948	.35	10.00
81,735,000	1948 S	.70	24.50
172,637,500	1948 D	.25	6.50
217,490,000	1949	.40	14.00
64,290,000	1949 S	.85	31.00
154,370,500	1949 D	.35	9.50
272,686,386	1950	.40	14.50
118,505,000	1950 S	.45	15.75
334,950,000	1950 D	.20	5.25
294,633,500	1951	.45	15.75
100,890,000	1951 S	.65	24.50
625,355,000	1951 D	.15	4.25
186,856,980	1952	.40	14.25
137,800,004	1952 S	.40	15.00
746,130,000	1952 D	.15	3.00
256,883,800	1953	.20	7.00
181,835,000	1953 S	.25	7.00
700,515,000	1953 D	.15	3.25
71,873,350	1954	.45	14.50
96,190,000	1954 S	.30	6.50
251,552,500	1954 D	.15	3.25
330,958,200	1955	.20	4.00
44,610,000	1955 S	.35	10.50
563,257,500	1955 D	.15	2.50
420,926,081	1956	.10	2.50
1,098,201,100	1956 D	.10	2.50
282,540,000	1957	.10	1.50
1,051,342,000	1957 D	.10	1.50
252,595,000	1958	.10	1.75
800,953,300	1958 D	.10	1.25
619,715,000	1959	.10	1.20
1,279,760,000	1959 D	.10	1.25
586,405,000	1960 Small Date	3.85	—
	1960 Large Date	.10	1.00
1,580,884,000	1960 D Small Date	.20	—
	1960 D Large Date	.10	1.25
756,373,244	1961	.10	1.00

LINCOLN CENTS

Quantity	Year	Uncirculated Single	Uncirculated Roll
1,753,266,700	1961 D	.10	1.00
609,263,019	1962	.10	1.00
1,793,148,400	1962 D	.05	1.00
757,185,645	1963	.05	1.00
1,774,020,400	1963 D	.05	1.00
2,652,525,762	1964	.05	1.00
3,799,071,500	1964 D	.05	1.00
1,497,224,900	1965	.05	1.00
2,188,147,783	1966	.05	1.00
3,048,667,100	1967	.05	1.00
1,707,880,970	1968	.05	1.00
2,886,296,600	1968 D	.05	1.00
261,311,510	1968 S	.05	1.00

Buying and Selling Coins

The best place to buy coins and sell them is by trading with a reputable dealer. Look in the "Yellow Pages" of your telephone directory under "Coin Dealers, Suppliers, etc." for a listing of dealers in your area. Leading department stores also sell coins, and almost all have special departments where coins are on display. But you'll find prices are more attractive when you purchase from dealers, men who devote themselves exclusively to coins.

You can also buy and sell by mail. There are countless dealers who specialize in mail order only. The coin publications (pages 52–3) carry their advertisements.

The mail-order side of the coin business operates with a good degree of integrity. As you scan dealer advertisements, you will notice almost all offer credentials in the form of affiliations or memberships. Some are members of the Professional Numismatic Guild, an organization that screens prospective members and sets ethical standards that they must follow. The Retail Coin Dealers Association is another and similar dealer's group. Many of the most noted international coin dealers are members of the International Association of Professional Numismatists.

Some dealers do not belong to dealer organizations, but instead are affiliated with coin clubs in their area or such primarily collector-oriented organizations as the American Numismatic Association, the American Numismatic Society or the Organization of International Numismatists.

Some dealers, in addition to holding membership in one or more dealer organizations, strive to establish their reputability with such statements as "This is my 254th ad" or "I have been a coin dealer for 24 years." You should convince yourself of the dealer's integrity before you buy or sell, and such statements do help.

If you are dealing exclusively in uncirculated rolls, you will have less problems with grading than the average collector. Even so, uncirculated coins can vary in quality. Tiny scratches, oxidation and attempts to clean the coins can diminish values. Learn as much as you can about grading before you enter the mail-order market.

Coin shows and conventions give an excellent opportunity to shop for coins, or simply to become more informed about current prices. Usually conventions are hosted by area numismatic organizations, and attract dealers who rent booth space. A recent convention in New York City displayed the wares of more than fifty dealers from the United States and several foreign countries. The coin column in your local daily newspaper is sure to give advance notice of local exhibitions and shows.

Many shows offer a coin auction as the featured event. Some auctions take floor bids only, but others accept mail bids as well, so it is possible to compete without actually being in attendance.

A good number of dealers offer coins through mail bids solely. If you want to bid by mail, the dealer may ask you to send along a 25 percent deposit in the amount of your bid. Mail bids are accepted in the order received. In the case of identical bids, the one with the earliest postmark is awarded the lot.

Auction catalogs are an excellent source of information about coins and particularly helpful in establishing values. Never throw one away. Most dealers prepare a "price realized" list after the auction which gives the "knockdown price" for each lot. Such lists are also to be valued as information sources.

A Long Island, New York, lawyer, Stanley Apfelbaum, recently launched First Coinvestors, Inc., a company that helps investors build portfolios of rare coins. FCI invites prospects to fill out a short application form and mail it with $12.50 to company headquarters in Albertson, New York. In return, the prospect receives an approval package of coins.

The prospect then agrees to invest $50, $100, $200 or $500 per month and for each payment receives a coin-approval package. He examines the coins and only after he's convinced that it is a worthwhile package is the monthly payment actually due.

The program compares to a mutual fund in that the investor is employing a specialist to do his research for him. Another similarity is that the amount of the monthly payment can be either reduced or increased at any time, or the investor can cancel the plan.

FCI was founded in 1969 and is now a publicly owned firm. The company anticipated 5,000 subscribers by the end of 1970.

Apfelbaum has found that physicians are the most avid buyers. Housewives and military personnel are the next most-important customer classifications. "We even ship a few packages to Vitenam each month," he says.

FCI also provides subscribers with a monthly market advisory letter and gives information on how to store and preserve coins. For more information, write: First Coinvestors, Inc., FCI Building, 16 McKinley Ave., Albertson, N. Y. 11507.

You can buy unsorted coins, too. Many vending-machine companies supply them. The First National Vending Machine Company (5322 West Belmont, Chicago, Ill. 60641) has been furnishing "guaranteed unpicked" coins from its vending machines to collectors for years. A sack containing 5,000 cents cost $55. Ten sacks, a total of 50,000 cents, are $530.

So-called "silver" coins are also available from vending-machine companies. The Acmc Vending Machine Company (1696 West Washington Boulevard, Los Angeles, Calif. 90007) offers bags of "guaranteed numismatically untouched coins"—1,000 nickels, 500 dimes or 200 quarters at $52 a bag. They arc shipped freight collect.

Proof Sets

Proof sets have won wide acclaim for their investment potential, yet many experts in the field believe them to be almost a purely speculative buy. "I'm afraid of them," a Philadelphia coin dealer told me. "Some are definitely overpriced. One day the bottom is going to fall out."

Proof sets used to be sold by the Philadelphia mint. Each set consisted of one coin of each denomination produced during the year of issue, and could only be ordered during that year. The price was $2.10 a set. From 1955 through 1964, the proof sets were sold in plastic containers bearing the mint's seal.

When the country was struck with a coin shortage in 1964, the production of proof sets was suspended. But trading in the sets continues and the market is extremely active.

Some sets have soared in value. The 1950 proof set sold for $57 in 1956 and $70 early in 1963. But before the end of the year, its price had zoomed to $130.

Other sets have also demonstrated similar sudden price jumps, but almost all sets have been subject to long periods when little or no price change has been recorded.

"I have avoided them as investments," said Louis A. Newitt in a recent issue of *Coin World*, and he pointed to the erratic nature of their price rises as his reason. "If you do invest in proof sets," said Mr. Newitt, "invest in the best rate of return—the 1950 sets."

Coin Oddities and Errors

Many collectors specialize in coin oddities and errors. For example, some 1955 cents show a die break across Lincoln's head, and these coins have become known as the "cracked skull" cents. Oddity collectors gobble them up.

But such coins shouldn't interest you, if investment is your aim. It is often difficult to establish authentic oddities and more than a few coin experts refer to those who specialize in errors as "flyspeck collectors."

Generally, the only variations that should concern you are those that have attained recognition in recognized catalogs. These include the "plain," "D" and "S" mint issues of each coin, and certain overdates or double strikes. For example, some 1955 Lincoln cents were double struck. In very fine condition, the coin lists at $145. Authenticated oddities are rare, however. Let the catalog be your guide.

Numismatic "Finds"

You can never tell when you might turn up a rare coin. A Southern California bowler joined a team that collected a three-cent contribution for every missed space, the kitty to be used for a party at the end of the season. Lacking confidence in his spare-shooting skills, the bowler went to a bank and purchased a roll of pennies. Later he discovered the coins were the famous 1955 double-struck cents, a coin assessed at $400 in the 1969 Coin Redbook.

The story has a footnote. Before he made his discovery, the young man spent ten of the cents for a bottle of orange soda. "I figure I paid $4,000 for that orange soda," he says, "or about $250 a gulp. Today I *hate* orange soda."

Perhaps you're one of the millions of Americans who culls his pocket change in quest of valuable coins. If you are, keep a list of certain key dates handy.

Lincoln cents before 1935 are worth two and three times their face value, but they must be in fine condition or better (see above). The mint mark issues are particularly valuable, since they are the first coins young collectors strive to obtain. The 1931-S, in fine condition, is listed at $17.50 in the Bluebook. Cents from the dates 1934 with mintages below 50 million are worth saving, too. Generally, these are mint-marked coins.

Buffalo nickels have almost disappeared from general circulation. Watch for issues prior to 1929. They are particularly valuable if the date and mint marks are sharp and clear. Jefferson nickels with mintages of less than 10 million are almost certain to sharply increase in value.

Short issues of Mercury-head dimes are beginning to climb in price. The 1916-D is listed at $11 in fine condition. The 1919-D, 1921, 1921-D, 1926-S and 1931-D are others worth watching for.

Among the higher denominations, be on the lookout for "standing Liberty" quarters dated 1916, a coin which is listed at $275, 1918-S, listed at $250, 1919-D and S, 1921, 1923-S and 1927-S. Remember, they have to be fine or very fine.

For Washington quarters, the important dates are: 1932-D and S, 1936-D, 1937-S and 1955-D. Since these are relatively recent mintages, they should be very fine, not merely fine.

Once in a while you may come upon a Liberty "walking-type" half dollar. Almost any issue in very fine condition between 1916 and 1933, plus 1937-D and 1938-D, brings a premium price.

What about the Kennedy half dollar? The truth is that its investment potential is virtually nil. The Treasury Department turns out these coins by the hundreds of millions and people keep squirreling them away. Most of those who hoard Kennedy half dollars do so in the belief that the coins will be valuable one day as collectors' items. It's not likely. Value depends on rarity, and Kennedy half dollars are about as rare as roadside litter.

Other people feel these coins will be valuable because of their silver content. Another misconception. The Kennedy half dollar is 60 percent copper and only 40 percent silver. The precious metal content of the coin is a mere .148 ounce. The price of silver would have to skyrocket to $3.38 an ounce for the Kennedy coin to contain so much as 50 cents worth of silver.

The coins listed above are only a sampling of the "find" you might encounter. You can formulate a list of your own based on the mintage statistics and prices given in coin reference manuals.

An enterprising Texan has prepared a list of almost 600 of the "most valuable and widely circulated" U.S. coins, and printed it on wallet-size, plastic cards (like credit cards). One costs $1. Write Coin Card, P. O. Box 20546, Houston, Tex. 77035

Coin Books and Publications

As an investor in coins, there are two books you must own. The first is the *Handbook of United States Coins*, which is issued annually. Commonly called the ".Blue Book," it gives the average amount dealers will pay for individual coins, according to condition. It also gives the quantity minted each year for each series. This handbook costs $1.25 and is available at many coin dealers, or from Western Publishing Company, Inc. (Whitman Hobby Division, Racine, Wis.). Remember, a new edition is printed each year.

The other book you must own, a companion to the first, is *A Guide Book to United States Coins*, and it, too, is issued annually. Often referred to as the "Red Book," it gives the retail valuation of coins, that is, how much you can expect to pay. The Red Book is priced at $2.50, and can be purchased at coin dealers or from Western Publishing Company.

Your local library is sure to have available several books on the subject of coins and collecting. *America's Money, The Story of Coins and Currency*, is a recently published and colorful history. Order it at your local bookstore or from the publisher (Thomas Y. Crowell Company, 201 Park Avenue S., New York, N. Y. 10016). It costs $5.95.

There are a number of popular magazines and newspapers devoted to coin collecting. Obtain sample issues of each and decide which ones best suit your needs. They include:

Coin World (P. O. Box 150, Sidney, O. 45365), one year, 52 issues, $6; sample copy, 35¢.

Numismatic News (Iola, Wis. 54945), one year, 26 issues, $3; sample copy, 25¢.

COINage Magazine (16250 Ventura Blvd., Encino, Calif. 91316), one year, 12 issues, $4.75; sample copy, 60¢.

Coins Magazine (Iola, Wis. 54945), one year, 12 issues, $3; sample copy, 50¢.

The Numismatist (P. O. Box 2366, Colorado Springs, Colo. 80901), one year, 12 issues, $7.50; sample copy, 75¢.

Numismatic Scrapbook Magazine (P. O. Box 150, Sidney, O. 43565), one year, 12 issues, $5; sample copy, 50¢.

You can also increase your knowledge of coins by joining a collector's organization. The most noted one is the American Numismatic Association (818 North Cascade Blvd., Colorado Springs, Colo. 80901). The ANA is dedicated to the research and publication of articles about coins, coinage and the history of money; it maintains a library and museum, publishes *The Numismatist*, a monthly magazine, and holds annual conventions.

The American Numismatic Society (on Broadway between 155th and 156th streets, New York, N. Y. 10032) is another organization that can be of value. Its goal is "the advancement of numismatic knowledge" and it maintains the most comprehensive numismatic library in the world.

Summing Up

If you plan to invest in coins, tread carefully at first. Study the field thoroughly before you put your money down. Talk to dealers, read books on collecting, and subscribe to two or more of the publications that contain numismatic news. Follow these hints:

• In general, coin values depend on three factors: availability, quality or condition, and denomination.

• Limit your investment spending to uncirculated rolls or, in cases of critical scarcities, to uncirculated singles, of U.S. coins.

• Four series of U.S. coins offer the greatest investment potential. They are: Franklin half dollars, Roosevelt dimes, Jefferson nickels and Lincoln cents.

• Buy and sell through a local dealer or by mail, but in either case establish the dealer's reliability and integrity before you invest.

• Once you've made a purchase, don't store it away and forget it. Keep abreast of changing values.

RARE BOOKS

Are rare books a good investment medium? "They're the best investment you can make," says H. P. Kraus of New York, one of the nation's leading book dealers. "I'm now buying back books for five and six times the price I sold them for ten years ago."

There are solid reasons for the boom. The number of books available for investment purposes is gradually shrinking because of the nation's tax laws. Here's how one dealer explains what's happening: "After a wealthy person has built up a collection of rare books, he seldom sells them to a dealer. It's of much greater benefit to him to donate the books to an institution and get a tax write-off plus the gratification of doing something for his old alma mater. So most of the rare books of the world are ending up in universities or research libraries. Whatever's left is escalating in price bit by bit."

Another factor is that colleges and universities and even public libraries are buying first editions and rare books as never before. Even obscure little libraries are sending in orders to dealers.

Rare books are seldom found in curio shops or second-hand stores. Most rare book dealers are members of the Antiquarian Booksellers' Association of America, a nonprofit organization devoted to the "stimulation of interest in book collecting, and in the maintaining of high professional standards among its members."

Write to the ABAA (630 Fifth Ave., New York, N. Y. 10020) and request a copy of the organization's membership list. It's free. It gives the names and addresses of each of the organization's approximately 400 members, plus the speciality of each, such as "rare books, bindings, fine printings, first editions" or "natural history, ornithology, entomology, hunting, fishing and botany."

The next step is write the dealers of your choice and request a catalog from each. The catalogs are free, too.

Establishing Value

"If you're buying for investment, buy quality," says H. P. Kraus. "Buy the bluest of the blue chips."

Other dealers agree. "The books most sought after are the first editons of great books in literature, art and science," says the Antiquarian Booksellers' Association of America. "These are source books revealing the development of man, and are of intrinsic importance, their values being influenced by scarcity and the demand for them at any particular time."

A first edition is the first appearance of a book between covers, the first printing. In recent times publishers have taken to indicating a "first edition" on the reverse of the title page, and occasionally a publisher will identify an edition as a "second printing" or "second edition," but there is no standard practice of identification, a situation that presents the prospective investor with constant challenges but also works to make real finds eminently possible.

Not all books of a first edition may be exactly the same, and this can cause variations in value. For instance, a first edition may have several "issues," printings in which type changes have been made. There can also be differences within the various issues—a change in binding, for instance—and these are called "states."

Usually a work is a first edition if the date on the title page agrees with the copyright date (which normally appears on the reverse of the title page). But there are exceptions. Longfellow's *The Song of Hiawatha* was published in Boston in 1855, but not every copy bearing the 1855 date is a true first edition. The first issue of the first edition contains advertisements that bear the date November 1855, and this characteristic—called a "point"—renders this edition more valuable than any other.

The term point can also refer to a misspelled word, a typographical error, variations in the binding, differences in the end papers, etc. Any of these can significantly affect value. First copies of Stephen Crane's *The Red Badge of Courage* are worth $400-$500 in mint condition. When the first edition was being printed, the last line of type of page 225 was somehow damaged. Copies of the book with the damaged line are worth only $50, while copies with the line corrected—the correction has a slanting "d"—are worth no more than $30.

Rare book dealers will help you in your research and so will librarians. Fortunately, there is a wealth of bibliographic material available (see page 64).

Among first editions, many factors influence value. The literary merit of a book is almost always a prime consideration. Scan the catalogs of several book dealers and pick out the highest-priced volumes. The names of the authors of these books will read like a "Who's who of American literature."

There is, of course, a difference of opinion as to what constitutes literary merit, and the market can be subject to wide fluctuations. J. D. Salinger, much in vogue in the early 1960's, has been the victim of waning interest. Henry Wenning of C. A. Stonehills' in New Haven, Connecticut, recalls selling a copy of *Catcher in the Rye* at auction for $130 in 1960. "Today I'd sell a fine copy for $50," he says.

The books of other latter-day authors have been subject to price swings, too. John Barth's *The Sot-weed Factor* and *Giles Goat Boy* have shown sudden spurts in value. A first edition of Vladimir Nabokov's *Lolita* is priced at $50.

Some works of modern poetry are highly prized. It's worth your while to set aside first editions of Rod McKuen's works, and Robert Greeley and Robert Duncan are "hot."

The Red Badge
Of Courage

An Episode of the American Civil War

BY

Stephen Crane

New York
D·Appleton and Company
1895

A reproduction of the title page of THE RED BADGE OF COURAGE. First copies of the first edition in mint condition are worth $400-$500.

Early in the 1960's, it was possible to buy copies of John O'Hara's first book, *Appointment in Samarra* for $7 or $8. By the late 1960's, copies were selling for as much as $70. Despite the escalations, first editions, even by some of the most noted American authors, are still within the budget of virtually every collector-investor. Here are some sample prices from recently published catalogs:

AIKEN, Conrad. *Punch: The Immortal Liar. Documents in His History*. Spine faded, dust jacket, faded, chipped. New York: Alfred A. Knopf, 1921. First Edition. $20.

ALLEN, Hervey. *Anthony Adverse*. Decorations by Allan McNab. Dust jacket. New York: Farrar and Rinehart, Inc., 1933. First Edition. $15.

BULLFINCH, Thomas. *The Age of Fable; or, stories of Gods and Heroes*. 12mo, original cloth, inner spine defective. Boston: Sanborn, Carter and Bazin, 1855. First Edition. With A.L.S. laid in. $50.

CABELL, James Branch. *Jurgen.* 12mo, original cloth, dust jacket chipped, 1/2 morocco slipcase. New York: Robert M. McBride & Co., 1919. First Edition. $85.

CALDWELL, Erskine. *The Bastard.* New York, 1929. Tall 8vo., purple cloth, faded. With illustrations by Ty Mahon. One of 1000 copies of the author's first book. First Edition. $20.

CALDWELL, Erskine. *God's Little Acre.* New York, 1933, 8vo., cloth; bookplate and portion of publisher's announcement pasted in. Together with Modern Library Edition of 1934 which contains a new introduction by the author. Both copies first editions. $20.

CALDWELL, Erskine. *Journeyman.* Boxed, soiled. New York: Viking Press, 1935. First Edition. One of 1475 copies. $10.

CATHER, Willa. *A Lost Lady.* Dust jacket, spine chipped. New York: Alfred A. Knopf, 1923. First Edition. $25.

CATHER, Willa. *My Antonia.* Boston, 1918. 8vo., cloth. With illustrations by W. T. Benda. Enclosed in cloth slipcase. Inscription on endleaf. First Edition. $50.

COZZENS, James Gould. *Castaway.* Dust jacket, stained, chipped. New York: Random House, 1934. First Edition. $15.

CRANE, Stephen. *The Black Riders and Other Lines.* Boston: Copeland and Day, 1895. 16mo, full black morocco binding with original wrappers bound in. First Edition. $35.

DICKINSON, Emily. *Bolts of Melody.* Edited by Loomis Todd and Millicent Todd Bingham. Dust jacket, soiled. New York: Harper & Brothers, 1945. First Edition. $10.

DREISER, Theodore. *Chains, Lesser Novels and Stories.* New York, 1927. 8vo., batik boards and cloth. One of 440 copies signed by the author. First Edition. $10.

DREISER, Theodore. *A Gallery of Women.* New York, 1929. 8vo, cloth, 2 vols. First Edition. $10.

HEMINGWAY, Ernest. *Across the River and Into the Trees.* Dust jacket, spine torn. New York: Charles Scribner's Sons, 1950. First American Edition. $15.

HEMINGWAY, Ernest. *A Farewell to Arms.* Cloth, spine faded. London: Jonathan Cape. First English Edition. $20.

HEMINGWAY, Ernest. *Men Without Women.* New York, 1927. 8vo, cloth, with the earliest form of dust-wrapper. First Edition. $90.

HEMINGWAY, Ernest. *The Sun Also Rises.* New York, 1926. 8vo, cloth. With "stopped" line 26 on p. 181. First Issue. Fair condition. First Edition. $75.

HENRY, O. *Heart of the West.* 12mo, original cloth. New York: The McClure Co., 1907. First Edition. $35.

HENRY, O. *Options*. Illustrated. Cloth, spine faded. New York: Harper & Brothers, 1909. First Edition. $15.

HOLMES, Oliver Wendell. *A Mortal Antipathy*. Cloth, scuffed, cloth folder. Boston: Houghton, Mifflin & Co., 1885, First Edition. $10.

KILMER, Joyce. *Summer of Love* 12mo, cloth. New York: The Baker & Taylor Co., 1911. First Edition. Author's first book. $35.

LARDNER, Ring W. *Round Up*. Dust jacket, chipped, spine faded. New York: Charles Scribner's Sons, 1929. First Edition. $25.

O'HARA, John. *Hellbox*. Dust jacket, soiled. New York: Random House. First Edition. $10.

O'HARA, John. *Ten North Frederick*. Dust jacket, spine faded. New York: Random House. First Edition. $10.

PARKER, Dorothy. *After Such Pleasures*. New York, 1933. 8vo, cloth, slipcase. One of 250 copies signed by the author. First Edition. $15.

SAROYAN, William. *Don't Go Away Mad and other plays*. Cloth, dust jacket, slightly soiled. New York: Harcourt, Brace and Co. First Edition. $15.

SAROYAN, William. *Rock Wagram*. Cloth, dust jacket. New York: Doubleday & Co., Inc., 1951. First Edition. $10.

Keep in mind that whenever you purchase a book by a modern writer you are almost always engaging in speculation. Like summer showers, reputations come and go. Never forget that "old books" are purchased by second-hand bookshops (not be confused with rare book dealers) in bulk, at pennies per pound.

You cannot go wrong if you buy quality, however. "The market is tremendously steady for Hemingway," says one dealer. "He's the darling of the critics. He's easy to read. I think that in the long run Hemingway prices will pull ahead of just about everyone else."

Scarcity is another factor that has to be weighed. The first American edition of Herman Melville's *Moby Dick, or the Whale*, was almost entirely destroyed by a fire at the publishing house. One of the few remaining copies, in very fine condition, sold for $2,500 in 1967.

Historical value is important, too. *Uncle Tom's Cabin* by Harriet Beecher Stowe would win no prizes for literary artistry, but it has monumental importance as a historical document. No one knows for certain how many copies of the first edition exist, but it numbers in the thousands. There are several different types of first-edition bindings, including copies with cloth bindings. These are available at $500-$600 in fine condition.

Sometimes a book has value because of its literary influence.

Frank Norris' *McTeague, A Story of San Francisco*, is a case in point. The story of a dentist who allowed his life to become dominated by avarice, the book had a wide influence upon Norris' contemporaries. It is judged to be a landmark work in American fiction. A first edition in fine condition sells for about $200.

Don't overlook children's books as an investment medium. Although it can be difficult to find material of this type in really fine condition because of the handling and rude treatment it receives, some children's books are strictly blue chip. *The Wonderful Wizard of Oz* by L. Frank Baum, first published in 1900, has this status. There are many "states" or versions of the first edition, with prices ranging from $200 up to $1,000. The first American edition of *Alice's Adventures in Wonderland* by Lewis Carroll, published by D. Appleton and Company in 1866, is worth $500 in fine condition.

A book does not always have to be old to be valuable. *Flowers and Fruit Prints of the 18th and Early 19th Century* by Gordon Dunthorne has climbed steadily in price since first published in 1948. Copies of the first printing of 2,500 sold for $50-$100 up until 1960, but in recent years dealers have been cataloging the volume at $350 a copy.

There are other investment opportunities besides first editions. Americans, first instance. Books published before 1875 which deal with the exploration and development of the United States are considered potentially valuable by many experts. The subject matter of such works includes state, county and local history; Indian tribes, laws, wars and treaties; state laws and constitutions; railroads and canals; the Black Hills gold rush; the California gold rush; sports; natural history; the fur trade; Oklahoma and oil. Texas and cattle, etc., etc. Second, third or fourth editions of books on these subjects are often highly prized.

Books of this type, incidentally, can sometimes be obtained from nondealer sources. "Literally hundreds of valuable books are buried away across the country in old book shelves, boxes, trunks and other half-forgotten hiding places," says Van Allen Bradley in his book, *Gold In Your Attic* (Fleet Press, $8.95). Some, he says, are worth "fabulous" sums.

Of course, you must specialize. "As a focus for your collection, choose a subject that's close to your heart," says H. P. Kraus. "This could be a particular author, a branch of learning, an intellectual problem, a period of history. A few subjects very popular with collectors are the history of science, medicine, Americana (especially early works on the history of the West), atlases and maps, American literature in first editions, early printed books (particularly of the 15th century), Bibles in English and foreign languages, illuminated manuscripts, editions and translations of one of their favorite works in world literature, science or art. These are only some of the many possibilities."

"Books on the occult are in tremendous demand right now," says another dealer. "And we can sell almost anything on slavery or Africa."

Become a devoted student of whatever subject you choose. Then you'll be better able to recognize book bargains.

You can even specialize in one book. Take Izaac Walton's *The Complete Angler, or the Contemplative Man's Recreation*. The first edition, published in 1653, was revised and enlarged so many times it has provided a field day for collectors and dealers. Here, with 1970 prices, are a few examples of the many editions:

WALTON, Izaac. *The Complete Angler.* Sm 8vo,, full polished calf, gilt. London: J. G. for Rich. Marriot, 1661. $300.

WALTON, Izaac, and Charles Cotton. *The Complete Angler. . . . To Which are now prefixed The Lives of the Authors.* Frontispiece and plates. 8vo, full calf, spine cracked and chipped, boxed. London: Thomas Hope, 1760. $90.

WALTON, Izaac, and Charles Cotton. *The Complete Angler.* Frontispiece and plates. 8vo, full calf, front cover detached but present, spine cracked & chipped, slipcase. London: John Hawkins, 1792. Fifth Edition with additions. $30.

WALTON, Izaac. *The Complete Angler.* 24mo, full morocco by Riviere. London, William Pickering, 1825. $150.

WALTON, Izaac, and Charles Cotton. *The Complete Angler.* 2 vols., 8vo, 3/4 morocco, spine faded. New York: Wiley and Sons, 1880. Large paper copy. One of 100 copies. $90.

WALTON, Izaac. *The Complete Angler; or, the Contemplative Man's Recreation,* by . . . Being a facsimile reprint of the First Edition, published in 1653. Sm 8vo, 1/2 calf, boards. London: Elliot Stock. $10.

Most book dealers are specialists, limiting themselves to particular fields of interest. The listing of dealers published by the Antiquarian Booksellers Association of America gives the speciality for each member.

Selling Books

When you wish to sell a book, the first thing to do is consult a copy of *American Book Prices Current* at your local library, a reference source that reports on sales of books at dealers' auctions. Bear in mind that the prices listed are the dealers' or *wholesale* prices.

Once you have some idea of the book's value, take it to a dealer for an appraisal. If there is no dealer close at hand, select one from the ABAA's membership list and send him a description of the book. This is the information to send:

Author:
Title:
Size (length and width of pages in inches):
Type of Binding (full leather, one-half leather, cloth, paper):
Publishers and where published:
Date (if no date appears on title page, give copyright date):
Number of pages and illustrations:
Condition:

From this information, the dealer can decide whether the book has value. He then may ask you to send it to him. The ABAA recommends sending books by insured parcel post (book rate) or Railway Express prepaid.

A book's condition is always a critical factor in establishing value. "Mint" condition refers to a book that is as fresh and clean as when first issued. "Very fine" or "fine" are something less than perfect. "Very good" and "good" are other classifications used by dealers.

Even what seems to be a small defect can have a significant bearing upon value. One dealer had for sale two copies of Faulkner's novel, *Light in August*. One copy, just about in mint condition, was priced at $50. The other had no dust jacket and showed some "slight wear at the spinal extremities." It cost $12.50.

A rebound book is of little value no matter how rare it might be. A loosened group of pages is considered a serious defect. A missing page is even worse. "Fine original condition"—that is what bookmen seek.

It may be to your advantage to seek a private source when you sell, that is, to deal in the retail market. If this is your intent, seek out clubs and organizations that might have a special interest in the book. Query the membership list or place a classified advertisement in a publication that covers the field. A book on ornithology is of interest to members of the Audubon Society. Books and memorabilia concerning the American West are sought by the Sierra Club.

Recently a collector sold a copy of *The Gentleman's Farriery: or a practical treatise on the disease of horses* (published in London in 1754) to the owner of a large racing stable. He happened to see the man's name on the sport's pages. There is a long list of prospective buyers for virtually every rare book. It's up to you to use your imagination and ingenuity to seek them out.

College and public libraries seek to enrich their collections with noteworthy books and first editions. In tracking down organizations or individuals with possible interest in a particular book, consult *The Encyclopedia of Associations*, available at your local library. It will provide you with a comprehensive listing of organizations within the book's field of interest.

Museums and historical societies are other prospective markets. Ask at your local library for directories that list these. Individuals also buy and sell books by means of classified advertisements in collectors' magazines. These publications are listed on page 64.

Limited Editions Club Books

More than few dealers recommend purchase of the books issued by the Limited Editions Club as an investment medium. These dealers often support their contention stocking and trading in these volumes.

The Limited Editions Club, founded more than fifty years ago, prepares its own editions of the classics, printing them in handsome type, illustrating them with fine drawings, and putting them in elegant bindings. Membership in the club is kept to 1,500 persons, and on publication day each member receives a copy of each edition. A nonmember wishing a copy must appeal to a member to obtain one. Any member desiring a second copy must appeal to a fellow member.

In other words, the supply—like Rembrandt's paintings or the world's real estate—is firmly fixed. So there is a natural tendency for the books to rise in value. In the active resale market, some of the club's earlier books are priced at slightly below their initial cost, but literally hundreds of them have risen in value, and in some cases the increases have been spectacular. Dealers list a Limited Editions volume of *The Conquest of America* at $100. *The Poems of Robert Frost* is priced at $150. *Lysistrata*—signed by Picasso—at $500, is the most stunning gainer. For more evidence as to how Limited Edition's books have gained in value, obtain a copy of *Forty Years of Limited Editions Club Books, 1929-1969* (Catalog 192), issued by dealer Philip C. Duschnes (699 Madison Ave., New York, N. Y. 10021).

A person assigned a membership in the Limited Editions Club receives it on a permanent basis, but is permitted to relinquish the membership after purchasing twelve books, which constitutes a "series." Each book in the series is priced at $22.50.

Among the works in progress are:

Ah, Wilderness! by Eugene O'Neill, with an introduction by Walter Kerr; illustrated with paintings by Shannon Stirnweiss, designed by Adrian Wilson, and printed at The Stinehour Press, Lunenburg, Vermont.

The Captain's Daughter and Three Other Stories by Alexander Pushkin, translated from the Russian by Ivy and Tatiana Litvinov; illustrated with color lithographs by Charles Mozley and designed by Mr. Mozley, and printed at The Westerham Press, Westerham, England.

The Poems of Percy Bysshe Shelley, selected by Stephen Spender and with an introduction by Mr. Spender; illustrated with wood engravings by Richard Shirley Smith, designed by John Dreyfus, and printed at the University Printing House, Cambridge, England.

The Short Stories of Charles Dickens, selected and introduced by Walter Allen; illustrated with colored line drawings by Edward Ardizzone, designed by Joseph Blumenthal, and printed at the Spiral Press, New York.

The Stranger by Albert Camus, in the translation by Stuart Gilbert, with an introduction by Wallace Fowlie; illustrated with tempera paintings by Daniel Maffia, designed by Ward Ritchie, and printed at The Ward Ritchie Press, Los Angeles.

For more information concerning membership, write The Limited Editions Club, 207 West 25th St., New York, N. Y. 10001. Request a prospectus.

Reference Sources

Your local library is certain to contain scores of bibliographies and reference sources to help you in evaluating rare books. A few of the most important reference works are mentioned in the paragraphs that follow:

A Practical Guide to American Book Collecting (1666-1940) by Whitman Bennett (Bennett Book Studios, Inc., New York) describes in detail the most noteworthy of American books.

Bibliography of American Literature, by Jacob S. Blanck (Yale University Press), a four-volume work, is an exhaustive bibliographic study of American literature. Few reference sources are so valuable.

U.S-iana (1650-1950) by Wright Howes (R. R. Bowker & Co., New York) is rated by one bookman as "the most useful single work of bibliographical information in the Americana field." The most recent edition was published in 1963 and classifies more than 11,-000 different items.

American First Editions by Merle Johnson is the basic source on the identification of important editions.

Literary History of the United States by Robert E. Spiller (Macmillan Company, New York, 1953) is another basic guide to American literature.

The General Guide to Rare Americana by Stanley Wemyss contains price information that is out of date, but has descriptive information on some obscure books that is not to be found in other guidebooks.

The American Book Collector (18 West School Street, Chicago, Ill. 60657) is the principal magazine covering the book field. An annual subscription—10 issues—is $7.50.

MAGAZINES

Magazines are a collector's medium, not so much an investor's. There are a few exceptions, but generally the market for back issues is slim and erratic.

The exceptions include *Playboy*. The first issue, December 1954, can be sold to a secondhand magazine dealer for more or less than $50, the price figure depending on condition. The complete series is gold.

Old movie magazines are another "hot" item. Motion picture fans hold them in high esteem, and a *Photoplay* or *Silver Screen* of the 1930's, which originally cost 15 to 25 cents, is worth $25 to $35 today.

"Most people look upon movie magazines as trash and throw them out," says Ben Friedman of Midtown Magazines, Inc., Maywood, N.J. "They save copies of *The National Geographic* instead.

They look so nice lined up on a shelf. But it's the old movie magazines that are what's valuable today. *The National Geographic*
doesn't appreciate in price." There's a reason for this. As *The Wall
Street Journal* pointed our recently, *The National Geographic* sells
its own back issues and when there's a demand for a particular issue
they reprint it.

Magazines of a scientific or technical nature gain steadily in value
for the date of issue, although the yearly gains are small. *Scientific
American, Architectural Forum* and *Fortune* are examples of these.
There is a constant demand for magazines like *Life, Time,* and *The
New Yorker*, but it takes years for publications of this type to reach
even their respective cover prices in value.

Old comic books, on the other hand, have immense value. Issues
of *Batman, Superman, The Detective* and *Plastic Man* from the late
1930's and early 1940's can bring $100 to $150. The first issue of
Batman sells for $300.

Where do you purchase back issues of magazines? From subscribers who save them; from publishers who want to unload re-
turns from news dealers or surplus press runs, and occasionally
from libraries after they have put them on microfilm.

Where do you sell them? There's the rub. Secondhand magazine
dealers buy bulk quantities if the magazines are in good condition,
not cut or torn. But they pay little. Look in your Yellow Pages
under "Magazines-Back Number" for a listing of dealers in your
area.

The best prices are paid by collectors. Look in the classified
advertisements in the collectors' newspapers (listed on page 76) to
obtain the names and addresses of comic-book collectors and Shirley Temple fans. Libraries sometimes purchase individual magazines to replace issues that have been pilfered or damaged, but
librarians usually deal with the back issue stores. Magazines simply
aren't a worthwhile medium for the serious investor.

Old newspapers or, more specifically historic newspapers, are
collected, too. The most prized are those that carry significant
headlines or stories and are dated prior to 1900.

Dealers in the field include:

Harrington's, 33 Cognewaug Rd., Cos Cob, Conn. 06807
Americana Mail Auction, 4015 Kilmer Ave., Allentown, Pa.,
18104
George Kane, Box 187, Los Gatos, Calif. 95031

The only publication covering the field exclusively is *The Newspaper Collector's Gazette* (c/o Barbara Stuhmuller, 259 Y St., Newburgh, N. Y. 12550). An annual subscription, 12 issues, is $3.

Summing Up

Intrinsic importance, the degree of scarcity and condition are what determine a book's value. Follow these suggestions when investing:

• Buy and sell through a reputable rare-book dealer; usually this means he will be a member of the Antiquarian Booksellers' Association of America.
• Seek first editions of works that possess literary merit. These are the books with the greatest investment potential.
• Specialize; invest in the books of only one author or a particular field of interest.

AUTOGRAPHS

When it comes to inflation-proofing your money, the signatures of the world's notables, both past and present, are every bit as effective as stamps, coins, rare books or any other collectible you might name, as long as you invest intelligently. Prices are easy to establish and dealers never hesitate to buy quality material.

The best way to obtain signatures is to buy them from established dealers, who function in much the same way as rare-book dealers. But the field is unique in that you can also "create" valuable material. If you're canny and persistent, you can obtain prize autographs and the price of a postage stamp will be your only cost.

The word "autograph" is somewhat misleading, at least when applied to investing. Dealers are seldom interested in buying or selling mere signatures. Instead, they trade in autograph *material,* which refers to letters, documents, diaries, early hand-drawn maps, printed handbills, broadsides and inscribed books. A signature in an autograph book or on a scrap of paper has no value. The greatest value attaches to letters and documents of former U.S. presidents, the signers of the Declaration of Independence, noted statesmen, generals, authors, composers or scientists.

There are no rigid rules to follow, however. Sometimes the letters and documents of notable persons of the past are of relatively little value because they are plentiful or not sought. Henry Wadsworth Longfellow used to send out as many as 70 autographs a day to his admirers. Likewise, the autographs of Samuel F. B. Morse, James Russell Lowell, Henry Clay, Daniel Webster and William Cullen Bryant exist in relatively large supply and are not expensive. On the other hand, the letters of Poe, Melville, Mark Twain and Emily Dickinson are avidly sought. Only six signatures of William Shakespeare arc known to exist and each is worth a fortune.

Autograph material from persons relatively unknown can be valuable, too. The letters and documents of Thomas Lynch, Jr., one of the signers of the Declaration of Independence, and Joseph Smith, founder of the Mormon Church, are highly prized. So are the signatures of Daniel Boone, Edgar Allen Poe, Nathan Hale and John Paul Jones.

Among the autographs of American presidents, the most sought after are those of Washington and Lincoln, with Jefferson a close third. But even the autographs of Eisenhower, Johnson and Nixon have value, and it is a fact that a full handwritten letter of President Kennedy is worth more than a similar letter of George Washington.

Of small investment value are letters or signed photos of stage, opera, or movie and television stars, sports heroes, popular singers, and contemporary minor literary or political figures. Facsimiles never have the slightest value.

How to Invest

When buying for investment, buy the finest material, advises Charles Hamilton, one of the country's foremost dealers. Buy the letters of Washington, Lincoln, Napoleon, Poe, Melville, and Hawthorne.

"Never compromise on quality," Hamilton declares. "If you cannot afford a good Poe letter, buy a good Longfellow letter. If you cannot afford a choice Washington letter, buy an excellent letter of Philip Schuyler."

Lucius S. Ruder was one of the most canny investor-collectors of recent years. His collection brought $382,154 at auction in 1966. His holdings were remarkably diverse, and included material from American presidents, leaders of the Old Northwest and Confederate leaders and generals. Quality was another hallmark of the collection. Ruder purchased only premium material.

You can speculate in the autograph market by purchasing material you feel will have future value. Will John O'Hara or John

Barth come to have the stature of Poe or Hawthorne?

Speculation can involve politics, too. Who will be the presidential candidates in 1976? Who will be elected that year? Be careful. During 1947 and the early months of 1948, more than a few dealers stocked up on the letters of Thomas Dewey, certain that the New York governor would defeat Harry Truman in the presidential election of 1948. Today Tom Dewey's signature is no more valuable than Tom Seaver's.

Don't limit yourself to one field. Diversify; build several different collections—music, art, Americana, science, exploration, World War I or II, Napoleon, Lincoln, Washington, war generals, etc. Study each of your fields carefully. Then you'll be able to recognize value.

Beware of fads, of people who are currently popular who can slip into obscurity. Follow your taste in making judgments.

The best way to become knowledgeable about autographs and market prices is to obtain dealers' catalogs and study them. Here is a listing of the country's more noted dealers:

Autographs, Coins and Currency, Inc., 37 South 18th St., Philadelphia, Pa.

Conway Barker, 1231 Sunset Lane, Box 35, La Marque, Tex. 77568.

Robert Batchelder, 1 West Butler Ave., Ambler, Pa., 19002.

David Batten Autographs, P. O. Box 2212, Fresno, Calif. 93720.

Walter R. Benjamin Autographs, 790 Madison Ave., New York, N. Y. 10021.

Robert K. Black, 109 Lorain Ave., Upper Montclair, N. J.

Maury A. Bromsen, 195 Commonwealth Ave., Boston, Mass.

Emily Driscoll, 175 Fifth Ave., New York, N. Y. 10010.

Bruce Gimelson, Fort Washington Industrial Park, Fort Washington, Pa., 19034.

Goodspeed's Book Shop, Inc., 18 Beacon St., Boston, Mass. 02108.

Charles H. Hamilton Autographs, Inc., 25 East 53rd St., New York, N. Y. 10022.

Doris H. Harris Autographs, Room 422, 6381 Hollywood Blvd., Los Angeles, Calif. 90028.

Paul F. Hoag, P. O. Box 257 Weatogue, Conn.

King V. Hostick, 901 South College, Springfield, Ill. 62704.

Kenneth W. Rendell, Inc., 626 Bristol Rd., Somerville, Mass. 02144.

Paul C. Richards, 233 Harvard St., Brookline, Mass. 02146.
George Rinsland, 4015 Kilmer Ave., Allerton, Pa. 18104.
The Scriptorium, 933 North LaCienega Blvd., Los Angeles, Calif.
Charles Sessler, Inc., 1308 Walnut St., Philadelphia, Pa.

Dealers in Europe include:

Folio Fine Art Ltd., 6 Stratford Pl., London, England.
Winifred A. Myers, Ltd., 80 New Bond St., London, England.
J. A. Stargardt, Universitats-Strasse 27, 355 Marburg, Germany.

Dealer catalogs describe available material and give prices for each item. Here are some typical listings:*

Julian Huxley. Letter signed on U. N. stationery May 1, 1946, about nationality of his sons. $17.50.

Arturo Toscanini. 3 autograph notes signed on stamped picture postcards. In Italian. Each $27.50.

Enrico Caruso. Long, remarkable autograph letter signed, Sept. 9, 1904. Explanation of attack upon both his personal and artistic dignity. In Italian. $65.

Jean Cocteau. Autograph letter signed Oct. 25, 1958. Mentions his holy man's (healer's) directives. Framed with addressed envelope and portrait. $85.

Martin Van Buren. Large concluding portion of engraved document signed as president May 17, 1841. Framed with engraved portrait. $100.

George B. McClellan. Autograph letter signed by the Union general Oct. 13, [1863-65] to Gov. Horatio Seymour of N.Y. Praises and requests promotion for his former A.D.C., Capt. N. B. Sweitzer. $115.

Bernard Shaw. Autograph manuscript signed with initials Feb. 22, 1935. Four 4to pages of holograph penciled, typically Shavian, replies to typewritten questions pertaining to transportation and roads: "If the Minister of Transport were capable of taking the wisest course, he could never get elected . . ." $175.

James Monroe. Impressive vellum document with seal, signed as president May 25, 1824. $250.

Henri Matisse. Interesting autograph letter signed Apr. 3, 1950. Tells about copying a large El Greco in the Prado. $250.

*Abbreviations used in these listings are as follows: A.L.S. (Autograph Letter Signed); L.S. (Letter Signed); A.D.S. (Autograph Document Signed); D.S. (Document Signed); A.Ms.S. (Autograph Manuscript Signed); A.Q.S. (Autograph Quotation Signed); A.N.S. (Autograph Note Signed); folio (a large sheet) 4to (about 8" x 10"); 8vo (about 5" by 7"); 16mo or 24mo (a small sheet).

Claude Monet. Unusual autograph letter signed Nov. 27, 1880, before his great fame. Makes a gracious plea for postponement of an already overdue payment. $275.

Theodore Roosevelt. Chatty, informal letter signed as president on White House stationery June 2, 1907. With corrections in his hand. $285.

Andrew Jackson. Highly important official document with perfect embossed presidential seal signed Mar. 21, 1829. Appoints his Tennessee friend Wm. B. Lewis (largely responsible for the Jackson-for-President movement) second auditor in the Treasury; making him a member of the famous Kitchen Cabinet. Countersigned by Jas. A. Hamilton, acting sec. of state. $475.

George Washington. Revolutionary War document signed June 8, 1783, discharges a corporal with 6 years of service. Countersigned by Jonathan Trumbull, Jr., with filled-in Badge of Merit. $1,575.

When you receive a catalog, scan the listings immediately and order at the earliest possible moment. The best material is often gone within 24 hours after the catalog is issued. But never take for granted that any item is sold. Always place an order if a particular item interests you.

When you buy from a reputable dealer, you don't have to be concerned about authenticity. Each item is guaranteed to be genuine.

Don't hesitate about patronizing the largest dealers. Often the biggest firms offer the best buys. A small dealer is more likely to overprice premium material. But a large firm is usually less in awe of quality items since it handles them more frequently.

The Charles Hamilton firm is the only one of its type in the United States to offer autographs at auction. Six or seven times a year dealers, collectors, and investors from every part of the world gather at New York's Waldorf Astoria Hotel to bid on material assembled by Mr. Hamilton and his staff.

An elaborate catalog describes each item in careful detail. A recent catalog listed 290 different items. Here are a few of the listings with the estimated prices for each item:

ADAMS, JOHN and John Marshall. Excessively rare manuscript vellum D.S. by both, 1 full page, oblong large folio, City of Washington, March 3, 1801. Appointment of Thomas Gibbon as judge of the district court of Georgia, "with the advice and consent of the Senate," boldly signed by Adams as President and by Marshall as acting secretary of state, with large U.S. paper seal. In extremely fine condition, this document was signed by Adams on the very day he left office as President and may well have been his last official act.   ($350.)

BURR, AARON. Vice-president; shot Alexander Hamilton in famous duel. A.L.S. "A. Burr," 1 full page, oblong small 4to, N(ew) York, July 17, 1817. To

R. W. Westcott of Philadelphia, with portion (about one-half) of integral address-leaf, ". . . no doubt the sale by Ross & Wilkins was a fraud; yet as I have actually paid about 14,000 in money, and as Field has often demanded of me the 1/2 of his . . . time etc. in attempting the settlement of those lands . . . I must participate in the benefit if any . . . We must therefore meet here . . . at 61 Vezey St. about 3 doors E. of Greenwich St; you will find in a small brick house, a small room & a most cordial welcome . . ." Worn, with transparent-paper repairs on blank verso, and a few small holes, but in very satisfactory condition. With an authentication by Walter R. Benjamin, 1936. Two pieces.   ($50.)

KENNEDY, JACQUELINE B. (ONASSIS). A.L.S. "Jacqueline Kennedy," as First Lady, 2 full pages, small 4to, on the blue-engraved stationery of The White House, Washington, June 28, (1962). To Miss Ellen Key Blunt of the *Washington Post*. With original White House envelope, addressed by Mrs. Kennedy, stamped and postmarked, Washington, D.C., June 29, 1962. Two pieces.   ($350.)

LINCOLN, ABRAHAM. Autograph Telegram Signed "A. Lincoln," as President, three-line on an oblong narrow 8vo sheet of printed stationery, Executive Mansion, Washington, June 13, 1863. To Major General (Joseph) HOOKER, marked "Cypher," in Lincoln's hand: "I was coming down this afternoon; but if you would prefer I should not, I shall blame you if you do not tell me so." Blank margins trimmed and lightly hinged to a 4to sheet.

The "A" of Lincoln's signature is scuffed and minutely retouched, else in extremely fine condition, the handwriting strong and dark. Published in Basler, Vol. VI, p. 271, wherein it is related that Hooker replied, "It may be well not to come," but that Lincoln had already departed and it was necessary for E. M. Stanton to order the tugboat stopped and Lincoln asked to return. An attractive display piece. ($1,200.)

NIXON, RICHARD M. President. L.S., almost 1 full page, 4to, on the engraved legal letterhead of Mudge, Stern, Baldwin & Todd, 20 Broad Street, New York City, October 29, 1963. To Martin W. Schwartz of the Student Center Policy Board of New York University, declining "to address the New York University student body . . . because of the heavy demands of my legal practice . . . I regret that this is the case because I know I would greatly enjoy the opportunity of being with you on the New York University campus . . ." Fine.   ($50.)

TRUMAN, HARRY S. L.S., about 3/4 page, small 4to, on his engraved letterhead, Independence, Missouri, September 27, 1963. To Walter B. Smalley, sending thanks for a clipping about Senator Strom Thurmond, ". . . who preferred to stand at his own desk when he found out he was going to stand at the one formerly used by me. He was the Senator who got up and left the room when I came in as President of the United States. So, you see he grew up with a discourteous dispostion. United States Senators really should be the most courteous of all public servants . . ." Very slightly soiled, with recipient's docket in blue ink on face, else fine.   ($50.)

Sincerely yours,

Harry Truman

Don't fail to obtain these auction catalogs. Keep them for reference along with the "list of prices realized" for each auction, which is available for $1 following the sale.

Autographs sold at auction by the Hamilton firm are "unconditionally guaranteed to be genuine." This is not likely to be the case, however, when you buy through a conventional auction house, like Parke-Bernet, for example. Most auction material is sold "as is." There is no guarantee that any item is genuine. If you're not an expert and unable to establish an item's authenticity yourself, it might be wise to let an autograph dealer bid for you. He will then guarantee the item. The charge for this service is usually ten percent of the purchase price.

At the Hamilton auction sales, some buyers use arcane methods to signal their bids, but the usual method is to simply raise your hand. The auctioneer will not let you bid against yourself.

You can also bid by mail. The Hamilton catalog features a bid sheet on which you can list the items you want and the highest amount you will bid for each. If this amount is not exceeded by a floor bid, the item is yours. You also "win" in the event your mail bid is equaled but not exceeded by floor bid.

If you have never bid by mail, you are required to send a 25 percent deposit with your bid, or furnish suitable references. No merchandise is shipped until full payment is received.

J. A. Stargardt (Universitats-Strasse 27, 355 Marburg, Germany), the largest autograph dealer in Europe, also conducts auction sales of worldwide importance. The firm accepts mail bids.

Their impressive catalog is almost the size of *Fortune* magazine. Write and request one.

Besides established dealers, there are a number of other sources you can utilize in obtaining signed material. These include rare book dealers, auction houses, and antique and curio dealers, but autograph dealers are your best source of supply.

Acquiring Autograph Material

Autographs that you obtain directly from famous people have investment value, too. The exact value depends on who signs what.

Says Charles Hamilton: "The collector-investor should use his imagination to get the subject to write a letter or sign a document, to do something that will give the signature historical value. A case in point is the signature of the late General Douglas MacArthur. "MacArthur lived a long life," says Mr. Hamilton, "and invariably presented his signature to anyone who requested it." It is not a rarity. But at one of his auctions, Hamilton offered MacArthur's signature on a typescript of the "Instrument of Surrender, Tokyo Bay, Japan, September 2, 1945." It brought $700.

President Lyndon Johnson's signature on the Gulf of Tonkin Resolution or a letter from Mrs. Marguerite Oswald containing comments about her son—this is the type of material that has value. The signature of a professional baseball player is about as worthwhile as an autograph from your milkman, but a New York dealer was able to offer Joe DiMaggio's signature at a nice price recently because it appeared on a souvenir card from the Baseball Hall of Fame.

Congressman Seymour Halpern of Forest Hills, New York, began collecting autographs as a youngster. His play is to draw a pen-and-ink sketch of the celebrity and request that it be signed. Few celebrities refuse him and many add humorous comments.

Halpern was aboard Air Force One on its flight from Dallas to Washington following the assassination of President Kennedy. He asked a secretary to type out a copy of the presidential oath on the plane's official stationery. He then requested President Johnson to sign the document. After some hesitation, Johnson did, and Congressman Halpern had a glittering prize. Again, what was signed was every bit as important as who signed it.

In writing and requesting autographs, Mr. Hamilton suggests that you learn something about the subject first. Your letter should then ask a question or make a request. If you're writing a well-known author, ask what advice he might give to young writers, or how he happened to start as an author. You could ask him to make some pointed comments about one of his more noted books.

Not everyone you write to is going to answer, of course. But a surprising number will. Poet Allan Ginsburg and novelist Henry Miller are likely to reply. Harry Truman is another who sometimes fulfills autograph requests. Eddie Rickenbacker does. German admiral Karl Doenitz is a prolific letter writer. Sometimes Picasso can be prevailed upon to reply, and even the tiniest of his sketches has immense value. The Nazi war criminals write. Salvador Dali is cooperative. Dr. Jonas Salk responds with handwritten notes.

"Don't worry about how you phrase the letter," says Charles Hamilton. "Just be honest and you will probably be successful."

Collectors of autographs, presidential autographs in particular, have to be wary of material produced by the Autopen, a robot device that has become the bane of collectors and dealers. A secretary or staff member operates the machine by depressing a foot pedal, which leaves the hands free to feed letters, documents or photos into the device.

According to Charles Hamilton, the Autopen was used by John F. Kennedy's staff many thousands of times. Richard Nixon, Lyndon Johnson, Mrs. Johnson, Vice-President Hubert Humphrey, Robert Kennedy, Edward Kennedy, and New York Governor Rockefeller allowed their aides to "sign" their correspondence by means of the Autopen. Hamilton reported on his investigations concerning the device in his book, *The Robot that Helped to Make a President*.

Each signature produced by the Autopen has minute variations, and therefore only the most able experts can distinguish a robot autograph from the real thing. But Autopen signatures are valueless.

PERIODICALS AND BOOKS

Manuscripts (1023 Amherst Dr., Tyler, Tex. 75701) is the leading publication for autograph collectors. It is a quarterly magazine with the same general dimensions as the *Reader's Digest*, and features articles that are somewhat scholarly in nature. "The Grant-Lee Surrender Correspondence" and "The Lure of Musical Autographs" were recent articles.

You can also enhance your knowledge of the field by becoming a member of the Manuscript Society, an organization of approximately one thousand collectors. One of its purposes is to "encourage the meeting of autograph collectors and stimulate and aid them in their various collection specialities."

Membership dues are $10 a year. For more information, write: Kenneth W. Duckett, Executive Secretary, The Manuscript Society, Morris Library, Southern Illinois University, Carbondale, Ill. 62901.

These books will be of interest if you're planning to invest in autographs:

Collecting Autographs and Manuscripts by Chares Hamilton (University of Oklahoma Press, $8.95). This is a comprehensive discussion of every aspect of buying, selling and collecting. It contains close to one thousand facsimile signatures.

Scribblers and Scoundrels by Charles Hamilton (Paul S. Erikson, Inc., New York, N. Y. $6.95). Mr. Hamilton's adventures as a dealer are covered here, but it also discusses buying from dealers, buying at auction and how to collect for investment profit.

Autograph Collector, a New Guide by Robert Notlep (Crown Publishers, $4.95).

From the White House Inkwell; American Presidential Autographs by John M. Taylor (Charles Tuttle & Co., Rutland, Vt. $10).

Summing Up

When investing in autograph material—letters, documents and other items of historical importance—follow these tips:

* Specialize in several different fields.
* Write for dealers' catalogs and study them carefully.
* Buy quality material.
* Buy from established dealers. Be sure your purchases are guaranteed to be authentic.

OTHER COLLECTIBLES

I know a young man in Springfield, Massachusetts, who has been collecting German military orders and badges for more than ten years. He's been extremely clever in building up his collection, avoiding dealers in the United States and the high prices he feels they charge, and buying instead from German war veterans whom he has been successful in contacting through classified advertisements he's placed in obscure, right-wing German newspapers. In the last few years he's seen most of the thousands of items in his collection double in value and they will probably double again in the next few years. If he had put his money into blue-chip stocks, he would not have done as well.

As this suggests, there are other items, besides stamps, coins, books and autographs that do offer investment potential. They include:

Indian artifacts
barbed wire
bottles and jars
tokens and medals
electric insulators
guns and ammunition
clocks and watches
buttons and badges
dolls
costumes
antique automobiles
military relics
minerals and gemstones
swords and edged weapons

This is only a partial list. While most of these do offer investment opportunity, they are more for the collector, the hobbyist, the person who gains pleasure from simply owning and treasuring such objects, and is not necessarily interested in their dollar value. For the most part, these items do not meet the criteria set down in the opening paragraphs of this chapter.

If you are interested in any of the above-listed fields, consult a collector's publication for more information. These include:

Collectors' Den (Box 5525, San Antonio, Tex. 78201), one year, 12 issues, $3.

Collectors News (Box 156, Grundy Center, Ia. 50638), one year, 12 issues, $3.

Collector's Weekly (Kermit, Tex. 79745), one year, 52 issues, $4; sample copy, 35¢.

The Flea Marketeer (800 W. 7 Mile Rd., Detroit, Mich. 48023), one year, 12 issues, $2.50; sample copy, 35¢.

Hobbies, The Magazine for Collectors (1006 So. Michigan Ave., Chicago, Ill. 60605), one year, 12 issues, $5; sample copy, 50¢.

Below are listed collectors' publications of a specialized nature:

Antique Automobile, (West Derry Rd., Hershey, Pa. 17033), the official publication of the Antique Automobile Club of America, one year, six issues, $5.

Car Classics (Western Trails Publishing Company, 6660 Reseda Blvd., Reseda, Calif. 91335), one year, six issues, $3.

Doll Castle News (Castle Press Publications, Brass Castle, Washington, N. J. 07882) one year, six issues, $2.50.

Gem and Minerals (P. O. Box 687, Mentone, Calif. 92359), one year, 12 issues, $4.50.

Just Buttons (Sally Lewis House, Southington, Conn. 06489), one year, 12 issues, $3.50.

The Medal Collector (500A Guys Run Rd., RD #2, Cheswick, Pa. 15024), official publication of the Orders and Medals Society of America, one year, 12 issues, $7.

The Pontil (c/o Don Smith, 4624 T St., Sacramento, Calif. 95819), official publication of the Antique Bottle Collectors Association, sample copy free on request.

Shotgun News (Snell Publishing Co., Columbus, Neb. 68601) one year, 24 issues, $3.

3 • Art and Antiques

Late in February 1970 at an auction at Parke-Bernet Galleries in New York City, buyers spent $5,852,250 for 72 impressionist and modern paintings. The biggest sale was Von Gogh's *Le Cypres en l'Arbre en Fleurs,* a relatively small canvas—20 ¼ by 25 ½ inches —and not one of the artist's more highly regarded works. Yet it went for $1.3 million, more than three times the previous record for a Van Gogh. A sum of $230,000, which was paid for a minor Matisse, *Fête de Fleurs a Nice,* was more than double the record price set for a Matisse only a year before.

It is not just the work of the French Impressionists that is skyrocketing in value. According to *The London Times*-Sotheby art index (which is based on the prices paid at the auction houses of Sotheby's, Christie's, Parke-Bernet and when possible, the Paris sales rooms), the prices of British eighteenth- and nineteenth-century paintings multiplied more than ten times between 1951 and 1968; the twentieth-century European paintings, 19 ½ times; and the seventeenth-century Italian paintings, 33 times.

Thus ruthless demand for fine art, apparent for decades now, shows no sign of weakening. One reason for this is that more Americans are art conscious today than ever before. Before World War II, there were about twenty art museums in the country; today there are about ten times that number. But the overriding factor is that the available supply of art cannot be replenished. When what remains is gone, there will be no more. It's as simple as that.

The Learning Process

You do not have to be backed by the Mellon family to invest in art. Not at all. There are countless opportunities for people with modest budgets. What you do have to have is an eye for art. You must train yourself to be able to recognize style, method and detail. You must be able to perceive quality.

As a young man, Joseph Duveen, who was to become the world's most renowned art dealer, once asked permission of his Uncle Henry to make a presentation to J. Pierpont Morgan. The uncle, aware of Morgan's astuteness, gave grudging approval.

The youthful Joseph assembled a group of thirty miniatures, six of the finest quality and twenty-four of only modest value. He scattered the fine ones among those of little merit, hoping to sell them all. Morgan examined the collection casually and asked how much for the entire lot. As soon as Joseph named the price, Morgan quickly picked out the six choice miniatures and slipped them into his pocket. Then—calculating aloud—he divided Joseph's price by thirty, multiplied by six, and announced that that was the amount he was paying. The chagrined Joseph could only agree.

To develop the discerning eye of J. P. Morgan, map out an educational program for yourself. Begin at your local museums. Plan visits in advance. Read about the artists or exhibitions featured. Inquire as to when lecture tours are scheduled and check on the availability of Audio-Guide tours, those tape-recorded lectures that can be rented for about fifty cents.

You'll reap a great many benefits from a museum membership. Usually they are of modest cost, ranging from $15 to $25. Besides the opportunity to enjoy the permanent collection and traveling exhibitions, a membership often includes special lectures and film programs and the chance to purchase catalogs and museum-published books at substantially reduced sums. Often a membership also includes a free subscription to the museum's monthly bulletin.

Many museums offer special services to those interested in purchasing art, such as lectures by art experts and advice by museum curators on what to buy. Some museums go further and help to organize collectors' clubs. Members receive a wide array of benefits to help them make wise art purchases.

More and more museums are selling art. Although you will rarely see a price on a museum-exhibited painting, one that is labeled "lent by the artist" or "on loan from XYZ Gallery" is invariably for sale. Of course, some museums have their own galleries—the Museum of Modern Art is one—where original art of high quality is on display and unabashedly offered for purchase. Sometimes the works can be rented with an option to buy.

The Handbook of American Museums, published by the American Association of Museums (Smithsonian Institution, Washington, D. C. 20560) gives comprehensive descriptions of both the art and science museums in the United States, and can prove a useful reference book to museums in your own community and also to those in cities you may be planning to visit. It's a bargain at $8.

The Traveler's Guide to America's Art by Jane and Theodore Norman ($8.95 Meredith Press, 250 Park Ave., New York, N. Y. 10017) is similarly helpful. In the case of New York City, obtain a copy of *Museums of New York City,* published by the City's Museums Council. It's free. Request a copy from the Office of the Secretary, The American Museum of Natural History, Central Park West at 79th St., New York, N. Y. 10024.

Visiting galleries is another way to increase your knowledge. "Don't forget," says Joanna Eagle in *Buying Art on a Budget* "that galleries are basically stores with merchandise to sell." As in any store, you're entirely welcome. Occasionally a gallery will charge a small fee, usually in the case of a special exhibition, but almost all have no admission charge.

In some ways galleries can be of even more value to you than museums. For one thing the dealer will be happy to give you information about prices. Don't hesitate to ask what things cost.

Be frank with the dealer. He can be a valuable contact. If you're only on an information-gathering expedition, tell him. He may recommend other sources of information. If you are planning on making a purchase, tell him how much money you have to spend.

Whenever you visit a gallery, be sure to sign the register so you will be placed in the gallery's mailing list to receive announcements of forthcoming exhibitions. Or ask the dealer to put you on the list to receive such notices.

Slide reproductions offer you another method of getting to know great art. The best of these show each work in its original size and reproduce colors with outstanding fidelity. McGraw-Hill Company, Inc. (330 West 42nd St., New York, N. Y. 10036) is one of the leading companies in this field. Inquire about their color-slide program for art enjoyment.

Exhibition catalogs are another way of becoming more informed about the art field. Scan the art magazines (pages 100–1) for news of exhibitions and write for the catalogs you feel will be the most helpful. Save the catalogs. They're important reference sources.

Buying for Investment

Prices for oil paintings are almost always quite steep, and unless you are an exception you are not going to be buying "names." But that really doesn't matter. There are countless investment opportunities if you're willing to do your homework, then search and shop.

There are works of Dutch painters of the seventeenth century available at reasonable prices. Many of them, from the all-important aspect of quality, rank very high.

Works by artists of the mid-nineteenth-century French Barbizon school are expected to sharply appreciate in value over the next decade. Prices are now in the $1,000 to $7,500 range.

More than one dealer will tell you there are "sleepers" to be found among the artists representing the Italian baroque period of the late sixteenth and seventeenth centuries. Caravaggio, the Carracis and Cavallino were among the giants of this school, but there are scores of unpublicized but greatly skilled artists of this period whose paintings can be purchased for modest sums.

The market for British painters of the eighteenth century was relatively quiet during the 1960's. This period includes great portraitists like Gainsborough, Reynolds, Romney, Lawrence and Hoppner, and brilliant landscapists—Constable, Crome and Wilson. While the works of these artists are priced at high levels, there are paintings by their contemporaries available at nominal prices.

Last, there are splendid opportunities in nineteenth-century and early twentieth-century American art. The landscapes by members of the Hudson River School and other regional artists are an example. The works of American Prairies Painters, best typified by the action-filled paintings of Frederic Remington, and the American primitives, are steadily escalating in value.

The contemporary field of art is the biggest of all and presents the greatest challenge to your taste and judgment. Be wary. Too many collectors are overinfluenced by what is fashionable. Styles of contemporary art, like Christmas, come and go. It is generally agreed that Pop was the most important art movement of the 1960's. (There were also optical art, color-field painting, minimal sculpture, kinetic sculpture and earth works.) But by the end of the decade, critic John Canaday of *The New York Times* declared, "Pop in its pure form is said to be a goner . . . ." Stay away from whatever is faddish.

There should be some diversity in the way you invest. Don't put your entire budget into one work of art. Acquire several.

While there is nothing wrong in specializing in one medium, it's wrong to buy the works of only one artist. Like schoolteachers and vacuum-cleaner salesmen, artists occasionally have bad days. Select the best from a number of artists.

When seeking to establish a painting's value, the first question to ask is, "Who painted it?" Establishing the name of the artist is only one aspect of this matter, however. The painting should also truly characterize the artist in order to bring a top price.

Renoir was renowned for his skill as a colorist, but his later paintings do not always show this particular talent and they are generally less valuable than the others. Or take Gauguin. The paintings he executed in Tahiti which depict Tahitian women against bright backgrounds are regarded as the most typically Gauguin. Earlier paintings that he did in France are much less colorful, thus less "Gauguin-ish," and not so highly prized.

Almost as important as who painted it and how typical of the artist is the painting is the attribute of quality. "Quality is the essence of art value," says Richard H. Rush in *Art as an Investment.* "For a painting to be worth anything it must have quality. A fine painting speaks for itself. It radiates beauty and beauty is an integral part of quality. It exhibits a mastery that cannot fail to be recognized."

Recently I spoke to a collector who esteems the work of American artist Jacob Lawrence. "Lawrence hasn't been promoted like many American artists and his paintings are not at all expensive," the collector pointed out. "Yet Lawrence is original; he makes a statement. His work has quality. Someday Lawrence will be held in high esteem. It *has* to happen."

It makes no difference whether the work is executed by a "name" artist. The selling price is not significant. Where or when the work was executed is not important. If it has quality, it will show through.

The subject matter and size of a painting are also important in establishing value. Generally, pictures with bright, pleasant colors sell faster than do those with dark and somber tones. Fine landscapes, flower paintings, still lifes, genre paintings, nudes, scenes from mythology—these subjects have universal appeal, or, at least, no discernible prejudices.

But scenes depicting funerals or cemeteries, or pictures of birds or slain animals, hurt a painting's value. In the case of portraits, those of the smallest value are ones in which the sitter is of no historical importance and the artist is unknown. At the other end of the scale are portraits of famous men or women painted by great artists. Rembrandt's self-portrait is the best example.

When it comes to the matter of size, a painting with the dimensions of 30 x 36 inches, or a bit smaller or larger, is the most desirable. Outsize paintings, too large to hang in an apartment or house, are not held in high esteem, although there are many exceptions.

Naturally, condition is a significant factor. If the painting has been damaged, restored or overcleaned its value is lessened.

It goes without saying that the painting must be established as authentic. And whether or not it bears the artist's signature is another factor. Artists of the seventeenth-century Dutch School usually signed their paintings, but Italian artists of the same century did not. An authentic signature adds greatly to a painting's value.

PRINTS AND OTHER MEDIUMS

If you are an investor with limited funds, consider the print field. Original lithographs, etchings, engravings, woodcuts and other works produced by artists in limited editions are probably the most available of all forms of art, and in recent years the investment potential of prints has been just as great as that of paintings.

At a Parke-Bernet auction of prints late in 1969, the top price was paid for a harsh-black-and-white Matisse lithograph. Titled "le Renard," it sold for $9,500. Five years before it could have been purchased for $750. Picasso's 100-etching edition of Vollard Suite, available in 1964 for $24,000, went for $140,000 at the same auction. Marked increases were apparent at the other end of the price scale, too. A Redon print being offered for $200-$300 in 1966 sold for $750.

The interest in prints has triggered a boom in printmaking, and there are said to be more than three thousand artists at work in the field. Each year brings an increased number of print exhibitions and competitions. More books are being published on the subject than ever before, and galleries devoted exclusively to prints are springing up everywhere.

In spite of the surging interest in prints, there still exists confusion as to what a print is. First of all, a print is a work of art, created and executed by the artist with all the originality and imagination that go into a painting or piece of sculpture. Such giants of art as Rembrandt, Botticelli, Brueghel, Rubens, Goya, Picasso and Klee are known primarily as painters, but they were printmakers as well. More than one art expert has said that Rembrandt's genius is most apparent in his etchings, which are types of prints.

In making a print the artist takes special inks or printmaking tools and draws a picture or an image directly onto stone, wood or metal. He then applies ink to the "plate" and transfers the image to paper or perhaps cloth, a task he may do himself or turn over to another professional. The last stage is when the artist inspects each print drawn from the plate and signs and numbers those that pass his inspection.

Each impression pulled from the stone, block or plate is an original. It is this concept of "multiple originals" that often confuses the novice art buyer.

Prints are not originals if they are mechanically reproduced. Mechanical reproductions of Picasso prints have flooded the country in recent years. You see them in frame shops, gift shops and Woolworth's—everywhere. Because modern printing methods are so sophisticated, it is sometimes difficult for the novice to tell an original print from a mechanical reproduction. That some artists, particularly contemporary printmakers, sign mechanically reproduced copies of their work adds to the confusion.

An artist uses one of four basic methods to create an original print, each one of which has an array of variations. Contemporary printmakers in particular have evolved new processes which have produced stunning effects.

Virtually everyone is familiar with the incised, or intaglio, process of printmaking. The printing areas are furrows or indentations cut or carved into the plate surface. The grooves fill with ink to form the image. Engraving, etching, mezzotint and aquatint are examples of the intaglio process.

The relief process is exactly the opposite. Here the surface material is cut away so as to project the image and provide the printing surface. The most familiar examples of the relief process are woodcuts and wood engravings, but linoleum, poster board and lucite are also used.

Lithography is a third method used to create prints. A relatively new printing process, lithography involves printing from a plane or flat surface which is neither raised or depressed. The image is drawn on a specially prepared stone or plate in such a way that it will absorb and print with special inks.

Virtually everyone is familiar with the fourth method used in printmaking—the stencil process. Inks or paints are applied to specially treated paper or other impervious material with perforations or cutout sections. The image comes through the perforations or cutouts to be printed on the surface against which the sheet rests. In printmaking, the process is known as serigraphy, and it is commonly referred to as the silk-screen process.

By way of summary, let me repeat the definition of a print as given by The Print Council of America. The council stresses that a print is a work of art and states that it must meet these three criteria:

• the creation of a master image by the artist alone on the plate, stone, woodblock or other material.

• the execution of the print by the artist or pursuant to his directions.

• the approval of the finished work by the artist himself.

Once you become knowledgeable about prints, you can buy from printmakers in your area. Call and make an appointment to visit the artist at his studio. This is no problem if you live in a large city. About one-half of the market for prints is in New York, while Los Angeles, Chicago, Philadelphia, San Francisco, Washington, D. C., Boston and Dallas account for most of the rest of the activity.

Old master prints are available in good supply, and even a Hogarth or a Daumier can be obtained for less than $50. Goya prints, pulled after his death, are priced in that general area, too.

Prices on most of the old master prints have not risen nearly as dramatically as more modern works. In some cases plates still exist and reprintings have been made from time to time, an obvious reason why values have remained depressed. There are aesthetic reasons, too. Many old master prints are limited in size, color, and have less visual appeal than modern prints. But the demand is increasing and the value is there.

The master American landscapists Winslow Homer and George Innes left a legacy of prints and drawings. So did American frontier painter George Catlin, impressionist Mary Cassatt, artists of social protest like Everett Shin and Arthur B. Carles, and landscape painters representative of the Hudson River School.

Some of the most innovative work in prints in recent years has involved lithography. The Tamarind Lithography Workshop, Inc. (112 N. Tamarind Ave., Los Angeles, Calif. 90038) and the

Tatyana Grosman Workshop (5 Skidmore Pl., West Islip, N. Y.), are among the most technically advanced lithographic printmakers in the country. Each has a wide following.

For more information and advice about prints and print buying, consult the many organizations devoted to the medium. The Print Council (575 Madison Ave., New York, N. Y. 10022) distributes a free pamphlet entitled, *What Is a Print,* publishes a listing of print exhibitions throughout the country three times a year, and distributes a roster of U.S. print dealers. The Print Council also publishes some excellent reference books on prints. The FAR Gallery (746 Madison Ave., New York, N. Y. 10022) distributes a helpful essay on prints entitled, *An Introduction to Fine Prints—A Guide for the Layman.* It's free.

The Associated American Artists (663 Fifth Ave., New York, N. Y. 10022) commissions prints from leading international printmakers and makes them available to members under a print-of-the-month-club type policy. Under the AAA's membership program, each sponsor member makes a $100 deposit, all of which is applicable to purchases from the association's offerings—past, present or future—for a membership year. Two signed prints are given free to each new member. Membership also includes a free subscription to the *Print Collector's Newsletter* and advance copies of all catalogs. The prints offered cover a wide range, from realistic and traditional to abstract and expressionistic.

There are scores of books available about prints and printmaking. Those mentioned below, written by experts, are among the most highly recommended titles:

The Book of Fine Prints by Carl Zigrosser (Crown Publishers) traces the development of prints from the earliest times to the present. It's a first rate introduction to the study of graphic arts. *Modern Prints and Drawings* by Paul J. Sachs (Macmillan) is also historical in nature and features splendid illustrations and an informative text.

The technical aspects of printmaking are covered in Gabor Peterdi's *Printmaking Methods Old and New* (The Macmillan Company), considered to be classic in the field, and S. W. Hayter's *About Printmaking* (Oxford University Press), which emphasizes modern techniques.

Drawings are another excellent investment medium for anyone with a limited budget. It's still possible to purchase a drawing by a famous artist for a tiny fraction of what one of his paintings would bring.

A drawing is any delineation of form with or without reference to color. There are many types. They range from delicate pencil lines to rough-toned charcoal. Drawings can also be executed in pen and ink, grease pencil, pastel crayons, colored chalk and sanguine pencil, and there are brush drawings, too.

A problem with drawings is that they are sometimes difficult to authenticate. In centuries past, it was not the practice to sign drawings.

For more information about collecting drawings, write to the Master Drawings Association (33 East 36th St., New York, N. Y. 10016). This is a membership association. One of the advantages of joining is the magazine, *Master Drawings*, a thorough and reliable review of the field that is published quarterly.

Sculpture is the art of producing works of art in three dimensions. Modeling and carving are the traditional types of sculpture, with wood and stone the traditional mediums. Modern-day sculptors are likely to weld or cast using one of a variety of metals or plastics.

Sculpture is generally expensive, but one way to circumvent the high prices is to concentrate on maquettes, the diminutive studies the scupltor creates in preparing the final work. A maquette is similar to the sketches or drawings a painter prepares before executing the finished version of his work. Sometimes a sculptor will prepare a whole series of maquettes, each one displaying the technical skill and aesthetic quality of the completed work.

The Art Dealers Association of America

No matter what type of art interests you, prints, paintings or sculpture, buy from a responsible dealer, a man or woman with an established reputation in the art field.

When buying a piece of art, it's common practice to have the dealer write detailed information as to what has been purchased on the bill of sale. This includes the name of the artist, the medium, the year the work was executed and any other pertinent details. (This also pertains to the purchase of antiques.) This is your *guarantee*. If the object turns out to be something less than was represented, the dealer is obliged to take the article back and refund your money.

Before making a purchase, establish that the dealer is a member of the Art Dealers Association of America. This assures that you will be buying from a gallery that has been in operation for at least five years, and has won a reputation for honesty and integrity in dealing with the general public, museums, artists and other dealers. Further, the member-gallery will have had established itself as a true *art* dealer rather than merely a dealer in "pictures."

Here is a list of the members of the Art Dealers Association of America:

A.C.A. GALLERIES
63 East 57th St.
New York, N. Y. 10022

Representational American paintings and drawings: contemporary as well as late 19th and early 20th centuries

ACQUAVELLA GALLERIES, INC.
18 East 79th St.
New York, N. Y. 10021

Old master, impressionist, post-impressionist and contemporary paintings

ASSOCIATED AMERICAN ARTISTS, INC.
663 Fifth Ave.
New York, N. Y. 10022

Original etchings, lithographs and woodcuts, 15th through 20th centuries

BABCOCK GALLERIES
805 Madison Ave.
New York, N. Y. 10021

American painting of the 19th and 20th centuries

BODLEY GALLERY
787 Madison Ave.
New York, N. Y. 10021

Contemporary works of art; modern master drawings; works by surrealist masters

LA BOETIE, INC.
1042 Madison Ave.
New York, N. Y. 10021

20th-century European and American paintings, sculpture and drawings; international native art; graphics by masters

GALERIA BONINO, LTD.
7 West 57th St.
New York, N. Y. 10019

Contemporary paintings and sculpture

BORGENICHT GALLERY
1018 Madison Ave.
New York, N. Y. 10021

Contemporary painting and sculpture

LEO CASTELLI GALLERY
4 East 77th St.
New York, N. Y. 10021

Vanguard American painting and sculpture

GALERIE CHALETTE
9 East 88th St.
New York, N. Y. 10028

20th-century European and American paintings, drawings and sculpture

CORDIER & EKSTROM, INC.
980 Madison Ave.
New York, N. Y. 10 21

Contemporary painting and sculpture

DAVIS GALLERIES
231 East 60th St.
New York, N. Y. 10022

19th- and 20th-century American works of art; 19th-century English watercolors and drawings

PETER DEITSCH GALLERY
24 East 81st St.
New York, N. Y. 10028

Rare original prints and drawings 19th and 20th centuries

TIBOR de NAGY GALLERY
29 West 57th St.
New York, N. Y. 10019

Contemporary art, both abstract and representational

THE DOWNTOWN GALLERY
465 Park Ave.
New York, N. Y. 10022

Modern American masters' paintings, sculpture and graphics; American folk art

DWAN GALLERY, INC.
29 West 57th St.
New York, N. Y. 10019

Contemporary paintings and sculpture

ROBERT ELKON GALLERY
1063 Madison Ave.
New York, N. Y. 10028

Contemporary painting and sculpture; 20th-century masters

ANDRE EMMERICH GALLERY, INC.
41 East 57th Street
New York, N. Y. 10022

Contemporary American and European art; pre-Columbian art; ancient Greek art

FAIRWEATHER-HARDIN GALLERY
101 East Ontario St.
Chicago, Ill. 60611

Contemporary paintings, sculpture and graphics

FAR GALLERIES, INC.
746 Madison Ave.
New York, N. Y. 10021

Graphic art—original lithographs, etchings, woodcuts, etc.; drawings, sculpture and paintings by contemporary European and American artists

JOSEPH FAULKNER
MAIN STREET GALLERIES
646 North Michigan Ave.
Chicago, Ill. 60611

Turn-of-the-century and 20th-century American and European paintings and sculpture; ethnic art; graphics

RICHARD L. FEIGEN & CO., INC.
27 East 79th St.
New York, N. Y. 10021

Masters of the 19th and 20th centuries, and the new generation

FINDLAY GALLERIES
11-13 East 57th St.
New York, N. Y. 10022

European painting of the 19th and 20th centuries

FLAIR GALLERY
113 West 4th St.
Cincinnati, O. 45202

20th-century American and European painting, sculpture and graphics

FORUM GALLERY
1018 Madison Ave.
New York, N. Y. 10021

American paintings and sculpture

LUCIEN GOLDSCHMIDT, INC.
1117 Madison Ave.
New York, N. Y. 10028

Drawings, prints, illustrated books

JAMES GOODMAN GALLERY
55 East 86th St.
Apt #15B
The Park Lane
33 Gates Circle
Buffalo, N. Y. 14209

20th-century American and European drawings, watercolors and sculpture

GRAND CENTRAL
ART GALLERIES, INC.
Hotel Biltmore
40 Vanderbilt Ave.
New York, N. Y. 10017

Principally 19th-and 20th-century realistic American art

RICHARD GRAY GALLERY
620 North Michigan Ave.
Chicago, Ill. 60611

19th and 20th centuries and new generation paintings, sculpture and drawings; architectural sculpture

STEPHEN HAHN GALLERY
960 Madison Ave.
New York, N. Y. 10021

French paintings of the 19th and 20th centuries

DALZELL HATFIELD GALLERIES
Ambassador Hotel
Ambassador Station, Box K
Los Angeles, Calif. 90070

French and German painting of the 19th and 20th centuries; American art; sculpture and 20th-century graphics; modern Aubusson tapestries

B. C. HOLLAND, INC.
224 East Ontario St.
Chicago, Ill. 60611

19th- and 20th-century paintings, drawings and sculpture

HUTTON-HUTSCHNECKER GALLERY, INC.
967 Madison Ave.
New York, N. Y. 10021

Specializing in Fauves, German and Russian expressionists; sculpture

IRVING GALLERIES, INC.
400 East Wisconsin Ave.
Milwaukee, Wis. 53202

Contemporary American and European paintings, sculpture and original graphics

MARTHA JACKSON GALLERY
32 East 69th St.
New York, N. Y. 10021

International contemporary paintings, sculpture and graphics

SIDNEY JANIS GALLERY
15 East 57th St.
New York, N. Y. 10022

Three generations of modern art from cubism to pop

KENNEDY GALLERIES, INC.
20 East 56th St.
New York, N. Y. 10022

American paintings, sculpture and graphics of the 18th, 19th, and 20th centuries

M. KNOEDLER & CO. INC.
14 East 57th St.
New York, N. Y. 10022

Paintings and sculpture of all periods

KRAUSHAAR GALLER-   Paintings, sculpture and drawings by
IES   20th-century American artists
1055 Madison Ave.
New York, N. Y. 10028

LANDAU-ALAN GALLERY   Contemporary American paintings,
766 Madison Ave.   sculpture, drawings and collages
New York, N. Y. 10021

FELIX LANDAU GAL-   European and American 20th-century
LERY   painting and sculpture
702 North LaCienega Blvd.
Los Angeles, Calif. 90069

LEFEBRE GALLERY   Contemporary painting and sculpture
47 East 77th St.
New York, N. Y. 10021

R.M. LIGHT &CO., INC.   Fine prints and drawings
190 Marlborough St.
Boston, Mass. 02116

LOCK GALLERIES   Fine paintings of all schools
20 East 67th St.
New York, N. Y. 10021

ALBERT LOEB & KRUGIER   Painting and sculpture of the 19th and
GALLERY   20th centuries; contemporary Ameri-
119 East 57th St.   can and European art
New York, N. Y. 10022

MAKLER GALLERY   Paintings, sculpture and graphics
1716 Locust St.
Philadelphia, Pa. 19103

MARLBOROUGH-GERSON GAL-   American and European paintings;
LERY, INC.   drawings and sculpture of all periods;
41 East 57th St.   graphics of contemporary masters
New York, N. Y. 10022

PIERRE MATISSE GALLERY   Contemporary paintings and sculpture
CORP.
41 East 57th St.
New York, N. Y. 10022

MIDTOWN GALLERIES
11 East 57th St.
New York, N. Y. 10022

Contemporary American art; paintings, sculpture and graphics

THE MILCH GALLERY
1014 Madison Ave.
New York, N. Y. 10021

American paintings and watercolors of the 19th and 20th centuries

BORIS MIRSKI GALLERY
166 Newbury St.
Boston, Mass. 02116

Contemporary American art; European sculpture of the 19th and 20th centuries; Asiatic and primitive art

FREDERICK MONT, INC.
465 Park Ave.
New York, N. Y. 10022

Fine paintings by old masters

DONALD MORRIS GALLERY
20082 Livernois
Detroit, Mich. 48221

20th-century American and European art

NEWHOUSE GALLERIES, INC.
15 East 57th St.
New York, N. Y. 10022

Fine paintings

ODYSSIA
41 East 57th St.
New York, N. Y. 10022

Contemporary painting and sculpture

OEHLSCHLAEGER GALLERIES
107 East Oak St.
Chicago, Ill. 60611

Contemporary American and European paintings and sculpture

PACE GALLERY OF NEW YORK,
INC.
32 East 57th St.
New York, N. Y. 10022

Contemporary painting and sculpture

BETTY PARSONS GALLERY
24 West 57th St.
New York, N. Y. 10019

Contemporary painting, sculpture and prints

PERIDOT GALLERY
820 Madison Ave.
New York, N. Y. 10021

Contemporary American paintings and sculpture; contemporary master drawings

PERLS GALLERIES
1016 Madison Ave.
New York, N. Y. 10021

Paintings and sculptures by 20th-century French and American masters

FRANK PERLS
9777 Wilshire Blvd.
Beverly Hills, Calif. 90212

Contemporary paintings, drawings, sculpture, graphics

POINDEXTER GALLERY
21 West 56th St.
New York, N. Y. 10019

Contemporary painting and sculpture, primarily American

FRANK REHN GALLERY
655 Madison Ave.
New York, N. Y. 10021

Contemporary American paintings, watercolors and drawings

PAUL ROSENBERG & CO.
20 East 79th St.
New York, N. Y. 10021

French paintings of the 19th and 20th centuries; contemporary American and European paintings and sculpture

ROSENBERG & STIEBEL, INC.
32 East 57th St.
New York, N. Y. 10022

Paintings and other works of art; furniture; porcelains

SAIDENBERG GALLERY
1035 Madison Ave.
New York, N. Y. 10021

20th-century European and American paintings; sculpture and graphic art

BERTHA SCHAEFER GALLERY
41 East 57th St.
New York, N. Y. 10022

Contemporary American and European painting and sculpture

ROBERT SCHOELKOPF GALLERY
825 Madison Ave.
New York, N. Y. 10021

19th- and 20th-century American paintings, sculpture and photography

SEIFERHELD AND COMPANY, INC.
158 East 64th St.
New York, N. Y. 10021

Old-master drawings, paintings and other works of art

CHARLES E. SLATKIN, INC., GALLERIES
115 East 92nd St.
New York, N. Y. 10028

Old- and modern-master drawings; French paintings of 19th and 20th centuries; modern sculpture; French and American tapestries

STAEMPFLI GALLERY, INC.
47 East 77th St.
New York, N. Y. 10021

Contemporary American and European painting and sculpture

DAVID STUART GALLERIES
807 North LaCienega Blvd.
Los Angeles, Calif. 90069

Contemporary painting and sculpture; pre-Columbian, ancient and primitive art

E. V. THAW & CO., INC.
525 Park Ave.
New York, N. Y. 10021

Master paintings and drawing of all periods

VALLEY HOUSE GALLERY
6616 Spring Valley Rd.
Dallas, Tex. 65240

Paintings and sculpture of the 19th and 20th centuries

WEYHE GALLERY
794 Lexington Ave.
New York, N. Y. 10021

Specialists in fine prints; sculpture, drawings and paintings

WILLARD GALLERY, INC.
29 East 72nd St.
New York, N. Y. 10021

Painting and sculpture, chiefly contemporary American

HOWARD WISE GALLERY
50 West 57th St.
New York, N. Y. 10019

Contemporary art with emphasis on kinetic and light art

ZABRISKIE GALLERY
699 Madison Ave.
New York, N. Y. 10021

Contemporary painting and sculpture; earlier American painting and sculpture

Buying at Auctions

Auctions are another good way to buy art—as long as you follow certain tried and proven techniques.

Your local newspaper and the art publications mentioned on pages 100–1 contain information about upcoming auctions, and most auction firms (listed in your Yellow Pages under "Auction-eers") send out bulletins announcing sales.

Another good source of news is the magazine *Auction*. A monthly publication, it presents articles on painting, prints, books and antique furniture by specialists in each field. In addition, it gives prices received at recent auctions, both in this country and in Europe. A yearly subscription is $8. To order, write Parke-Bernet Galleries, Inc., 980 Madison Ave., New York, N. Y. 10021.

Art-auction catalogs are an unrivaled source of information. At Parke-Bernet, each catalog is prepared with meticulous care and features detailed descriptions of each work. Parke-Bernet's cata-logs, incidentally, are available individually or by annual subscrip-tion. Write for an order form. These catalogs have become so popular among dealers and collectors they now represent from 15 to 20 percent of the gallery's annual income.

Don't hesitate about attending auctions at the larger and more noted galleries. At Parke-Bernet, which offers the country's most elegant art-auction facilities, almost two-thirds of all pieces sold at auction go for less than $300, and 15 percent for under $50.

Once you become interested in a specific sale, obtain a catalog in advance of the sale date. Then visit the auction house in the days before the sale to examine the objects. Personnel of the auction house will be on hand to answer your questions and give you estimates of the anticipated prices on each object. Be sure to obtain an estimate for each item that interests you. "The pre-sale estimates are guides to bidding," says Parke-Bernet. "They are the Galleries' approximate valuations but should not be misconstrued as 'prices,' for the final bid may be less than, or more than, the quoted esti-mate."

In almost every case, the objects being auctioned are from private sources, with the auction house serving merely as the sales agent, the middleman. And while every effort is made to authenticate each object, you receive no guarantee of authenticity when you buy at auction. It is strictly a case of *caveat emptor*.

Parke-Bernet expresses its policy in these terms: "The Galleries . . . assume no risk, liability or responsibility for the authenticity of any property identified in this catalogue. . . . All property is sold 'as is' and neither the Galleries nor the Consignor makes any warranties or representation of any bid with respect to the prop-erty. . . ."

Auction bidding is frequently exciting and it's easy to become caught up in the unfolding drama, bidding more than you intended.

Set a ceiling price for every item that interests you. Jot it down in your catalog so you won't forget it.

The bidding opens when the auctioneer announces the opening bid and someone meets it. To enter a bid, you simply raise your hand, although many dealers and experienced bidders use elaborate signal systems. Parke-Bernet gives this advice to new bidders:

Take a seat; make yourself comfortable. Follow the auctioneer's lead on units of advance. Raise your hand in a definite signal when you wish to enter a bid, directing the signal either to the auctioneer in the rostrum or to one of the attendants in the salesroom—it's their job to relay bids to the rostrum. Bit promptly, right from the beginning. We won't let you bid against yourself.

There's no necessity to bid from the start, and the more experienced bidders often wait until they have a "feel" of how the bidding is going before jumping in. You can delay bidding right up until the auctioneer announces, "Fair warning," the indication that he is about to "knock down" the object and declare it "Sold!"

If you're unable to attend an auction sale in person, you can leave an "order bid" with the dealer. He will then execute the bid in competition with others he may have received and with those submitted in the auction room at the time of the sale. Your bid will not be exceeded, and if the bidding does not reach the amount of your order, you will be awarded the item for less.

Getting Appraisals

When you are contemplating the purchase of a high-priced piece of art or an antique, it's wise to get an objective, authoritative opinion. You can do this by contacting a member of the Appraiser's Association of America, Inc., an organization of 530 experts in 125 cities in 30 states, each of whom devotes a good part of his or her (there are 30 women members) time answering the question, "What is this worth?"

Association members offer their opinions in fields largely confined to furnishings and the fine and decorative arts, but their expertise can also cover more than 150 different classifications, ranging from engraved tableware and pressed glass to mahogany highboys. They appraise Buffalo pottery, Indian relics and antique automobiles, virtually anything.

Members of the association are chosen on the basis of their professional and personal integrity as well as for their expert knowledge. The great majority have long years of experience in buying and selling in their field, and many are scholars as well as collectors.

How much does it cost to have an object appraised? It depends —on the size and value of the object, and the amount of time and travel involved. Some appraisers work on a per diem basis of $100. Fees in the East are higher than in the Midwest. Some appraisers have refused a fee when the object under scrutiny has turned out to be valueless.

The appraiser's association was established in 1947 by Jules S. Schwimmer, now secretary-treasurer. Prior to that time anyone who felt he knew more than the average person about a particular field could establish himself as an appraiser since there was no licensing.

The services of a professional appraiser are useful in a number of ways. They help to establish values for insurance purposes, or depreciation losses in connection with tax or insurance claims. Often his services are sought before a liquidation, not just a contemplated purchase.

For a list of members write the association's office, 663 Fifth Ave., New York, N.Y. 10022, and request a catalog. It costs $1.

Factory Art

The burgeoning market in art has spawned an outpouring of original inexpensive paintings, some of which may be on sale at your local five-and-ten or even the supermarket. Some refer to this as commercial art; others call it shlock art. Whatever the name, stay away from it.

This mass-produced art is turned out by one of a growing number of art "factories," some in this country but most abroad. They do produce "original" paintings, if by the word original you mean not a copy. But there is nothing at all creative about such works. Usually each piece of commercial art represents the labor of several specialists—one man sketches in the basic design in charcoal, another paints in the lakes and anything else of a marine nature, a third does the mountains and other features of the landscape, and a fourth fashions any living creatures that might be necessary. (Humans are rare; ducks, horses and cows are very popular.) Then somebody signs the canvas to give it "authenticity."

According to a recent article in *New York Magazine,* a commercial art factory in Leopoldsburg, Belgium, employs almost one hundred artists and "manufactures" some 6,000 paintings every week.

They cost from 50 cents to $15 to produce. There's likely to be an outlet in your community selling them from $5 to $150.

During 1968, Original Oil Paintings, Inc., one of the dozen or so American distributors of commercial art, delivered approximately 60,000 canvases to its distributors in forty states. The following year the figure zoomed upward as the company contracted to sell its purchases through the National Tea Company and Grand Union Stores, both supermarket chains, and E. J. Korvette, a major discounter.

The field has recently attracted the franchisers. For a $12,000 investment you can be established in your own art gallery, complete with a custom-frame operation and all the "signed original paintings" you can ever handle.

"They are selling worthless merchandise," says William Bendig, editor and publisher of *The Art Gallery*. "The commercial galleries take artists who wouldn't have a chance in the legitimate art world. Neither the owners nor their customers know very much about art."

Unfortunately, thousands of people have been confused and misled by the commercial galleries and have snapped up paintings for their investment value. More than a few stores encourage this, displaying newspaper stories that tell of the mushrooming prices being paid for the works of Van Gogh, Matisse, et al. But commercial art resembles the works of the impressionists in about the same way play money compares to a certificate for a share of AT & T stock.

Part of the problem is in the word "original." To many Americans there is a magic to it. Any original piece of art is valuable, they figure.

But commercial art has no value and it never will. If you like a factory painting because the canvas is just the right size for that space over your bookcase and the colors blend nicely with the wall covering, then buy it. But if it's an investment you're seeking, go to a reputable dealer. He'll show you a sketch or a lithograph that won't cost you any more than the mass-produced art. It will have real value. And if you buy wisely, its value may appreciate.

Getting Information and Advice

There are many organizations within the art field that give invaluable assistance to art buyers. Suppose you're interested in purchasing the work of certain painters. You can write either the

Metropolitan Museum of Art (Fifth Ave. and 82nd St., New York, N. Y. 10021) or the Museum of Modern Art (11 West 53rd St., New York, N. Y. 10022) and obtain a list of reputable galleries that handle the artists. If your interest is in a contemporary painter, write the Art Information Center (11 West 56th St., New York, N. Y. 10022) for a gallery list.

George Wittenborn, Inc. (1018 Madison Ave., New York, N. Y. 10021) is a leading publisher of books and periodicals on the fine arts. The firm makes available book lists on a variety of subjects—medieval art, primitive art, modern art, architecture, archeology, and so on. Write and request that your name be placed on the mailing list to receive book catalogs concerning your field of interest.

Art books can be extremely expensive—some are priced as high as $300—so have a good idea of what you're buying before you make a purchase. The cost of an art book is often directly related to the amount of color work it contains. If you're a novice in the art world and seek to increase your knowledge, you'll be better served by textual material than color reproductions. The reproductions are important, of course, but study them in a library. The books listed below are basic guidebooks for the collector-investor:

Art as an Investment by Richard Rush (Prentice Hall, $14.95) is a comprehensive how-to-do-it guide for the fledgling investor.

Art Collecting by Ted Farah (Cornerstone Library, $1) is a basic, informative guide for the beginner.

Buying Art on a Budget by Joanna Eagle (Award Books), $1.25.

Collecting Original Art by Jeffrey Loria (Harper & Row), $5.95.

Gardner's Guide to Antiques and Art Buying in New York by Aaron Gardner (Bobbs Merrill Co.), $5.95.

Here is a listing of the principal publications covering the world of art:

American Artist (2160 Patterson St., Cincinnati, O. 45214): one year, 11 issues, $10; sample copy, $1.

The Art Bulletin, a quarterly published by the College Arts Association of America (432 Park Ave. S., New York, N. Y. 10016). Write for information regarding membership and subscription prices.

Arts Canada (129 Adelaide St. W., Toronto 1, Canada): one year, six issues, $10 (Canada), $12 (U.S.); sample copy, $2 (Canada), $2.50 (U.S.).

Art Forum (667 Madison Ave., New York, N. Y. 10021): one year, 10 issues, $15.

Art in America (150 E. 58th St., New York, N. Y. 10022): one year, six issues, $15; sample copy, $2.75.

Art Journal, published by the College Art Association of America (432 Park Ave. S., New York, N. Y. 10016): one year, four issues, $5; sample copy, $1.50.

Arts Magazine (23 E. 26th St., New York, N. Y. 10010): one year, eight issues, $9.50; sample copy, $1.25.

Art News (444 Madison Ave., New York, N. Y. 10022): one year, 10 issues, $13.

The Art Trader (Box 43, Cambridge, Mass. 02138): one year, 10 issues, $10.

Craft Horizons, published by the American Crafts Council (16 E. 52nd St., New York, N. Y. 10022): one year, six issues, $10; sample copy, $2.

Print; America's Graphic Design Magazine (19 W. 44th St., New York, N. Y.): one year, six issues, $12.50; sample copy, $2.50.

Several national magazines cover the art world regularly. Both *Time* and *Newsweek,* for instance. The *New Yorker* reviews many New York City exhibitions and gives a comprehensive listing of exhibitions in each weekly issue. So do *New York Magazine* and *Cue.*

If you live in a metropolitan area, your local newspaper is likely to cover the subject of art extensively each Sunday. The Sunday *New York Times* is a first-rate source of information and its critics are judged to be among the nation's best. All of these publications are good supplements to the books and magazines I've mentioned, and will help to keep you knowledgeable about art-world trends.

Summing Up

Embark on an art-education program before you begin investing. Visit museums and galleries. Talk to museum curators and art dealers.

When appraising a painting for possible purchase, ask yourself these questions:

- Who is the artist?
- Does the work display quality?

• Is the subject matter pleasant? Is the painting bright and color-ful?

• Is the work of convenient size and is it in good condition?

If your budget is limited, consider investing in prints or drawings. No matter what field you invest in, buy from a responsible dealer or recognized auction house. Don't hesitate to have expensive pieces of art appraised before purchasing.

ANTIQUES

What is an antique? It is, according to one expert, a "man-made object of a kind no longer made that is valuable because of its age and historic implications."

This definition may be adequate if you are merely a collector, but if you're planning to invest in antiques you should be thinking in more specific terms. During World War II, the Office of Price Administration issued a regulation concerning antiques which defined them in these terms: "Antiques for the purpose of this exemption are (1) old objects such as furniture, tableware, household articles, etc. (if an article is less than 75 years old it will ordinarily not be considered an antique within the meaning of this exemption) which (2) tend to increase rather than decrease in value because of age; which (3) are purchased primarily because of their authenticity, age, rarity, style, etc., rather than for utility; and which (4) are commonly known and dealt in as antiques by the trade."

This definition is unquestionably valid today—except for the date reference. Furniture made later than 1830 is not usually con-sidered important by those who deal in antiques. When you are thinking in terms of investment, objects should be at least as old as the dates given below:

CERAMICS
European, *ca.* 1830
Chinese export, *ca.* 1840
Staffordshire, *ca.* 1850
American ceramics, *ca.* 1890

GLASS
Blown glass bottles and flasks, *ca.* 1860
Pressed glass,*ca.* 1840–1900
Opaque, *ca.* 1870–90

Paperweights, *ca.* 1915
Cut glass, *ca.* 1915
Art glass, *ca.* 1840
Iridescent glass, *ca.* 1926

SILVER
American, *ca.* 1815–30
European, *ca.* 1800

PEWTER
English, *ca.* 1750-1800
European, 1750–90
Oriental, before 1750
American, before 1860
English Britannia, before 1790
American Britannia, before 1860

FRENCH FURNITURE
Louis XIII, 1610–43
Louis XIV, 1643–1715
Regence, 1715–23
Louis XV, 1723–93
Louis XVI, 1774–93
Directoire, 1793–99
Empire, 1800–15

ENGLISH FURNITURE
Jacobean, 1608–88
William and Mary, 1689–1702
Chippendale, 1740–79
Heppelwhite, 1770–88
Adam, 1760–1812
Sheraton, 1790–1804
Regency, 1810–20

AMERICAN FURNITURE
Pilgrim, 1650–1710
William and Mary, 1710–40
Chippendale, 1760–75
Heppelwhite, 1780–90
Sheraton, 1790–1810
Duncan Phyfe, 1785–1835

Of course, there are dozens of other types and styles of antiques, but there are stable markets chiefly in those listed above. Shortages exist in every single one of these categories and prices are rising steadily.

During the 1970's dealers expect sharp price increases in fine authentic eighteenth-century American furniture. Some even predict it will become as highly prized as fine eighteenth-century French furniture was during the mid-1960's. Duncan Phyfe, in particular, is expected to spiral in value. Fine eighteenth-century English furniture will also show meaningful increases in value in the decade to come, say the experts.

Don't rush in. Pick a speciality. Study it carefully. What are its leading characteristics? Who were the foremost craftsmen? Bone up on the historical period involved. You should boast dealerlike knowledge before you enter the field.

Establishing Value

No matter what type of antique you collect, its value will be based upon certain standards. The greatest value attaches to those antiques that best typify the style of the creator or the period the piece represents. Style is always of overriding importance.

The value of a piece of furniture is greatly enhanced if the maker can be readily identified, either by the workmanship displayed in the piece or by virtue of a tag or stamp which bears the maker's name. In the case of American furniture, such names as Duncan Phyfe, Townsand or Goddard attached to a piece can double its value.

Size has an effect upon value, too. Although there are many exceptions, the smaller pieces have greater relative value than larger ones. There is a good reason for this: The larger pieces are less wanted because they occupy so much more space in apartments or today's smaller houses.

It is almost always true that the more elaborate the piece the greater its value. Ormolu, marquetry and parquetry mountings on a Louis XV commode make it worth significantly more money than a plain one.

There is also the matter of the history of the piece. If it has been connected in any way with an important, unusual or interesting event, it is more valuable.

Condition is of critical importance. The closer a piece comes to its original condition, the greater its value. Defects cover a tremendous range, from surface stains, dents and cuts to alterations or additions that can change the size or appearance of the piece.

Many objects that seem to be antiques at first glance are really frauds. Before you make your first purchase, you should know the various types of flimflam and be able to recognize each.

There is, first of all, the outright fake, the object that has been created to look like something it is not. Every antique is subject to imitation, but those that are most likely to be faked range from the relatively inexpensive, attractive items to pieces bearing moderately high prices. There is less likelihood of really expensive merchandise being faked since it is usually the object of careful scrutiny. But any object is liable to be counterfeited if the difference between the selling prices and the product cost makes the venture worthwhile.

Reproductions are fakes, but they are honest ones. There is no attempt made to deceive the buyer. Williamsburg, the Colonial capital of Virginia which has been restored to its original pre-Revolutionary style, is awash with reproductions, and some museums display them. But from an investment standpoint, they are worth about as much as the reproduction of a Picasso oil or a facsimile of Abraham Lincoln's signature. They are wholly without value.

Another type of antique to avoid is the object that has been transformed from its original state by a hammer and saw or a paintbrush. Unfortunately, there are uncounted examples of such attempts at glorification—the small reed organ that has been converted into a desk, or the Rogers-group Indian that has received a shining coat of antique red. This is sabotage; it destroys all value.

Where to Buy

There are an estimated 20,000 antique shops throughout the United States, and the quality of what they offer covers the widest possible range. Some experts say that there are only about 100 shops in which you can buy the highest quality cabinetware; others say the list numbers no more than 50.

There are two organizations that can be helpful to you in making antique purchases. Both are meant to assure high-principled trading practices. The dealer you buy from should be a member of one.

The National Antique and Art Dealers Association of America, formerly the New York Antique and Art Dealers Association, Inc., (42 E. 57th St., New York, N. Y. 10022) is a nonprofit membership of dealers mutually pledged to safeguard the interests of those who buy, sell or collect works of antiques and art. The Art and Antique

Dealers League of America, Inc. (136 E. 55th St., New York, N. Y. 10022) is a similar organization with similar aims. Both organizations will send you on request a free booklet containing the names of their members plus useful information on antique buying.

The auction house, of course, is another excellent hunting ground for the antique buyer. Buying at auction is covered earlier in this chapter.

Antique shows are a third source. There are now more then 2,000 shows scheduled each year, some of enormous size. The National Antiques show, held annually at New York's Madison Square Garden, is the biggest of all. Its 1970 edition offered the wares of over 300 dealers, collectors and connoisseurs.

Some people frequent secondhand stores, thrift shops or just plain junk stores in search of finds. Almost always this is a waste of time, at least from the standpoint of investment. The shopkeepers, especially in large cities, know what they're selling. Anything of real value has long since been redeemed.

Source Material

For an excellent listing of books on antiques, obtain the free antique-book catalog distributed by the Mid-America Book Company (Main St., Leon, Ia. 50144). The size of a tabloid newspaper, it has catalog pictures and describes many hundreds of volumes.

The following are among the recommended reference books:

The Concise Encyclopedia of Antiques (compiled by *The Connoisseur*) gives essential, primary knowledge supplied by experts on furniture, English glass, portrait miniatures, and so on.

The Concise Encyclopedia of American Antiques, edited by Helen Comstock (Hawthorn Books, Inc.), is a two-volume illustrated work containing descriptive information on such subjects as "Period Stoves," "Pottery and Porcelain," "Quilts and Coverlets," and "Figured Bottles and Flasks."

Know Your Antiques by Ralph and Terry Kovel (Crown Publishers, Inc.) is a new book on how to recognize and evaluate almost any antique. The authors conduct a syndicated column which bears the same title as the book.

The International Antiques Yearbook by Philip Wilson (Walker & Company, $5.95) is a collector's guide to the antiques and art trade in the United States and Europe.

Antiques as an Investment by Richard Rush (Prentice Hall, Inc.,

$14.95) is an excellent guide for both the beginner and experienced collector. It features authoritative and detailed price information.

The Official Guide to Popular Antiques and Curios ($5) is written by dealers, collectors and specialists in virtually every field of antiques, and contains authoritative price information on thousands of items.

The Complete Antiques Price List by Ralph and Terry Koval (Crown Publishers, Inc., $5.95) is just what its name implies. Its 512 pages contain 300 photos and 28,000 price entries.

Doubleday & Company has published several useful volumes in a series of collectors' guides; for example, *The Collector's Guide to Antique American Ceramics* and *The Collector's Guide to Antique American Glass.* Each is priced at $4.95.

Storing and caring for your antiques is no easy matter. Books covering this subject are easily available, however. In addition, the American Association of State and Local History (1315 Eighth Ave. S., Nashville, Tenn. 37203) has available—at fifty cents each —a fine selection of technical leaflets on this subject. They include:

Number	Title
1	*Leather: Its Understanding and Care*
2	*Caring for Your Collections: Textiles, China, Ceramics and Glass*
5	*Storing Your Collections: Problems and Solutions*
8	*Caring for Your Collections: Manuscripts and Related Materials*
9	*Safeguarding Works of Art: Transportation, Records and Insurance*
10	*Caring for Your Collections: Conservation of Metals*
40	*The Care of Antique Silver*
47	*Caring for Clocks*
50	*Insuring Against Loss*

Newspapers and magazines devoted to antiques include:

Antiques (551 Fifth Ave., New York, N. Y. 10017), one year, 12 issues, $14; sample copy, $1.75.

Antique Monthly (Box 440, Tuscaloosa, Ala. 35401); one year, 12 issues, $4.

The Antique Trader (Dubuque, Ia. 52001); one year, 52 issues, $4.

The Mid-Atlantic Antique Journal (P.O. Box 2092, Falls Church, Va. 22042); one year, 26 issues, $4.

Spinning Wheel (Exchange Pl., Hanover, Pa. 17331); one year, 10 issues, $6; sample copy, 75¢.

Yankee (Yankee, Inc., Dublin, N. H. 03444) one year, 12 issues, $4; sample copy, 50¢.

Also refer to the list of collectors' publications on pages 76–7.

Summing Up

When investing in antiques, first choose a field of specialization. Study it thoroughly. In making a purchase, evaluate the piece as to style, workmanship, ornamentation, size, historical significance and condition. Learn to recognize fakes and reproductions.

Buy from a reputable dealer—a member of the National Antique and Art Dealers Association of America or the Art and Antique Dealers League of America. Auctions and antique shows are other good sources.

4·Growth Stocks

Ownership of property of some type is the most effective—some say the only—inflation hedge. We've established that. But not all types of equity investment are practical for every person. If you live in Dubuque, Iowa, you are not going to have much of an opportunity to buy and sell impressionist prints or Andy Warhol serigraphs. A Manhattanite, unless he happens to be especially wealthy, is hardly going to speculate in real estate.

Common stocks are the perfect compromise. They're the most practical and convenient form of property ownership.

To invest in common stocks, you must have a basic belief that the country's economy, over the long term, is on an uptrend, and that the nation is vigorous and expanding. There are ample facts to support this. In 1967, the Joint Economic Committee of Congress completed an in-depth study that stated that the U.S. economy had a potential growth rate of 5½ percent or 6½ percent a year from 1965 to 1975. The 5½ percent projection was based on a real growth of 4 percent a year in the Gross National Product, combined with a 1½ percent annual rise in prices; the 6½ percent growth on a real growth of 4½ percent a year in the GNP with a 2 percent annual price rise. What's important to consider is that in the past such assumptions have proved conservative.

What about the 1970's? What about the slump early in the decade? Despite the recessive nature of the economy in the first months of 1970, the consensus of the most respected economists is that real growth in the present will approach 4.5 percent a year.

There are some fundamental reasons for this optimism. One is population. Look at the country's population curve and you'll see an enormous upswing for the decade right after World War II. This crop of war babies was 10 to 14 years old during the ten years between 1960 and 1970. They will be 20 to 24 during 1970–80; this means they will be getting married, having families, buying homes, establishing households, purchasing automobiles and, in general, stirring the economy to new levels.

A second basic factor is wages. They're up, way up. Not only is gross income increasing, but real income, the dollars available to make purchases, have increased at a greater rate than prices. In 1947, only 39 percent of the population had real incomes above $5,000. By 1966, the figure had risen to 67 percent.

Admittedly, the country's economy and Wall Street's reflection of it are subject to periods of gloom. There were declines in stock values in 1957, 1960, 1962 and 1966, and what happened in 1970, when the Dow Jones Industrial Averages plunged to a seven-year low, is fresh in everyone's memory. These downtrends produced an uneasiness but never any real alarm. Even the periods of sharpest and most prolonged decline did not cause anyone to forecast "another 1929." There is really no basis for comparing what happened then with events of a more recent nature. America's banks are sound; they weren't in 1929. And when prices skidded in 1970, it was not because of speculation and heavy margin buying, as was the case in 1929.

The peaks and the valleys average out. Not too long ago the Center for Research in Security Prices released the results of a study that showed an investment in a random cross-section of stocks on the New York Stock Exchange over a 40-year period would have increased in value at a rate that would have given a return of 9 percent compounded annually.

What Stocks?

Late in 1966 the stock market went on a rampage, and the Dow Jones Industrial Average shot up from 744.32 to 948.08 in slightly less than a year's time. The year 1968 saw a similar pattern, with the average rising from 825.13 early in the year to 985.21 in December. During these two periods, almost any stock chosen at random would have served as an inflation hedge. But there were some stocks that were much more effective than others in this regard, stocks that outpaced the market averages.

These were stocks of companies in expanding industries—companies whose sales were expanding enormously. These companies were also characterized by sound management. *Enlightened* management is a better description. They were companies whose management prepared for the future. They had a policy for, to use an overworked word, growth.

Burton Crane in his book *The Sophisticated Investor* says that his favorite definition of a growth stock is a "stock that someone is trying to sell you." It can be true. More than a few advisory services and a good number of brokers will use the term growth anytime they feel it can be an effective sales weapon. And the reason that it is effective is that few investors are able to establish the "why" for increases in prices and earnings. It may, indeed, be the result of fundamental causes, but it also may merely be a reflection of the upward thrust of the business cycle. Another problem is that once a company is tagged a "growth company" it is likely to retain that label long after its period of rapid growth has ceased.

But there are several tried and proven criteria for selecting growth stocks. I regard the following as especially significant:

• The stock should show a continual expansion of sales at the rate of 12 percent compounded annually.

• Net earnings should also be increasing at the rate of 12 percent a year compounded.

• An energetic program of research and development is another vital characteristic. And, in general, research and development expenditures should go toward the creation of new products rather than the improvement of products or techniques that already exist. The chemical field is a good example of an industry that is oriented toward new product development, while steel companies are much more concerned with improving existing processes.

One way to judge an emphasis on research and development is by evaluating "plowback." Growth companies seldom pay out more than 40 percent of their net cash in one year. Instead, the money is reinvested, thus expanding future earning power.

• Check the company's price-earnings ratio, a figure that is computed by dividing the price of the stock by its actual or indicated earnings per share. For instance, a stock selling at 40 with earnings of $2 a share would have a price-earnings ratio of 20.

What is an attractive price-to-earnings ratio? It depends on the market averages in general. Just before Christmas in 1965, the Dow

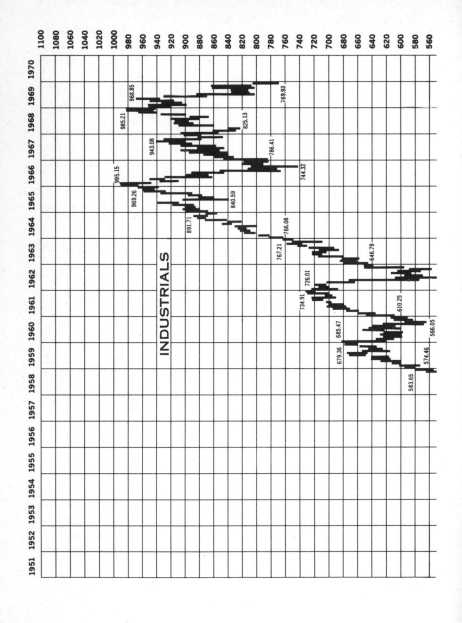

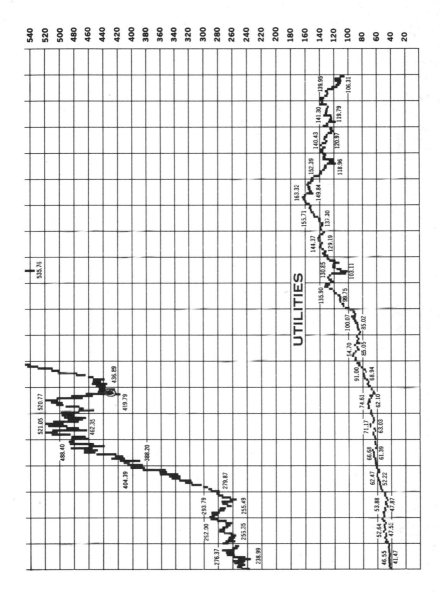

UTILITIES

Jones industrial average brushed 1000, establishing an all-time stock-market high. While many analysts were predicting the market would streak to 1200 and even beyond during 1966, the pressure of the country's involvement in Vietnam began to be felt. Instead of surging ahead, the market slumped. By the fall of 1966 it was below 750.

From that point through mid-1970, the market made six attempts to reach the magic 1000 mark again and failed each time. The most stirring try came late in 1968 when Wall Streeters seemed convinced that better days were just ahead. Richard Nixon had just been elected and the end of hostilities in Vietnam seemed somewhat assured. This euphoria sent the Dow to 981.

Then came what some observers call the "Nixon market" of 1969 and 1970. In an attempt to halt inflation, the administration put severe restrictions on money and credit, policies that depressed the economy. Corporation profits moved downward; unemployment increased. The stock market fell to sickening lows.

With the market fluctuating so, it is almost impossible to establish an attractive price-to-earnings ratio. Within the past few years, the 30 Dow stocks have sold for as much as 22.5 times earnings. When the market slumped drastically, the stocks were selling at not much more than 10 or 11 times earnings. Many analysts will tell you the "normal" price-to-earnings ratio for a given stock should be about 17 or 18, but whatever the figure, it has to be related to the market averages at the time.

• Examine the company's equity-to-date ratio. To find this, divide the total market value of the company's stock (the total number of common shares times the market value of one share) by the total value of bonds outstanding. A company with $45 million worth of stock and $15 million in bonds would be said to have an equity-to-debt ratio of three to one. Such a company would be regarded as being financially unsound. Anytime the ratio falls below five to one, analysts are wary. The ratio of current assets to current liabilities also gives a clue as to a company's financial stability or lack of it. Assets should be at least two to three times liabilities.

• The company's market must be assured. Some firms are thwarted in their attempts to take advantage of the fruits of their research. Boeing and McDonnell-Douglas, for example, have excellent research and development programs, but their only sizeable customer is the federal government. Or take the drug industry.

Competition is so keen that no company can hold an edge for very long.

• Freedom from government control is another characteristic a growth industry should have. It's normal for virtually any regulatory agency to have a depressing effect upon a company's volume. Probably the best example of this is what happened to the railroads under the overrule of the ICC.

• Management is always a crucial factor. The executive group that establishes company policy will, in the final analysis, set the pattern for growth. If these men are imaginative and innovative, if they are alert to shifting social and economic trends, the company will boast those characteristics, too.

Growth Industries

In the 1920's, automotive and radio stocks might have been chosen for their growth. During the 1950's, chemicals, airlines and frozen foods were the growth industries. What about the 1970's? What industries will expand at the fastest rate in the decade ahead? This section tells.

Pollution Control

The problem of pollution—air and water; aural and visual—is certain to be of increasing concern to Americans during the 1970's. No matter whose statistics you consult, the situation is grave. Air pollution alone is said to be ruining $11 billion in property in the United States each year. Our larger rivers and lakes are choking with contamination, with solid wastes being produced at the alarming rate of 3.5 billion tons each year.

No one knows how many billions of dollars will be spent in the decade ahead to control air and water pollution and to dispose of solid wastes, but everyone agrees the amount will be significant. In 1970, an estimated $8 billion was expended, with about 80 percent of the total going for water and waste-water treatment plants. The balance was used for air-pollution control equipment and cooling towers to combat thermal pollution.

In a policy that was in sharp contrast to that of previous administrations, Congress, in 1970, appropriated $800 million for air and water-pollution control action during the fiscal year, an almost fourfold increase in such expenditures. President Nixon has proposed that $10 billion be spent on a "nationwide clean waters program" over the next five years.

The hot war on pollution has been a great boon to hundreds of companies, perhaps thousands of them. Indeed, it has given rise to a pollution-control industry, a field that was almost wholly unknown, or at least without significance, only four or five years ago.

The public's apprehension can also be made manifest in a negative way. Because motor vehicles have been accused of causing more then one-half of the air pollution, the automobile industry is developing engine modifications and control devices to curtail carbon monoxide, unburned hydrocarbons and nitrogen oxide spewed out by the gasoline combustion engine. The phasing out of leaded gasoline has had an adverse affect on some petrochemical companies, and the manufacturers of synthetic detergents are under attack.

In evaluating companies in the pollution-control field, it's important to establish the degree to which pollution-control activities influence sales and earnings. Is the company deeply involved or is its role merely passive? Can the firm deliver complete systems or is it simply a parts supplier? Appraise the management for its knowledge of the industry.

The companies heavily concentrated in the manufacture and sale of pollution-control equipment are few. In 1969 and early in 1970, the shares of many of them were in high favor. Thus, long-term growth is now their principal attraction. These firms can be looked on as the industry's prospective growth leaders:

American Air Filter. With its full line of air-handling equipment, including units for cooling, filtering and ventilating, American Air Filter ranks as one of the foremost companies in the pollution-control industry. It has long held a commanding position in the production of wet scrubbers and fabric filters, and the purchase, in 1969, of a majority interest in Elex, a Swiss-based manufacturer of electrostatic precipitators, rounded out its product line. AAF's defense business, or lack of it, hurt earnings to the rate of 16 cents a share in 1969, but difficulties in this area seem to have been resolved. Backlog orders for pollution-control equipment are high and rising, and management anticipates future increases in sales and net.

Betz Laboratories. The manufacture of chemicals and the providing of technical services in the treatment of water and liquid wastes is an important segment of the antipollution industry. Betz Laboratories is one of the foremost companies in this field. With a customer list that includes paper manufacturers, oil refiners, public utilities and chemical and metallurgical companies, Betz offers 7000 items meant to control scale and corrosion, prevent fungicidal deterioration, and other treatment of water to facilitate recycling and the pretreatment of industrial wastes for discharge into municipal systems. The company has shown an outstanding growth record in recent years. Sales were up 93 percent and net income virtually doubled between 1965 and 1969.

Marley Company. Control of thermal pollution is Marley's field. The company manufactures and sells cooling towers for industrial, utility and commercial use. Benefiting from its design capability and a large and experienced sales force and service organization, the firm has become one of the industry leaders. Problems of what seem to be a nonrecurring nature beset the company in 1969 and, with rising material and labor costs, worked to depress earnings. But now contracts provide for escalations in material costs and labor rates, and management has predicted solid gains.

Slick Corporation. Through its aggressive acquisition program during the late 1960's, Slick Corporation attained a leadership role in the pollution-control field. Approximately 90 percent of the company's net income and 30 percent of its sales were derived from water-treatment chemicals and air-pollution equipment during 1969. Through its Pulverizing Machinery Division, Slick manufactures dust-collection units and reduction equipment, and recently entered the filter-bag market through the acquisition of Menardi & Company. Slick's net income picture has been darkened by its food-speciality business, but sluggish prices in this area are expected to be more than offset by income gains in the pollution-control fields.

Wheelabrator Corporation. With a broad product line in air-pollution control, and an annual sales volume of approximately $90 million, Wheelabrator Corporation is already one of the industry leaders, and the restructuring and expansion policies now being carried out should further enhance its position. In 1965, Wheelabrator entered into a licensing agreement with the largest European manufacturer of electrostatic precipitators. The company also markets a complete line of wet scrubbers and fabric collectors. Early in 1970, Wheelabrator was negotiating the sale of its airframe division, with the proceeds to go toward acquisitions in the pollution-control field or debt reduction. The company is 80 percent owned by Bell International.

Zurn Industries. In 1969 as much as 75 percent of Zurn's estimated sales were classified as "environmental control systems," making the company one of the relatively few with a major stake in pollution control. Zurn boasts a "total systems" approach, beginning with feasibility and research studies, and carrying through the design, engineering and construction phases. The company is able to provide these functions in air-pollution control (it markets scrubbers and mechanical collectors), incineration and solid-waste handling, and water and sewage treatment. The company's past earnings record has been quite ordinary, however. High costs, unfavorable contracts and problems with acquired companies caused the difficulties, but management forecasts are brightening earnings pictures.

Home Sewing

The rising prices of ready-to-wear clothing combined with the increasing leisure time most Americans have to pursue their avocations have combined to trigger a period of surging growth in the industries that serve home sewers. During 1970, the industry volume was expected to rise by 15 percent over the $3 billion registered in 1969. The years ahead are filled with promise for, as the industry enjoys pointing out, five out of every six female teen-agers who now sew can be expected to become permanent additions to the market which now numbers close to 50 million women. Among the growth companies are:

Singer. Surely the best-known name in the home-sewing field, Singer sold over one million new sewing machines in 1969, and forecast a 10 percent increase for 1970. What's even more important is that the company has close to two-thirds of its 1,500 Singer sewing centers converted into one-stop shops, selling fabrics, decorative trimmings, and a bright array of sewing sundries. Be aware, however, that these operations accounted for only 45 percent of Singer's sales in 1969. Sales volume was also derived from industrial products (21 percent); office equipment (13 percent); defense and space systems (13 percent) and education and training products (8 percent).

Belding Hemingway. By virtue of its acquisitions, Belding Hemingway has become a leader in the home-sewing field in recent years. The company, once dominant in industrial thread, now markets a full selection of fashion and staple buttons, and a wide range of sewing notions, items like needles, tape measures and iron-on patches. Belding Hemingway has not overlooked the fabric market and is becoming well known for its fiber glass, printed dress and sports fabrics, which are marketed under the Belding Corticelli label. Earnings for 1969 jumped to $1.61 a share from $1.35 the year previous.

Housing

People have been calling housing a potential growth industry for more than ten years, but any evident growth has been scanty and erratic. Take 1969, for example. It was forecast that two to three million housing units would be constructed. Yet only 1 ½ million units were actually built, a figure that constituted the annual average during the 1960's.

This sluggishness in the home-building industry combined with an expanding population and the fact that the federal government classifics approximately 15 million housing units as substandard have made for a critical housing shortage. There is a period of growth ahead; there *has* to be.

Most housing experts believe that the early 1970's will see the beginning of the boom period. Perhaps it will start in 1971, or the year after. But don't envisage the results as neat little split-levels or ranch-types—three or four to the acre. The day of the single-family home may be going the way of the hula hoop. New patterns in housing are ahead, say the experts.

Drive through the fringe areas outside any large American city and you can perceive the trend that is beginning to develop. The older suburbs made up of single houses on postage-stamp size lots are being bulldozed and high-rise apartment houses are going up in their place. In block after block of New York City's borough of Queens, the high risers stand shoulder to shoulder. They loom high above New York from the New Jersey palisades, and they ring Los Angeles, Chicago and Dallas.

But this is only one part of the trend. Garden apartments and town houses—known as row houses a generation ago—are another reflection of what's happening and what's going to continue to happen.

Multiunit construction—that's the wave of the future. Mortage rates—at the highest levels in the country's history early in 1970

—and the limited acreage available in urban and suburban areas have forced the trend. "Why should I put two or three houses on an acre of land," says a Long Island builder, "when I can put ten or twelve town houses there. It's the most practical way to operate today."

The trend is already well established. Said *Forbes* recently: "By 1971—or 1972 at the latest—the United States will for the first time in its history be building more multiunit housing than single family homes."

Combined with this new approach toward home building, will come technical advances in construction—that is, mass production methods. The federal government's Department of Housing and Urban Development is sponsoring Operation Breakthrough, a major effort to persuade private industry to use its technological skills and capital to produce quality housing on a mass scale. The program is supported by a $15 million budget for grants and the construction of prototypes. The first results of the competition were announced in February 1970.

To some degree, past efforts to establish assembly-line techniques in home construction have been stymied by organized labor. Carpenters and bricklayers see themselves being supplanted by factory workers who would fabricate complete rooms which would be trucked to construction sites for assembly. This system, incidentally, has been practiced in Europe for more than two decades. But craft-union opposition shows signs of easing.

The companies involved in any surge in home building would cover a very wide range. They include mortgage brokers and savings and loan associations, landowners and developers, and builders and manufacturers of prefabricated sections, plus the suppliers of the basic raw materials. Some of the companies with attractive growth potential in the industry include:

American Standard. While building products—plumbing and heating products, principally—represented 84 percent of American Standard's volume as recently as 1966, the figure slipped to 48 percent in 1969, a diversification achieved through acquisition. But don't be misled by these statistics. Company policy has dictated a strengthening of its position in the housing field. For example, in 1968, American Standard acquired the William Lyon Development Company, a land developer and builder of multiunit structures. This course, plus the new and aggressive management team that took control in 1966, should make American Standard a principal beneficiary in the anticipated increase in home construction.

Boise Cascade. Not too many years ago, Boise Cascade was a relatively small company known only for its lumber products. By means of a vigorous acquisition program and internal growth, the company mushroomed in size, and in 1969 attained sales of more than $1.7 billion. Its major holdings are still the building materials field, however, where the company sells everything from raw lumber to fiberboard, and from structural sheathing to plywood. In addition, Boise Cascade is involved in land development, on-site home construction and in recent years has shown particular interest in urban-development programs. During 1969, the company showed a 23.3 price-earnings ratio.

Kaiser Cement and Gypsum. Recent years have seen earnings skid for Kaiser Cement and Gypsum, with sagging prices for gypsum products the prime reason. Cement prices were down, too, but reversed themselves in 1969. Similar action on the part of gypsum prices, plus an upswing in home building which accounts for more than two-thirds of the company's gypsum sales, would provide the opportunity for significant earnings gains.

Masonite Corporation. Hardboard—paneling, siding and partitions—represents about three-fourths of Masonite's sales volume. The company is the largest producer of the product, accounting for about 45 percent of the U.S. market. In recent years, Masonite has put a solid emphasis on research, developing an attractive line of hard-wood specialty products. The company's earning record is consistently brighter than most of the other large firms in the building industry.

Owens-Corning-Fiberglas. In 1969, Owens-Cornings' sales totaled $487 million, with construction materials accounting for two-thirds of the total. Sales of Fiberglas products made up the bulk of this total, but in recent years the company has strengthened its position in the building materials field with the introduction of such products as reinforced plastic tub-showers, suspended ceilings for the home remodeling market, and duct systems for commercial buildings. The company etched out an erratic pattern of growth during the late 1960's, but any uptrend in the home-building industry could trigger an impressive earnings gain.

Potlatch Forests. The word "Forests" in this name is somewhat misleading. Although the company does market a wide array of forest products—lumber, plywood and a great variety of paper products—it also has substantial ranking as a land developer and home builder. For instance, one Potlatch subsidiary, the Speedspace Corporation, constructs modular, transportable structures, and in 1969 accounted for about 5 percent of Potlatch's total volume. The company owns approximately 1 1/3 million acres of timberland, an inflation-proof raw materials source. Profit margins in recent years have not excited Wall Streeters, but significant increases have been registered since the lows struck by the company in 1962. The management is dedicated to extending and improving its record of gains.

Tappan Company. An energetic research and development policy has put the Tappen Company in an excellent position to benefit from any upsurge in home construction. Once known almost exclusively for its home ranges, the company now markets range hoods, cabinetry, disposers, refrigerators and dishwashers. That's only part of the Tappan story. Aware that low-cost, multi-unit, mass-produced home construction may be the shape of things to come, the company has developed a one-piece, kitchen-wall module that contains water taps and appliances and boasts a single plumbing and electrical connection. It has won builders' raves. Tappan's price-earnings ratio for 1969 was a modest 12.1.

Crime Prevention

If you think the cost-of-living index has shot skyward in recent years, take a look at J. Edgar Hoover's crime-rate charts. There's real growth there. The FBI director says that during 1969 larcenies were up 21 percent, armed robberies increased 16 percent and crimes against property rose by 11 percent. Only a cynic would say that crime is a growth industry, but crime *prevention* certainly is.

The names of the crime-fighting companies may not come to you immediately. But think a minute. There's Pinkerton's and William J. Burns International, companies that provide guards and investigators to banks, factories and large retailers. There's American District Telegraph, which manufactures alarm systems, and Walter Kidde Inc., whose Globe Security Division is noted for its electronic detection devices.

Among the companies in the crime-prevention field that show growth potential are:

Wackenhut Corporation. One of the largest of the armed-guard companies, Wackenhut has recently added investigative work and electronic surveillance to its services. An earnings increase of 15 percent was projected for 1970.

American District Telegraph. The initials "ADT" are familiar to most of us. They're universally seen on alarm systems—both fire and burglary—that alert central stations to emergencies. The company enjoys stability by virtue of the five-year contracts its clients must sign, and growth potential because of rate increases and the insertion of an escalator clause in new agreements.

Life Insurance

During the 1960's, life-insurance companies lagged behind industrial firms in growth and development. But the situation is fast changing, and many life-insurance companies now present bright opportunities for growth.

A primary reason for my optimism is the increased investment income life-insurance companies are expected to enjoy as a result of rising interest levels. During the 1962-67 period, life-insurance companies showed an average annual earnings growth of about 7 percent. During 1969, average earnings growth was expected to average 11 percent with the increase traceable to investments at the higher interest rates that prevailed in the late 1960's. Industry investment income contributes close to 50 percent of total pretax earnings as compared to approximately 25 percent a decade ago.

Life insurance companies used to follow about the same investment policies as those recommended for widows and orphans. Not any longer. Many life firms work aggressively and creatively to develop new methods of boosting earnings. For example, the industry is increasing its holdings in real estate, but not merely in a passive way. Their investments nowadays emphasize equity and income participation. In other words, they tend to be inflation-proof.

Some companies will not commit long-term mortgage money unless a small percentage of the gross income is guaranteed. Lease-back arrangements are becoming popular. The insurance company purchases the land, then leases it back to the developer. The mortgage terms in the resulting leasehold provide the company with a percentage of the income besides the usual ground rent. Some insurance firms are preparing their mortgage contracts with warrants, granting the company the option to buy stock in the borrower's income property. Imaginative arrangements of these types have already begun to have a stimulating influence on insurance-company earnings, and since mortgage loans represent approximately 35 percent of all insurance-company assets, the future

impact of company inventiveness should be of the highest significance.

Another factor certain to have a beneficial effect upon life insurance stocks is the new and uniform adjustment methods which, in
effect, revamp industry accounting methods and make it easier to
discern earnings and growth. In the past, only the most erudite of
analysts could readily compare the "operating earnings" and "book
values" of life-insurance companies with those of other industries.
Aware of this and other shortcomings stemming from industry
accounting methods the Association of Insurance and Financial
Analysts appointed a committee to set forth adjustments in the
methods of arriving at earnings and asset statistics. I am not going
into the complexities of the problem, but the solution has been
reached, and it cannot help but stimulate investor interest in insurance stocks.

These developments in the life insurance field are being played
out against a background of increased life sales. For 1969, ordinary
life sales totaled $92.6 billion, an increase of 7.9 percent over 1968.
First-year premium volume also showed a healthy increase.

Among the insurance companies with good growth potential are:

Great Commonwealth Life Insurance Company. Founded in
1962, and with its business concentrated in life and endowment
insurance, this Dallas-based firm has shown consistent and rapid
growth, with insurance-in-force increasing from $100 million in
1962 to approximately nine times that amount at the end of 1969.
Assets rose from $7 million to approximately $40 million during
the same period. The net-earnings picture has remained depressed,
however, because of the costs involved in building a roster of
policyholders. But a bright renewal record plus income from invested reserves has set the stage for increased investor interest.

American National Insurance. Another Texas Company, American National Insurance, boasts assets of approximately $1 ½ bil-
lion, and thus ranks as one of the insurance firms likely to achieve
rising investment income over the next few years. Earnings were
66 cents per share in 1968 and could conceivably double or even
triple by 1973.

Computers

Are computers a growth industry? Consider this: In 1960, computer sales totaled $4 billion. In 1970, the figure increased to almost

$12 billion and, according to Diebold, Inc., will soar to $27 billion by 1975. The number of computers in use will surge from 90,000, the mid-1970 figure, to 160,000 by 1975.

This is exciting growth, but don't go out and buy IBM or National Cash Register—not for growth, anyway. These companies, along with Honeywell, Burroughs, and Control Data, are mainframe makers; that is, they manufacture the basic gray steel box and all that goes inside. The sales and earnings for the mainframe makers should continue to grow, but the most vigorous growth will be in computer "peripherals" and "software."

The computer peripheral market is expected to increase in size by 75 percent during the next five years, with the greatest increases to be registered by those firms that manufacture and market remote-data terminals, the devices that enable the user to transmit and receive from a distant point. The swing to computer time sharing and remote batch processing assures an increasing demand for these units.

In the early 1970's the computer peripheral industry was a crowded one, and some of the smaller firms seemed destined to be shunted aside. In selecting a stock in this field, look for a company with experienced management, a broad product line and solid sales and service organizations. Among the firms showing signs of both stability and growth are.

Ampex. The magnetic recording field, in which Ampex holds a dominant position, is closely tied to the computer peripheral industry. Ampex's per share earnings went from 80 cents in 1968 to $1.25 in 1969, and continued growth seems assured.

Gerber Scientific Instrument. Expansion has been the keynote at Gerber Scientific, with the company now able to offer a wide selection of new products. In the 1968-69 period, the firm's rate of growth was slightly more than 30 percent.

The software segment of the computer industry is considered to have an even greater growth potential than the peripheral equipment field. Software refers to computer services, to the programs that get the wanted information out of the computer.

Even though electronic data processing is already a major factor in business record keeping, scientific and engineering computation and industrial process control, there is important expansion ahead. It is anticipated that software firms will be called upon to provide information on the availability of jobs in various parts of the country, and match job applicants with the openings. The results of the

1970 census must be tabulated and studied in depth. There's a great deal to be done in Wall Street in providing quotations and other information (the over-the-counter market itself provides enormous opportunities in this regard) and EDP could aid in researching individual stock issues. The field of medical diagnosis and credit ratings represent potential. And there are many other fields.

It used to be that IBM and the other mainframe manufacturers provided their customers with many software products plus the services of their systems engineers at no cost. Several manufacturers, IBM included, reversed this policy as of January 1, 1970, a fact that cannot help but improve prospects for software independents. But even before the policy change, users consistently found that software packages developed by the independents were more efficient. This may seem remarkable at first glance, but such conditions aren't limited to the computer field. There is a burgeoning industry in the installation of telephone systems by independents, specialists who do it better and more economically than the local representative of "Mother Bell," whose services are gratis.

Quantum Science Corporation predicts that the computer software field will grow by 130 percent in the first half of the 1970's. Among the first that show good growth potential are *Planning Research Corporation, URS Systems Inc.* and *Science Management.*

Leisure-time Industry

In his book *The Year 2000* Herman Kahn predicts a 30-hour workweek and 13-week vacations for the American worker. A trend in that direction is already well-established, a fact that has made for bullish predictions concerning firms in the so-called leisure-time industry. One survey declares that spending on leisure-related goods and services is likely to grow at the rate of about 7 percent annually from now through 1980, and a Merrill Lynch study on leisure predicts that the market will grow from $150 billion to $250 billion by 1975.

The increased leisure that Americans have stems from several factors. The total number of working hours per week is declining, although the rate of decline in the past decade or so has been quite modest. People also have much longer vacations today. More than 60 percent of workers with ten years of service now get at least three weeks vacation a year. Early retirement is a third consideration. Over one-half the work force now retires before age 65; the figure was a mere 12 percent in 1956.

There are literally thousands of companies with a stake in the leisure-time industry, but only about 300 of them derive a significant amount of income from leisure-related industries. The field includes companies that manufacture sporting goods, recreation vehicles and photographic equipment; also firms that market musical instruments, toys and games and food service firms, as in the case of "prol-food" chains.

In choosing companies in the field with the greatest growth potential, look for those firms with a better-than-average research and development awareness. New products are often the road to sales and earnings increases in the leisure-time industry. Polaroid, which patented the in-camera development process, is the classic example. And American Machine and Foundry Company, the firm that introduced the automatic pinspotter to the bowling industry, saw its stock skyrocket in price.

There are any number of examples of a more recent nature. The development of steel and aluminum tennis rackets, the introduction of snowmobiles and the many advances in consumer electronics—cassette tape recorders, for example—were all of significance to the individual companies involved. Sometimes a new development can trigger industrywide growth. When machinery for artificial snow making came into widespread use in the mid-1960's it had a broadening effect upon the entire ski-equipment market.

The companies that have the capacity to innovate—and whose development skills are supported by manufacturing capacity and a national sales organization—are the firms that should show a competitive edge in the leisure-time field. As this statement implies, bigness is to be preferred to smallness.

What other fields promise growth? There's oceanography, another perennial growth favorite among Wall Street analysts. One day during the decade to come the field of ocean resources *will* boom. As plans now stand, a subsidiary of the Tenneco Company will begin dredging manganese nodules from the ocean floor off the California coast early in 1974, and this could be the first important commercial breakthrough. Eventually, hundreds of millions of dollars will be spent to exploit the sea.

Many investment experts call the drug field a growth industry. Most companies get good marks for research and their ability to diversify into drug-related markets. Government-sponsored medical-care programs and the development of new, disease-preventing drugs, plus the awakening market in underdeveloped countries, should provide impetus. But the increased involvement of the

federal government in the industry's pricing policies—a direct result of the government-supported Medicare and Medicaid programs—and the growing competition from European
manufacturers may offset industry gains. I have a wait-and-see
attitude about the drug industry.

It's not difficult to find industries that do have the stamp of
growth. Pick up your daily newspaper and scan the headlines or
glance at the contents page of a national magazine.

The nation's next major developments may come in the industries profiled above. It may be in communications or education, in
agriculture or transportation. Stay alert. Keep informed. Do your
homework. Tomorrow's Xerox is your reward.

Dollar-Cost Averaging

No one can mastermind the stock market and even the most
celebrated experts make bad judgments. Yet there is a tried and
proven investment policy that will help to protect you against the
market's price swings, and help you to achieve success on a long-
term basis. It's called dollar-cost averaging. It simply means that
you purchase a fixed-dollar amount of the same stock at regular
intervals.

Dollar-cost averaging has proven advantageous because you acquire more shares with your money when the price of the stock is
low. Then, when the stock rises, you make a gain on all the shares
you've obtained. The Monthly Investment Plan, offered by all
member firms of the New York Stock Exchange, enables you to
invest on this basis, contributing a set sum every month or every
quarter to be used in acquiring shares.

If you're investing small sums, less than $100 a month, the MIP
plan has its disadvantages. At low levels commission rates are
proportionately higher. It's wiser to set up your own program,
accumulating, say, $300 in a savings account each quarter and then
making your stock purchase.

Dollar-cost averaging will work to your advantage in both rising
and falling markets. Suppose, in a rising market, you made four
purchases of $100 each at regular intervals, and the price per share
was $5, $6, $8 and $10. With the first buy you would have
purchased 20 shares; with the second 16.7, on the third 12.5
and on the last 10 shares. This would have given you a total of 59.2
shares.

Your average cost per share is $6.76 ($400 divided by 59.2). But the average price during the same period ($5 plus $6 plus $8 plus $10 divided by 4) was $7.25.

Suppose you make the purchases in a declining market. This time you invest $100 at regular intervals at prices of $9, $7, $5 and $4. You would have acquired 70.4 shares at an average cost of $5.68. The average price during the period would have been $6.25.

The essence of the system is your tenacity, your ability to keep to your plan when stock prices skid. When market prices do become depressed an aura of pessimism prevails and people begin to look for other investment mediums. But dollar-cost averaging won't work unless you have the stick-to-itiveness to buy when others are saying market investment is pure folly. The system is entirely based on the fact that over the long term the trend of prices has always been upward, that no bear market lasts forever.

Stock Maintenance

Once you've made a stock purchase, watch over it carefully. Buy a security-record book, available at almost any stationery store, and keep it up to date.

Keep each stock certificate in a bank safe-deposit box or allow your broker to hold your certificates. Even though your name is registered with the issuing company, replacing a lost or destroyed certificate can be a long and even costly piece of business.

Always file the broker's statement with each certificate. You may need this documentation to validate information on your federal tax return.

For each purchase, your stock-record book should contain the following information:

• The company and number of shares.
• The certificate number (the serial number printed on the certificate).
• The date of purchase and the total cost, including the broker's commission.
• The date sold and the total amount received. Deduct the amount paid as a broker's commission.
• Your gain or loss on the transaction.

Your records should also reflect dividend payments, both cash dividends and those received in the form of additional stock. Get into the habit of entering dividends as soon as they are received.

You may also receive "rights" to buy new securities before they are issued at a figure that is below the market price. This option will have to be exercised before a certain date. Read the accompanying instructions carefully. Usually you can sell the rights if you do not choose to buy the new issue.

Warrants are somewhat the same as rights but usually they establish a buying price that is well above the stock's market level. They also have a much longer life than rights. You can either hold the warrants, hoping the market price will rise, or sell them. Enter all information relating to rights or warrants in your stock-record book.

Be sure to read any information received from the company. The annual report deserves a careful going over, especially the financial statistics. It's always wise to compare one year's assets, liabilities, capital surplus and so on with those of previous years. Such comparisons are much more revealing than the financial statistics for any one year.

If you have purchased stock in a company because of its heavy involvement in a particular growth industry, be sure to check whether that part of the company's business continues to represent a substantial portion of its total operation. Some companies lack in tenacity. If profits do not come quickly from a particular field, switch to something else.

Getting Information and Advice

In selecting growth stocks, learn to supplement your own investigations with the information and advice from some of the sources profiled in this section. Two publications that you must appraise are Standard & Poor's *200 Rapid Growth Stocks* and *America's Fastest Growing Companies*, which is published by John S. Herold, Inc. Both are published monthly.

Standard & Poor's, in developing its list of growth stocks, uses these criteria:

• "If the growth in share earning over the past five years has been steady, it must have amounted to at least 7 percent per annum, compounded;

• "If the growth has been interruped in only one year and the decline in that year has been less than 5 percent, annual growth must have been at least 10 percent;

• "If the growth has been interrupted in more than one year, or in one year has declined more than 5 percent, annual growth rate must have been at least 12 percent.

In addition, Standard & Poor's choices are limited generally to those issues with more than 500,000 shares outstanding and those with earning of at least 25 cents a share in the last full year.

Using electronic data-processing methods, Standard & Poor's screens approximately 6,000 issues to evolve its list of 200. For each, it determines a "growth premium." By definition this is the "extent to which the price of a given issue is judged to be in excess of the general level of stock valuation, as measured by the price-earnings ratio of the Standard & Poor's 425 industrials based on estimated current year earnings."

To determine the growth premium, divide the price-earnings ratio of the stock by the price-earnings ratio of the Standard & Poor's industrials and multiply the result by 100 to get the percentage. Says Standard & Poor's: "The difference between the percentage and 100 percent is the indicated premium (if a plus figure) or discount (if a minus figure)."

A subscription to *The Standard & Poor's 200 Rapid Growth Stocks* is $65 annually for 12 issues. A quarter trial subscription— three issues—is $18. The company address is 345 Hudson St. New York, N. Y. 10014.

America's Fastest Growing Companies is a relatively new publication, having been introduced in 1958, but it has won a wide following. The publication lists some 150 companies each month that have shown exceptional past earnings—an uninterrupted growth rate of 10 percent annually over the most recent three years. To reduce what is termed "downside margin of error," the publisher, John S. Herold, takes these precautions:

• Earnings are projected on the basis of either a five-year historical growth rate or the most recent growth rate, whichever is lower.

• Projections into the future are limited to three years.

• Growth projections are revised and checked every time earnings are reported.

Mr. Herold also gives the subscriber the mathematical tools for figuring the value of $1 at rates from 10 percent through 200 percent for periods of up to seven years. He also provides formulas for arriving at "prudent" values and "prudent" capitalization for growth stocks.

A one-year subscription to *America's Fastest Growing Companies*, 12 issues, is $68. Write John S. Herold, Inc., 25 Greenwich Ave., Greenwich, Conn. 06830.

A third publication you might want to consult is *Forbes Guide to Profits in Growth Stocks*. Published annually, it recommends 40 common-stock issues and gives background information and statistics on each. It costs $15. Order from the Investors Advisory Institute, 70 Fifth Ave., New York, N. Y. 10001.

In appraising any particular stock, two firms provide the great bulk of background information and financial data used by investors and the investment community in general. They are Standard & Poor's (345 Hudson St., New York, N. Y. 10014) and Moody's Investors Service (99 Church St., New York, N. Y. 10007). Much of the statistical information provided by one firm is also furnished by the other, so consulting the output of one is usually sufficient. The major differences are in the method of presentation.

The basic financial reference books concerning publicly owned corporations in the United States are Standard & Poor's *Corporation Records* and Moody's *Manuals*. Both are multivolume works with thousands of pages. For each company they give a brief history and comprehensive statistical information concerning assets, income, earnings, dividends and stock prices.

Information on each company is updated when new annual reports are issued or important developments occur which change the company's financial profile. Such reports are indispensable to the person seeking investments with growth potential.

It costs several hundred dollars a year to subscribe to either *Corporation Records* or *Manuals*, but you can forgo this expense by following one of a number of alternatives. Your broker has these reference books on hand at his office and you can consult one or both of them there. Or there's the public library. According to a recent issue of *The Library Journal*, Moody's *Manuals* is the most widely purchased of all stock-market reference books among libraries of the country, and is available virtually everywhere.

Another course is to ask your broker to obtain a copy of a Standard & Poor's or Moody's bulletin on a particular company for you. These bulletins contain all of the basic financial facts about a company and also make an evaluation as to the worth of the company's stock.

Standard & Poor's also publishes a *Stock Guide*, a monthly manual about the size of a pocket-sized book that contains an incredible amount of information on stock fluctuations, assets, earnings and dividends on companies listed on the New York and American Stock exchanges. Sometimes brokers give free copies of the *Stock Guide* to their customers.

Besides reading *The Wall Street Journal* or a daily newspaper with a well-regarded financial section, you should also keep abreast of market conditions by reading one or more of the several publications that cover the investment and business fields. Many of these, like *Forbes* or *Business Week*, may be well known to you. Others that you may wish to consider include:

Barron's National Business and Financial Weekly (Dow Jones & Co., Inc., 44 Broad St., New York, N. Y. 10004) is valuable for its articles on market trends and its studies of investment values. It also gives news and comment on political and economic developments affecting the financial scene. Its statistical section offers a comprehensive "status-at-a-glance" of stock listings, financial indicators and production and trade indexes. One year, 52 issues, $14.

The Wall Street Transcript (54 Wall St., New York, N. Y. 10005) is a tabloid-size newspaper containing company studies, industry surveys and other reports and articles prepared by brokers, analysts and individuals. One year, 52 issues, $210; trial subscription, 6 weekly issues, $11.95.

Dow Digest (Dow Research, Box 8132, Kansas City, Mo. 64112) is best described by its subtitle, "the best of the month's stockmarket reports." Published monthly; 14 issues, $11.50. Sample copy, $1.

The Value Line Investment Survey (5 East 44th St., New York, N. Y. 10017) gives weekly evaluations on each of 1,400 stocks, and reports comprehensively on these stocks four times a year. Trial subscription: 3 months, $44.

The Dines Letter (37 Wall St., New York, N. Y. 10005) contains specific recommendations based upon a point and figure methodology, and also gives general information for traders and investors. Trial subscription: four weeks, $9.

United Business Service (210 Newbury St., Boston, Mass. 02116) imparts business information, investment reports and stock recommendations. Trial subscription: 7 months, 28 issues, $49.

Babson's Reports (Wellesley Hills, Mass. 02181) contains the opinions and advice of Babson's economists and investment specialists. One year, 52 issues, $180.

In addition to these sources of information, there are the chart services. They include the following:

Trendline Daily Basis Stock Charts (Trendline Division, Standard & Poor's Corporation, 345 Hudson St., New York, N. Y. 10014) presents large, easy-to-read bar charts for 744 leading stocks, 72 "velocity stocks" and 14 market indicators and indexes. One year, 12 issues, $68.

Mansfield NYSE or ASE Stock Chart Services (R. W. Mansfield Company, 26 Journal Square, Jersey City, N. J. 07306) offers good-sized bar charts on all NYSE (or ASE) listed stocks, and also gives good general market information—stock and group averages, technical indicators, statistical barometers and analytical comments. One year, 12 issues (NYSE only), $80; 26 issues, $155; 52 issues, $275.

I. Q. Trends (Value Trends Analysis, P.O. Box 12160, San Diego, Calif. 92112) places 250 selected blue-chip stocks into overvalued and undervalued categories based on the relationship of historic yields with current yields. Makes specific recommendations which combine long-term gains with maximum safety. Well presented; easy to understand. One year, 24 issues, $75.

Wyckoff Charting Service (Wyckoff Stock Market Institute, Inc., 778 Busse Highway, Park Ridge, Ill., 60068) presents large, carefully prepared point and figure charts and vertical line charts on 200 selected listed stocks. One year, 52 issues, $240.

Paflibe (Dines Chart Corporation, 37 Wall St., New York, N. Y. 10005) offers approximately 2,000 point and figure charts per issue, plus charts of 60 technical indicators. One year, 12 issues, $95.

The Contrary Investor (James L. Fraser, Wells, Vt. 05774) uses personalized and psychological approaches in spotting neglected and often unusual stocks for investment and speculation. Goes against the "crown approach" to the market. One year, 26 issues, $27.50.

Some brokerage firms publish and distribute periodic forecasts and reviews of business and economic factors that influence the securities market. *Bache Review* is one such publication. Write Bache & Company (36 Wall St., New York, N. Y. 10005) for a free subscription.

The Chase Manhattan Bank (1 Chase Manhattan Plaza, New York, N. Y. 10015) publishes a bimonthly discussion of significant business and economic developments, *Business in Brief.* It's free.

Books

If you're not yet well-schooled in the fundamentals of buying stocks, you can get the necessary background information you need from the countless books and pamphlets available on the subject. Among the more highly regarded books are:

How to Buy Stocks by Louis Engel (the hardcover edition is published by Little, Brown & Co. and the paperback edition by Bantam Books). With chapters like "What You Should Know About Common Stocks," "What It Costs to Buy Stocks" and "How to Tell What the Market Is Doing," this is one of the most comprehensive and at the same time one of the most lucid books written on the subject of stock-market investment. It is available through Merrill Lynch, Pierce, Fenner and Smith, Inc. (70 Pine St., New York, N. Y. 10005).

The Stock Market by George L. Leffler and Loring C. Farwell (The Ronald Press Company, $8.50), a textbook, contains a wealth of background information on securities markets, investing practices and the operation of the stock markets.

The Sophisticated Investor by Burton Crane (Simon & Schuster, $2.45) contains advice for the more knowledgeable investor; for example, how to take advantage of upturns and downtrends, using charts, and so on.

Both the New York Stock Exchange (30 Broad St., New York, N. Y. 10005) and Merrill Lynch have available an array of booklets helpful to the new investor. Write each and ask for a list.

Two books that emphasize the selection of growth stocks are:

Choosing Tomorrow's Growth Stocks Today by John W. Hazard (Paperback Library, 95¢), and *Growth Opportunities in Common Stocks* by Winthrop Knowlton (Harper & Row, $3.95). Both are written for the fledgling investor.

Overseas Investing

If you are interested in trading in the shares of a foreign industrial company, check the over-the-counter market. The major exchanges list only a handful of foreign corporations.

You can also buy an interest in foreign companies by purchasing American Depository Receipts, commonly known as ADR's. These certificates are your documentation that a specified number of shares in a foreign company have been deposited to your credit in the foreign office of a U.S. bank.

The ADR is similar in many ways to an American stock certificate. You can, for instance, as a holder of an ADR, complete the sale of your holdings in the U.S. market simply by delivering the ADR endorsed in blank. To effect a sale of your underlying shares, merely surrender your ADR to the depositary, which cables its office or agent abroad instructing the release of the actual certificates to the buyer.

Dividends declared in deposited shares are collected by the foreign custodian and cabled to the depositary. The depositary, in turn, will send you a check for the dollar equivalent after deducting its fee.

For more information on ADR's write the Morgan Guaranty Trust Company of New York (140 Broadway, New York, N.Y. 10015) and request their booklet titled, *American Depository Receipts and Bearer Depository Receipts*.

Chase Manhattan Bank (1 Chase Manhattan Plaza, New York, N. Y. 10015) distributes two publications of interest to foreign investors. One, *Latin American Business Highlights*, is a 24-page quarterly review of business and economic trends in Latin America. The other, *Report on Western Europe*, profiles business trends in Western Europe, with an emphasis on developments in Common Market countries. It is a bimonthly, four-page pamphlet. Both publications are free.

International Financial News Survey is another useful publication—also free—concerning overseas investment. A weekly newsletter, it is available from the International Monetary Fund, 19th & H streets, N. W., Washington, D. C. 20431.

IMF also publishes *International Financial Statistics*, a standard source of statistical information on every aspect of international finance. A monthly publication, it costs $10 a year.

Summing Up

Common stocks are probably the most practical and convenient method of owning, of practicing equity investment. What common stocks are best? Those of soundly managed companies in expanding industries. Growth stocks bear these hallmarks:

• Both sales and net earnings should be expanding at not less than the rate of 12 percent per year compounded.

- Company policy should show a clear emphasis on research and development.
- The price-to-earnings ratio is only important in relation to the current market averages.
- The company's equity-to-date ratio should be five to one or above.
- The company should have an assured market for its products and be blessed with a forward-looking management team.

Watch over your stock purchases carefully, tabulating dividends received and keeping track of "rights" to buy new securities. Watch for changes in company policy that might signal disenchantment with a particular product or industry.

5·Growth Funds

Mutual funds can be another answer to the problem of inflation. Indeed, a large majority of the more than 600 different funds have as their prime object "growth of capital" or "stable current growth plus current income" or "long term capital growth," and so on.

Up until the latter months of 1969, funds were doing an exemplary job of achieving their goals. During the five years ending December 31, 1969, all but a few of the funds with assets in excess of $5 million outperformed the Dow Jones Industrial Averages, according to Wiesenberger Financial Services, the principal observer and reporter of the mutual-fund field. Some 188 funds, or 94 percent of those with five-year records, surpassed the Dow Jones average, while 154, or 77 percent, outperformed Standard & Poor's 500 Common Stock Index.

For the ten-year period ending in 1969, statistics were equally as impressive. Of the funds for which a ten-year record was available, 161, or 95 percent, outperformed the Dow Jones Average. Only 85 of these, however, did better than the Standard & Poor's Index.

Note well—these are *five year* figures. For 1969 itself, the picture was not nearly so sunny. The truth is that mutual funds as a group were down more than the standard market averages during 1969, much to the consternation of the nation's securities dealers.

Nevertheless, mutual funds do offer an effective buffer against the dollar's dwindling purchasing power. For many people there is no better way to acquire ownership.

When mutual funds first started becoming popular, it was commonly held that they were a long-term investment medium. In recent years, however, that notion became obscured, what with the publicity accorded the go-go funds (see below) and other funds of specialized nature. But what happened in 1969 reaffirmed the original idea of the funds: They are for the long pull.

The fact that funds can and do act in a disappointing fashion puts greater emphasis on selectivity. You have to choose with professional know-how.

By definition, a mutual fund is a company that issues redeemable shares; that is, those which normally must be liquidated by the fund on the demand of the shareholder. The shares are bought and sold on the basis of their exact net-asset value, a price that is determined by dividing the total value of the fund's holdings by the number of shares outstanding. The figure, of course, fluctuates with the fund's changing portfolio and changes in the stock and bond prices within the portfolio.

This definition also describes an open-end investment company, one that contrasts with a closed-end company. In the latter, shares are not redeemable, but are bought and sold on the various security exchanges or over-the-counter market just like other shares. Examples of a closed-end investment company are the Lehman Corporation and the Tricontinental Corporation, both traded on the New York Stock Exchange.

After you make a purchase in a mutual fund, you receive a certificate attesting to the amount of ownership you have on the diversified list of securities owned by the fund. Then you'll be sent, usually on a quarterly basis, the varying amounts of income received from dividends and interest on the fund's securities, after the deduction of operating expenses. The funds also distribute, usually annually, net long-term profits realized from the sale of portfolio securities when they occur.

Most funds offer plans for automatic reinvestment of investment dividends and capital gains distributions. There are also accumulation plans, either voluntary or contractual, wherein you can purchase fund shares regularly in an amount that suits your budget. A plan of this type is worth considering if your investment goals are long-range, if you're seeking to accumulate capital to send the youngsters to college or as a retirement fund.

If your investment objects are the opposite, to supplement your income for current needs, you can subscribe to a withdrawal plan. Herein you receive payments on a regular schedule. Generally, some of the principal must not be withdrawn to meet the payment schedule; it remains fully invested and at work.

As virtually everyone knows, mutual-fund shares have great liquidity. The fund is ready to buy them back at any time.

If you do get pressed for cash, consider using your fund shares as loan collateral rather than selling them. This may be the less-expensive course and there's always the chance your capital will be growing.

For reasons that have never been clearly established, few investors borrow on their mutual-fund shares. Yet most banks look upon them as proper collateral, and grant loans of up to 50 percent on the selling price of the shares.

Types of Funds

It used to be that the great majority of mutual funds were either common-stock funds, with their investments concentrated in blue-chip common stocks, or "balanced" funds, in which managers invested in common stocks and other fixed-income securities as well. A few other funds invested in only preferred stocks or bonds. But the late 1960's saw a rash of diversification and specialization as a wide array of new fund categories were established.

Most of these involved a high degree of risk. If your investment capital is limited, it's better to stay with the tried and proven methods of fund selection set down in the opening paragraphs of this chapter. Some of the newer types of funds include:

The Go-Go Funds. Essentially growth funds but with "maximum performance" as their objective and their investments in the more volatile stocks, the go-go funds were the great rage during the late 1960's. They performed sensationally for a time, and some achieved gains of 60 percent to 70 percent in a single year.

In almost every case, these funds were not large and thus it was easy for them to dart in and out of special situations. Often they put their money into new, unproven "glamour" companies. Once the go-go funds began to climb, they attracted an army of investors. But as their capital increased, their ability to maneuver decreased. Add to this the fact that virtually all glamour stocks experienced a cooling off during the latter months of 1968, and you have the principal reasons why their prices tumbled. The go-go funds are no longer in favor. They're simply too speculative. They're not for the investment amateur.

Specialized Funds. There have always been special-purpose funds, those that concentrate their investments in limited fields. Insurance and bond funds are two examples. But nowadays there are many more, and they have multiplied too quickly and their degree of specialization is much too high in many cases.

There are funds that are tied to specific industries, like the Chemical Fund (65 Broadway, New York, N. Y. 10006), with its portfolio, however diversified, concentrated in chemical stocks; the National Aviation Corporation (One Rockefeller Plaza, New York, N. Y. 10020), which has about 20 percent of its net assets in aeronautics and space companies, and approximately 20 percent in airlines; and the Oceanographic Fund (80 Broad St., New York, N. Y. 10004), which specialized in companies developing or utilizing ocean resources.

Other funds specialize in geographical areas. For example, there is the Florida Growth Fund (243 South County Rd., Palm Beach, Fla. 33480) with its holdings in companies that do business in Florida and the South; the Japan Fund (25 Broad St., New York, N. Y. 10004) with investments in Japanese companies; and Eurofund International (113 Astor St., Newark, N. J. 07114), which invests up to 80 percent of its net assets in foreign countries, with major holdings in Germany, Japan and the Netherlands.

A specialized fund may be a worthwhile investment, but the fact of its specialization is no guarantee of success. Before you decide on making a purchase, research the fund just as carefully as you would any other. Pay special attention to the fund's portfolio. Be certain that it offers plenty of diversification among the major companies of the industry involved (or industries, in the case of an area fund), so the fund will be in position to benefit from every major advance.

Dual-Purpose Funds. Most funds of this type were established in the late 1960's. They were intended for the investor seeking either current income *or* capital growth. Each has a definite life span, often 15 years.

Dual-purpose funds are established as closed-end investment companies and have two classes of stock. One class is the "income" or "preferred" stock; the other is the "capital" stock. If you decide to hold the income stock, you receive dividend income, a minimum of 6 percent a year in most cases. If the minimum amount is not paid in any one year, the deficit becomes a claim against the company.

If you hold capital shares, you do not receive dividend income.

Instead, your capital gains are reinvested and you receive the assets of the fund on the date it is terminated. The claims of the holders of the income stock are satisfied first, however.

In effect, when you invest in a dual-purpose fund your money does double duty. If you hold the income stock, you receive dividends from the income stock and from the capital stock as well. The drawback is that you do not share in any of the growth proceeds. The holder of the capital stock has a similar set of advantages and disadvantages. Most investment experts agree that the greatest benefits accrue to the investors who hold the capital shares.

Bear in mind that dual-purpose funds are not mutual funds in the accepted sense. As closed-end investment companies, their shares are bought and sold in the principal stock exchanges and in the over-the-counter market.

Since most of the dual-purpose funds have been in operation for only two or three years, it is difficult to make a judgment as to their investment value. They do bear watching, however.

Here is a list of the funds of the dual-purpose type:

American Dual Vest Fund; Haywood Management Corporation, 25 Broad St., New York, N. Y. 10005.

Gemini Fund; Wellington Management Company, 1630 Locust St., Philadelphia, Pa. 19103.

Income & Capital Shares; John P. Chase, Inc., 535 Boylston St., Boston, Mass. 02109.

Leverage Fund of Boston; Vance, Sanders & Company; 111 Devonshire St., Boston, Mass. 02109.

Scudder Duo-Vest Fund; Scudder, Stevens & Clark, 10 Post Office Square, Boston, Mass. 02109.

Hemisphere Fund; Tsai Management & Research Corporation, 680 Fifth Ave., New York, N. Y. 10019.

Putnam Duo Fund; Putnam Management Company, 265 Franklin St., Boston, Mass. 02110.

Hedge Funds. Dazzling sensations of 1968, but out of favor in 1969, hedge funds, often called "leverage" funds, utilize highly speculative techniques to boost capital values. A hedge fund may borrow against its own stock portfolio to buy more shares, or speculate on puts and calls or sell shares short. Using this they seek to profit from stock-price declines as well as rises; in other words, they "hedge."

Since these funds rely upon the speculative techniques of the professional trader, they're not for the small investor or amateur.

Letter Stock Funds. These, too, are extremely speculative, investing in "restricted" stock—securities not yet registered with the Securities & Exchange Commission for sale to the general public. It is stock that is generally sold by a small, recently established company to finance research, development or expansion, a company that does not wish to go through the travail and expense of a public issue. The buyer, the mutual fund, signs an "investment letter" agreeing not to resell the stock for a specified short-term period. It's from this practice that the term "letter stock" is derived.

Often such stock can be purchased by the fund at a sizeable discount. However, it may take years before the securities are registered and sold to the public. In other words, there is a high degree of risk here.

Fees

If you have never been solicited to buy a mutual fund, you are a rare person. They are sold by a vast army of full-time mutual fund salesmen, by stockbrokers and security dealers. In addition, there are uncounted thousands of part-time fund salesmen, people who come into contact with the general public, like letter carriers and service-station attendants.

Their incentive is the sales commission. The commissions range from 4½ when the purchase amounts to over $10,000 up to 8½ (the legal limit) in the case of small investments.

Each fund has its own schedule of fees which is listed in the prospectus; or you calculate the fee by checking the fund in the listings that appear in your local newspaper.

A typical listing will look like this:

	Bid	Asked
ABC Fund	$14.44	$15.46

This means that you must pay $15.46 per share to buy the fund, but receive only $14.44 per share for selling. The difference—$1.02 —is the commission per share.

The sales commission charge is called the "loading charge" or, simply, "load." Some funds are characterized by "front-end" loads. With this type, as much as one-half of your payments during the first year may go toward sales commissions and other selling expenses. Over the life of the contract, often ten to twelve years, the loading charges average out to the aforementioned eight or nine percent. It's just that they are assesssed early, or in "front." If you drop out of the plan before completion, you severely penalize yourself.

In addition to sales commissions, there is a management fee, usually one-half of one percent a year. It is deducted from the fund's profits before any distribution is made.

In recent years some funds have begun to assess fees over and above those mentioned above. These are called "performance" or "incentive" fees. In mid-1966, about twelve funds were charging performance fees, but by early 1970 the number had increased to over one hundred, according to the Arthur Lipper Corporation, a firm that compiles statistics on funds. Fund managers say that performance fees are necessary because of the higher cost of doing business, such as increased office-rental charges and mushrooming payrolls.

The Securities and Exchange Commission has decried the use of such fees. "Many of the performance fees now in use are unfair," said Hamer Budge, chairman of the SEC, in testimony before the House Committee considering mutual-fund legislation in March 1970. He pointed out that the performance-fee arrangement was a "one-way street." Fund holders never received a penalty payment, he noted, when fund performance was below that of the leading indexes.

The No-Load Funds

Maintaining a selling organization costs money, and in the case of mutual funds this expense is passed on to the customer in the form of a commission charge. This sales charge is called a "load."

There are, however, about 100 mutual funds in existence that have no salesmen or selling organizations. They do not charge commissions of any type. They are called "no-load" funds. The advantage of buying shares in a no-load fund is that virtually all of your investment goes toward the purchase of fund shares. Most of the no-load funds were developed by investment advisory services that originally managed the portfolios of large investors but were persuaded to open up fund sales to the general public.

The fact that there are funds that charge 8 percent or so in sales commissions and others that charge precisely zero may seem anomalous at first glance. But somewhat the same condition exists in many other industries. Compare dining at the Automat with that in a full-service restaurant. At the Automat you wait on yourself and it's not expensive. In the restuarant you are served by a maitre d', a captain and a covey of waiters, and it's reflected in your bill.

The financial pages of your newspaper will give you a tip-off as to which funds are the no-load type. When you scan the listings, look for funds in which the bid and asked prices are identical. These are the no-loads. In the load funds there is a difference in the two prices. This difference is the commission charge.

For years the no-loads were sneered at by the "regular" mutual-fund industry. They were considered small, of little importance. But in the late 1960's the no-loads changed their image.

At the end of 1967, about 418,160 people owned no-load funds. By the end of 1969, the figure had spiraled to 842,259—a 61 percent increase in two years.

While the no-load funds represent from 15 to 20 percent of the total number of funds, they account for only about five percent of the industry's assets, and a mere 3½ percent of the total number of fund owners, the reason being that there's no active selling effort on their behalf. Because there are no salesmen, you must use your own initiative in gathering together background information and making an evaluation.

It must be said at once that the no-load funds *do* offer the same professional guidance as the load funds, and you are assessed for this, usually one-half of one percent a year on your invested funds. The funds offer such features as periodic accumulation plans and income investment plans, just as the load funds do. The only difference is the no-load characteristic.

However, you should not invest in a mutual fund simply because it is a no-load fund. The no-load characteristic is a benefit, but the overriding consideration has to be performance. It is better to select an astutely managed load fund than a fund that performs below the market indexes but charges no sales commission.

Listed below are the names and addresses of a number of no-load funds, all of which have current income or long-term capital growth, or both, as their objectives. Each description includes the date the fund was founded (no funds organized before 1967 are listed), the assets (a $5 million minimum was another qualification), and statistics relating to recent management performance, specifically, the percentage increase or decrease in net assets per share for the five year period ending December 31, 1969.

American Investors Fund, 88 Field Point Rd., Greenwich, Conn. 06830 (1957)
 Assets: $295,300,000
 Objective: growth of capital.
 Five-year management results: + 77.5

David L. Babson Investment Fund, 301 West Eleventh St., Kansas City, Mo. 64105 (1959)
Assets: $29,700,000
Objective: long-term growth of capital and income.
Five-year management results: + 59.3

Consultants Mutual Investments, 211 S. Broadway, Philadelphia, Pa. 19107 (1962)
Assets: $14,300,000
Objective: long-term growth of capital and income.
Five-year management results: + 70.3

de Vegh Mutual Fund, 20 Exchange Pl., New York, N. Y. 10005 (1950)
Assets: $59,000,000
Objective: long-term growth of capital.
Five-year management results: +83.3

Drexel Equity Fund, 1500 Walnut St., Philadelphia, Pa. 19109 (1961)
Assets: $53,800,000
Objective: long-term growth of capital.

Energy Fund, 2 Broadway, New York, N. Y. 10004. (1952)
Assets: $135,400,000
Objective: long-term growth of capital in fields related to energy and its sources.
Five-year management results +60.0

Ivy Fund, 155 Berkeley St., Boston, Mass. 02116 (1960)
Assets: $65,500,000
Objective: long-term capital growth.
Five-year management results: + 150.7

Johnston Mutual Fund, 230 Park Ave., New York, N. Y. 10017 (1947)
Assets: $143,200,000
Objective: long-term capital growth.
Five-year management results: + 82.2

Mathers Fund, 135 S. LaSalle St., Chicago, Ill. 60603 (1965)
Assets: $47,200,000
Objective: growth of capital.

The Nassau Fund, 1 Palmer Square, Princeton, N. J. 08540 (1957)
Assets: $8,400,000
Objective: long-term growth of capital and income.
Five-year management results: + 16.1

National Industries Fund, 1800 Avenue of the Stars, Los Angeles, Calif. 90067 (1958)
Assets: $6,000,000
Objective: long-term growth of capital and income.
Five-year management results: + 46.0

Northeast Investors Trust, 50 Congress St., Boston, Mass. 02109 (1950)
Assets: $33,900,000
Objective: production of income.
Five-year management results: + 15.7

One William Street Fund, 1 William St., New York, N. Y. 10004 (1958)
Assets: $281,300,000
Objective: capital growth plus current income.
Five-year management results: + 44.5

Penn Square Mutual Fund, 451 Penn Square, Reading, Pa. 19601 (1958)
Assets: $149,500,000
Objective: growth of capital.
Five-year management results: + 30.6

Pine Street Fund, 20 Exchange Pl., New York, N. Y. 10005 (1949)
Assets: $47,400,000
Objective: stable capital growth plus current income.
Five-year management results: + 30.9

T. Rowe Price Growth Stock Fund, 1 Charles Center, Baltimore, Md. 21201 (1950)
Assets: $613,000,000
Objective: long-term growth of capital and income.
Five-year management results: + 74.9

Scudder, Stevens & Clark Common Stock Fund, 10 Post Office Square, Boston, Mass. 02109 (1929)
Assets: $155,600,000
Objective: long-term growth of capital.
Five-year management results: + 19.6

Stein Roe & Farnham Capital Opportunities Fund, 135 S. LaSalle St., Chicago, Ill. 60603 (1954)
Assets: $16,300,000
Objective: long-term growth of capital through investment in foreign as well as domestic securities.
Five-year management results: + 32.6

Stein Roe & Farnham Stock Fund, 135 S. LaSalle St., Chicago, Ill. 60603 (1958)
Assets: $124,700,000
Objective: long-term growth of capital.
Five-year management results: + 49.3

Closed-End Funds

The great majority of mutual-fund investors prefer open-end investment companies. But closed-end companies offer a splendid opportunity in these inflationary times.

A closed-end investment company is one whose shares are not redeemable but instead are bought and sold on the securities exchanges or in the over-the-counter market. Each of these companies has a fixed amount of stock which cannot be increased. Thus they are different from the open-end companies which can increase in capital value indefinitely.

What makes the closed-end companies so attractive is that many of them sell at discounts. Take the case of one such company, the United States & Foreign Securities Corporation. As of February 28, 1970, the company's stock was being offered at 30 3/8. But the company had a net asset value of $32.10. In other words the stock was selling at a discount of 5.3 percent—and in a depressed market.

Here is a list of some of the principal closed-end funds selling at discount prices, as of February 28, 1970:

> *Carriers & General Corporation*, 1 Wall St., New York, N. Y. 10005.
> Market price: 30¾.
> Asset value: $35.55.
> Discount: 13.5%.
> *Consolidated Investment Trust*, 35 Congress St., Boston, Mass. 02109.
> Market price: 11½.
> Asset value: $11.68.
> Discount: 1.5%.
> *The Dominick Fund, Inc*, 30 Broad St., New York, N. Y. 10004.
> Market price: 10¾.
> Asset value: $11.72.
> Discount: 8.2%.
> *Eurofund, Inc*, 113 Astor St., Newark, N. J. 07114.
> Market price: 18½.
> Asset value: $21.46.
> Discount: 13.7%.
> *General American Investors, Inc.*, 60 Broad St., New York, N. Y. 10004.
> Market price: 23⅛.
> Asset value: $23.18.
> Discount: .2%.
> *International Holdings Corporation*, 61 Broadway, New York, N. Y. 10006.
> Market price: 15¾.
> Asset value: $18.30.
> Discount: 13.9%.
> *National Aviation Corporation*, 1 Rockefeller Plaza, New York, N. Y. 10020.
> Market price: 22⅞.
> Asset value: $24.74.
> Discount: 7.5%.
> *SMC Investment Company*, City National Bank Building, Sixth & Olive Sts.,
>   Los Angeles, Calif. 90014.
> Market price: 9¼.
> Asset value: $14.81.
> Discount: 37.5%.

Tri-Continental Corporation, 65 Broadway, New York, N. Y. 10006.
Market price: 30⅛.
Asset value: $31.10.
Discount: 3.1%.
The United Corporation. 250 Park Ave., New York, N. Y. 10017.
Market price: 10.
Asset value:$11.76.
Discount: 14.9%.

Selecting Funds

Many people prefer to invest in mutual funds in preference to common stocks because this course relieves them of the responsibility of studying corporate reports and evaluating industries and, in general, spending time and effort in making an appraisal. "I'll buy a fund," they figure. "I'll let a professional do my work for me."

This attitude had a great deal more validity five or six years ago than it has today. Funds have proliferated so in recent years you must do some homework in order to make an intelligent choice.

Fund size is important. A large fund, one with a diverse and lengthy portfolio, is likely to grow steadily but moderately, and thus is preferred as an investment medium if your goals are long-term. A small fund is better able to concentrate its holdings on capital-gain situations.

The fund should have what one marketing corporation refers to as "visibility." It should be relatively well known. Securities dealers and brokerage firms should be making an effort to sell it. The fund should never be a secret.

The fund's investment record also has to be appraised. What gain (or loss) has the fund achieved? This information is easy to obtain. Indeed, when a fund salesman is attempting to win a new customer, he's likely to stress the return on investment his fund has achieved and dramatize his figures with elaborate charts and stunning visual aids.

But percentage figures that appear to give an insight into management success are not always reliable. Perhaps the fund has a limited portfolio and has benefited principally from two or three holdings that have performed brilliantly. Perhaps the fund was founded in the early days of the active bull market.

Your concern has to be with the way the fund performed from the time it was established to the present, year-by-year. Be sure to look at the figures for 1969, a year that some funds led the market averages on the downside. You want a management that does well in both good times and not so good.

Ask yourself how well the fund performed in comparison to other funds with similar investment objectives. Wiesenberger's *Investment Companies* and *FundScope* (see pages 153–4) provide statistics and charts which facilitate such comparisons.

In assessing a fund's management, look for a team of managers representing the industries in the fund's securities portfolio. Besides having the characteristic of diversity, management should reflect experience in research and development.

Avoid funds that are essentially one-man operations or with a limited number of management personnel. Avoid funds that list "name" personalities in key management roles. Also be wary of funds that performed well but then suffered a turnover in management. Assure yourself that you are "buying" the management which was responsible for the fund's gains.

Enterprise Fund, Value Line Special Situations, Axe Science Corporation and Harbor Fund are four mutual funds which have shown exceptional growth in the past five years and which also qualify for consideration in terms of portfolio and management. Each of these is profiled briefly in the paragraphs that follow.

Enterprise Fund. Shareholders Management Co., 606 South Olive St., Los Angeles, Calif. 90014.
    Assets: $770,800,000

Enterprise Fund was founded in 1953 as the California Mutual Fund. New management assumed control in 1962, and the name Enterprise Fund was adopted soon after. Enterprise seeks to achieve capital growth for its shareholders by investing in growth common stocks, preferred stocks and convertible bonds. As of December 31, 1969, 12.7 percent of its portfolio consisted of stocks representing broadly based, diversified companies; 12.4 percent represented consumer products and services; 10.7 percent finance, banking and insurance; 9.3 percent general industrial companies; 6.9 percent retail trade companies; 5.8 percent business services, and 5.1 percent in natural resources and related fields.

When buying Enterprise Fund, your minimum purchase has to be $500, except in the case of a purchase made under the terms of one of the various investment plans the fund offers. Then the amount might be as low as $50.

The fund assesses a sales charge of 8.5 percent in the case of investments of less than $25,000. The charge is 6.9 percent for investments of $25,000 to $50,000.

During the past five years (1964 through 1969), only one other fund (Price New Horizons) performed better than Enterprise Fund, according to Wiesenberger Financial Services. Enterprise showed a 243.5 percent gain in net assets per share for the period, including capital gains and income dividends. For the year 1968, the increase was 44.3 percent; for 1969, Enterprise recorded a net asset loss of 25.9 percent.

Value Line Special Situations Fund, Inc. Value Line Securities, Inc., 5 East 44th St., New York, N. Y. 10017.
    Assets: $249,500,000

Value Line Special Situations seeks capital appreciation through investment in "special situations." These, according to the fund's prospectus, are securities of companies in which "unusual and possibly non-repetitive developments are taking place," developments, it is judged, that will probably cause the securities to attain a higher market value. What can cause a special situation? It can be a reorganization, recapitalization, merger, liquidation or distribution of cash, securities or other assets, a technological improvement or important discovery or acquisition, a new or changed management, or material changes in management policies.

As of December 31, 1969, the fund's investment portfolio consisted of 3.1 percent government agency securities, 3.6 percent corporate bonds, 4.3 percent warrants and 88.1 percent common stocks. Of these, 9.6 percent were electronic stocks; 8.9 percent metallurgy and mining; 6.3 percent computer services; 5.9 percent insurrance; 5.1 percent conglomerates; 5.1 percent machinery, and 4.8 percent financial.

The fund's sales charge is 8.75 percent for purchases under $15,-000, and 7.75 percent for purchases of from $15,000 to $25,000.

In terms of performance, Value Line Special Situations ranked fourth among all funds during the 1965-69 period. For 1969, the fund showed a 23.1 percent gain in net assets per share, and in 1969 a new asset loss of 33 percent per share.

Axe Science Corporation. Axe Securities Corporation, 400 Benedict Ave., Tarrytown, N. Y. 10591.
    Assets: $50,400,000

Axe Science Corporation stresses investment in companies that are expected to benefit from new scientific developments. Management relies upon a battery of scientific advisers to evaluate these developments and their impact upon specific industries.

Harbor Fund, Inc., 606 South Olive St., Los Angeles, Calif. 90014.
　　Assets: $109,600,000

Harbor Fund, organized in 1956, was originally known as the Kerr Income Fund. Its name was later changed to Convertible Securities Fund, and then, in 1969, to Harbor Fund, Inc.

The fund, according to its prospectus, seeks to "provide income, reasonable protection of capital and potential growth of capital." To accomplish this threefold objective, Harbor Fund owns a portfolio that consists principally of convertible bonds and convertible preferred stock. It is the only mutual fund that so specializes.

In buying Harbor Fund, a minimum purchase of $500 is required, although purchases in units of $50 are possible by means of the fund's Shareholder Investment Account.

Harbor Fund assesses a sales charge of 8.5 percent for purchases under $25,000, and 6.9 percent for purchases from $25,000 to $50,000.

For the five-year period ending in 1969, Harbor Fund showed an 86.4 percent gain in net assets per share. For 1968, the gain was 28.9 percent per share. For 1969, the fund showed a loss of 20.2 percent per share.

> *Security Equity Fund.* Security Management Co., Inc., 700 Harrison St., Topeka, Kan. 66603.
> Objective: maximum capital gain.
> Assets: $138,500,000.
> Five-year net asset gain: 195.2%.
> *Ivy Fund.* Studley, Shupert & Co., Inc. 155 Berkeley St., Boston, Mass. 02116.
> Objective: maximum capital gain.
> Assets: $65,400,000.
> Five-year net asset gain: 150.7%.
> *Chase Fund of Boston, Inc.* Chase Distributors Corporation, 535 Boylston St., Boston, Mass. 02116.
> Objective: maximum capital gain.
> Assets: $113,100,000.
> Five-year net asset gain: 146.3%.
> *Channing Special Fund Inc.* Channing Company, Inc., 280 Park Ave., New York, N. Y. 10017.

Objective: maximum capital gain.

Assets: $165,600,000.

Five-year net asset gain: 140.6%.

Knickerbocker Growth Fund, Inc. Knickerbocker Shares, Inc., 20 Exchange Pl., New York, N. Y. 10005.

Objective: maximum capital gain.

Assets: $11,900,000.

Five-year net asset gain: 133.6%.

Crown Western Investments; Dallas Fund Series S 3. Box 1372, Houston, Tex. 70001.

Objective: maximum capital growth.

Assets: $13,600,000.

Five-year net asset gain: 124.2%.

Fund Information Sources

Your prime source of information in evaluating a mutual fund is the prospectus, the official circular that describes the company issuing the shares and gives definitive information as to the shares themselves. The prospectus is vital to your investigation. Write the fund and request one.

The prospectus explains the fund's investment objective and policy. It tells what rights and restrictions apply to shares and gives the fund policy on dividends, capital gains dividends and taxes.

The prospectus lists the fund's board of directors and any other person who is involved in instrumenting investment policy, and each man is profiled. It gives background information as to the fund's performance, and explains in detail how shares are purchased, redeemed and the commission rates. Special plans, like a periodic investment plan, are detailed. Last, the prospectus includes a financial statement setting down in detail the fund's assets and liabilities.

Always begin your fund appraisal with the prospectus. Then turn to one of the several advisory services available.

Most brokers and money managers consider Arthur Wiesenberger's *Investment Companies* the preeminent sourcebook on funds. An annual, it is published by the Wiesenberger Services Division of the Nuveen Corporation (61 Broadway, New York, N. Y. 10006). It costs $45, but it's likely you can consult the book at your public library, or surely at your broker's office.

FundScope (Suite 700, 1900 Avenue of the Stars, Los Angeles, Calif. 90067) is another splendid information source. The 1970 edition of the FundScope *Mutual Fund Guide* gives statistical records for 428 funds, such information as the net asset value per share, capital gain distributions per share, high and low offering prices, and so on.

The guidebook stresses performance and offers ratings that grade funds "above average" or "below average" in growth, income and overall stability. The *Mutual Fund Guide* costs $15.

FundScope also publishes a monthly magazine with news and features about funds. A 14-month subscription is $45. A trial subscription for three months, which includes a free copy of the *Mutual Fund Guide*, is $17.

Forbes (60 Fifth Ave., New York, N. Y. 10011) also rates funds in its annual *Mutual Fund Survey*. Its 1970 edition appraises more than 400 funds, including 56 no-loads, giving assets, dividends and expenses for each, and rates performance in relation to market fluctuations. It's free when you purchase a subscription to *Forbes*.

In the case of no-load funds, you can gain useful information from the *No-Load Fund Digest* (Box 61, Wayland, Mass. 01778). A monthly publication, the *Digest* analyzes more than 75 of the no-loads, giving performance summaries and charts for each. A trial copy is $2.

For background information on mutual funds, I suggest two books:

The Money Managers, published by McGraw-Hill Book Co. (330 West 42nd St., New York, N. Y. 10036) is a readable handbook explaining the funds and how they work, and gives a comprehensive picture of the industry as a whole. It costs $1.95.

A more objective view of the field is contained in *Investment Trust and Funds*, a 96-page booklet available for $1 from the American Institute of Economic Research (Great Barrington, Mass. 01230). It surveys funds with the same candor Consumers Union appraises television sets.

The 96-page *Mutual Fund Fact Book* also gives general background information on funds, including an array of charts and statistics. For a free copy write the Investment Company Institute (1775 K Street, N. W., Washington, D. C. 20006).

Summing Up

Mutual funds are a splendid inflation hedge, but bear in mind, when investing, that your goals should be more long-term than short-term. Don't trade back and forth; buy and hold.

Avoid go-go funds, funds that are overspecialized, hedge funds and letter-stock funds.

When evaluating a fund, be certain to check its prospectus. Give special attention to the fees charged, the size of the fund, its portfolio and the fund management. Appraise fund performance in relation to other funds and the market averages.

6 · The Bond Market

Inflation is self-generating and self-perpetuating. When people think prices are going to continue to increase, their buying decisions reflect their expectations. They are less likely to postpone purchases of home appliances or automobiles. Workers press for substantial wage increases to offset the rising cost of living. Wage increases lead to higher production costs and influence management to raise prices.

Inflation also diminishes the value of all fixed-income investments, including bonds. As prices edge downward, yields increase. Each week the Dow Jones staff prepares a municipal bond-yield index, an arithmetic average of the yields of 20 selected state and city bonds, all new issues with 20-year maturities. During 1969, the index ranged between a low of 4.82 percent for the week ending July 24 and high of 6.86 percent for the week ending December 19. It marked the first time the index shot above the 6 percent level since 1927, the year the average was first calculated.

Moreover, the 2.04 percent fluctuation was the sharpest for any single year. When translated into market prices, the swing meant that a bond costing $1,000 in July could have been bought for about $745 in mid-December.

It's not just local government bonds that are attractively priced. Consider this: On April 13, 1970, new American Telephone & Telegraph Company bonds were offered to shareholders at 8 3/4 percent. On May 5 that year the bonds were being traded at 95 1/2, a price that gave investors a return of 9.19 percent, a record for triple A (highest quality) corporate bonds.

It's already clear that millions of Americans have switched from the savings and loan to the bond window. In most years the general public has comprised between 10 and 20 percent of the bond market. But in 1969 individuals accounted for more than one-half of the government long-term issues, and on some corporate issues estimates of the general public's participation ran from 60 to 70 percent of the offering.

CORPORATION BONDS

Bonds—corporate bonds—are among the most conservative of all investments. They should not be considered inflation-proof. A bond is simply an I.O.U., a corporation's promissory note. It promises to pay you, the bondholder, a specified amount of interest periodically over a certain length of time and also repay the loan in full on the expiration date.

A bond is not an equity investment; you own nothing. It is not a growth security.

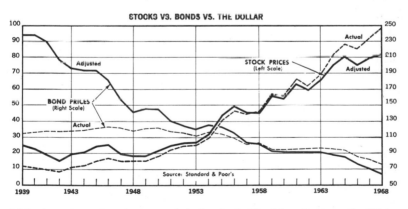

This chart shows how investments in bonds declined in value over the thirty year period, 1939-1969, while common stocks increased in value. The "adjusted" line takes into account increases in the cost of living. (*Copyright* FINANCIAL WORLD, *New York, N.Y., 1969*)

Why mention bonds? Because of their interest rates. Industrial bonds or utility bonds are a good investment substitute for a savings account. Eight or nine percent interest is better than five percent. It's as simple as that.

One other point. When buying bonds, it's no longer necessary to put your money away for 20 or 30 years. An increasing number of corporations are issuing five-year bonds. Bonds of this type were virtually unknown until 1969, but in the first nine months they were in use they accounted for about $1.3 billion in public financing.

Five-year bonds at eight and nine percent! No wonder they're high in the public's favor.

A word about bonds in general. The dictionary defines a bond as a "sealed instrument under which a person, corporation or government guarantees to pay a stated sum of money on or before a certain date." A bond, then, is similar to a promissory note or an I.O.U.

As most people realize, the market in bonds is dominated by banks, insurance companies, pension funds, and other large financial institutions. Thus it's a field in which the small investor has to be somewhat wary.

Bonds are usually issued in multiples of $1,000. After issue the price fluctuates. In the bond market, prices are quoted as a percentage of the face value, and the financial-page listings do not include the percentage sign. To figure the price of a $1,000 bond, simply multiply the quoted figure by 10. For example, early in 1970 bonds issued by the Great Northern Railway were quoted at 92, or $920; Sherwin Williams bonds were at 100 3/4, or $1,007.50.

Bonds have a fixed rate of interest, but this is only one aspect of their value. Actually, there are three methods of measuring what a bond is worth.

The *interest rate* on a bond is based on its face value. On a 5 ½ percent bond, you receive $55 a year (5 ½ percent of $1,000), and you receive this amount no matter how the price of the bond might fluctuate. Usually interest is paid every six months.

In the case of a coupon bond (a bond with interest coupons attached) the coupons are clipped as they come due and are presented to the issuer for payment of interest.

Current yield is the second way a bond's value is measured. Suppose you buy a bond at a price that is above or below the face value. It follows then that the fixed rate of interest is not a valid measure of the return you will be receiving. To figure a bond's current yield, simply divide the dollar amount of interest by the price you pay for the bond. A 5 ½ percent bond, one paying $55 in annual interest, that is purchased for $850 would have a current yield of 6.47 percent ($55 divided by $850).

A bond's third value indicator is *yield to maturity*. If you buy a bond at $850 and hold it to maturity, you stand to gain $150, for it will be redeemed at $1,000. If you buy a bond at $1,100, you are going to lose $100 at maturity. Yield to maturity takes into account a bond's gain or loss. It also considers the current yield. Those dealing in bonds use a set of bond-yield tables to determine yield to maturity (or you can use the instructions on page 164). It's vital to know this figure. It's the clearest indicator of what your money is going to earn.

Many bonds are subject to "call." This means they can be redeemed by the company before maturity.

If you own "bearer bonds," your name will not be listed on the company's books, and you will be notified of forthcoming redemptions by means of newspaper advertisements. Get in the habit of reading the call ads. If your broker subscribes to a service which reports calls, he can backstop you.

When you buy or sell bonds, deal with a "bond house." They usually own the bonds they sell. This means you won't have to pay any commission. The bond house's profit is the difference between the two sides of the market, the bid and the asked prices, or, to put it another way, the wholesale and the retail. A bond house purchases bonds at the wholesale price and sells them at the retail. The difference between the two prices, called the "spread," is normally two points, or $20 per $1,000 bond.

You can also trade through your securities broker but if he isn't a dealer he will assess a service charge over and above the spread.

Summing Up

In mid-1970, industrial and utility bonds were being offered at the most attractive rate in history. In purchasing such bonds, you are not necessarily protecting your savings against inflation, but bonds are a fine investment substitute for a savings account. First establish the bond's value in terms of interest rate, current yield and yield to maturity. Then get a clear idea of what fees are going to be involved in the transaction. Look for bonds with five year maturities.

CONVERTIBLE SECURITIES

A well-dressed middle-aged gentleman came into my office recently, introduced himself and we chatted. He told me that he had been extremely active in the market during the past ten years.

"How are you doing?" I asked.

He smiled. "You know," he said, "I've never lost on a single investment."

This is not the stunning achievement it seems at first glance. Limit yourself to the bond market and it's not likely you will lose. The problem is that you won't gain very much.

But then my visitor told me that his investments had brought him substantial month-to-month income plus large profits. Then I knew he could be investing in only one type of security—convertible bonds.

I recommend them without reservation.

The purchase of long-term bonds is seldom advised during times of inflation. But *convertible* bonds are different. By giving you all of the safety of a conventional bond, plus the possibility of the same capital gain you might get with a common stock, convertible bonds offer you the best of both possible worlds.

Convertible Bonds

What is a convertible bond? It's a bond with an extra. When you buy a convertible, the bond contract gives you the provision of converting the bond into a specified number of shares of the common stock of the issuing company. This means you are getting the security of the bond plus the right to participate in the growth of the company through the acquisition of common stock.

It must be said that convertible bonds are "junior" debt obligations and not quite the equal of the issuing company's other bonds from the standpoint of safety. Nevertheless, convertibles get extremely high marks in this respect. Unless the firm goes bankrupt, the convertible bond can always be redeemed at maturity for at least its face value.

Convertible bonds are issued in $1,000-dollar denominations as are conventional corporate bonds. The interest rate, sometimes called the "coupon" rate, is set as a percentage of the face amount. The issuing company promises to repay the principal—that is, redeem the bond—on a specified date, the maturity date. Many convertible bonds are callable, which means they can be redeemed by the issuing company before the maturity date, usually at a small premium—3 to 4 percent—over the face amount.

The bond's conversion feature is measured by how much the common stock has to rise before you can begin to make a profit on the conversion rights. Usually, the conversion figure is 10 to 15 percent above the current price of the stock. Naturally, the closer the conversion figure to the current price of the stock, the more appealing the bond. I suggest, as a general rule, that the conversion price be within 15 percent of the current stock price on any bond you purchase.

In practice, it works like this. Suppose you buy a 5 percent, $1,000 bond that can be converted into 20 shares of common stock. Assuming you paid the full face value for the bond, you would be getting the rights to convert at $50 a share. But at the time of your purchase, it's likely the stock would be selling at between $40 and $45 a share.

You're betting the stock will rise to, say, $50 or $60. In that event you make a profit by converting the bond into stock. If it did hit $60 and you sold, you'd get $1,200. (Actually, it's not always necessary to exercise the conversion rights. As the stock price begins to move upward, the bond itself will reflect the rise.)

Suppose the common stock declines. The bond is also going to decline. But its decline is not going to be as sharp, for as the bond price goes down, its yield rises and the bond does not lose in attractiveness.

If, for example, the bond should drop in price to 70—$700, the $50 of interest payable each year (5 percent of the $1,000 face value) is equivalent to a current yield of 7.01 ($50 divided by $700). Bond buyers could not help but be attracted to the issue.

So convertibles tend to resist declines even when other bonds are falling in value. Their convertibility feature imparts stability.

There are scores of different convertible bonds issued every year. Virtually every major U.S. corporation has relied upon this method of raising money at one time or another.

The foremost reason they are issued in preference to bonds of the more usual kind is that convertibles enable the issuing company to pay a lower interest rate. Because of the conversion feature, the corporation realizes that it can offer the bonds at ½ percent or even 1 percent lower than the current bond interest rates. This can mean a saving of many millions of dollars.

Convertibles are also issued when a corporation believes the price of its stock is on the rise. If their belief is right, then many bondholders will exercise their conversion rights and the corporation will not have to pay back the borrowed capital. Small corporations with substantial bond indebtedness but only a limited number of shareholders sometimes prefer convertibles in a rising market, too. Because the bonds are likely to be converted into stock, they not only avoid incurring additional indebtedness but also increase the number of stockholders.

Selecting Convertible Bonds

"Can and will the corporation repay the loan?" This is the first question to ask yourself when appraising a convertible issue. Don't buy simply because you are intrigued by the conversion feature of the security and/or because the interest rate is particularly high or both. As a matter of policy, never purchase a convertible from any corporation whose conventional bonds you would not buy.

The answer to the question concerning repayment is often provided by the answer to a second question, "Have previous loans been repaid?" Both Standard & Poor's and Moody's rate bonds according to the issuing company's ability to meet interest payments and redeem the securities, and the corporation's past repayment record is a vital factor in these evaluations.

The underwriter is another guide to quality. Be sure you are dealing with a major firm, one that does a major amount of underwriting on a year-to-year basis. An industry leader is not going to endanger his reputation by selling a risk-filled issue.

Investigate the issuing company's earnings and assets. The latter should be well in excess of the face value of the bonds being issued.

In almost every case, a convertible bond will sell at a lower yield than a nonconvertible bond issued by the same company. Compare the two. It is my opinion that the interest paid by the convertible should be within 1 percent of the nonconvertible interest.

Don't consider investing in convertible bonds unless you have both the time and inclination to watch over them. They require special attention.

Consider conversion privileges, for example. Some run to maturity. Others do not; they may run out in a specified number of years or they may change. American Machine & Foundry Company is offering 4 ¼ percent bonds to mature in 1982. The conversion rate is 18 shares per $1,000 bond. But this rate remains in effect only until March 1971, and in the years thereafter the rate is not quite so attractive.

You also have to keep aware of the bond's call features. If the issuing corporation decides to call your $960 bond for $1,050, you could make an adequate profit by turning in the bond for redemption. (It's likely you could also sell the bond profitably, for the market price will rise to within a fraction of the call price.)

But sometimes the bond's selling price is higher than the call price. What then? You must either sell or convert the security before the final date of the call.

Many convertibles are bearer bonds; they are not registered by owner on company records. To announce that a bond is being called in for redemption, the corporation schedules newspaper advertisements in the financial press. You must check the newspapers regularly to be aware of calls. When there has been a substantial sale of bonds in a particular region, the issuing corporation will advertise the redemption in the newspapers in that region. It's standard practice to publish the first call notice 30 days before the redemption day.

If you don't plan to check for call advertisements, put the bonds in your broker's hands. They will then be checked daily against a redemption list.

Computing Yields

Once issued, convertibles are traded on the New York Stock Exchange like other bonds. Financial newspapers report on bond sales each day. Here are sample listings:

Corporation	Type of Bond	High	Low	Last	Net Change
Alcoa	cv5 ¼ s91	97½	96	96	−1½
American Airlines	cv4 ¼ s92	66½	65½	66½	+ 1
American Machine & Foundry	cv4 ¼ s81	67	66½	66½	−¾
B & O Railroad	cv4 ½ s2010	47	46⅝	47	—
Commonwealth Oil	cv4 ¼ s92	85	85	85	−½
Del Monte	cv5 ¼ s94	75	75	75	—
Eastern Air Lines	cv8s95	109¼	108½	108½	—

Let's take a close-up look at one listing:

Alcoa	cv5 ¼ s91	97½	96	96	−1½

The "cv" indicates the bonds are convertible; the "5 ¼ s" is the coupon rate, the current interest (literally, five-and-one-quarter bonds). The "91" is the maturity date—1991.

The balance of the listing refers to the day's trading activity. Bonds are quoted in units of 100. The "97½" means the bond is selling at $950.

The newspaper listings give no indication of the conversion figure (except as it may be reflected in the price). You will have to get this information from your broker.

Remember, the newspaper listing gives you only the coupon rate, or the current interest rate. The figure that is more important to you is yield to maturity. This takes into consideration either the discount or the premium at which the bond is selling.

Your broker will give you the yield-to-maturity figure. Or you can come to a fairly close approximation by using this step-by-step method (the figures refer to a 5 percent, $1,000 bond that is selling at 96—$960).

1. Add the price paid to the redemption figure and divide by 2 to get the average value:

$$\frac{\$960 + \$1,000}{2} = \$980$$

2. Divide the discount (the face value minus the price paid) by the number of years to maturity. Let's suppose the bond has 10 years to run.

$$\$1,000 - \$940 = \$60 \qquad \frac{\$60}{10} = \$6$$

3. Add the result—$6—to the annual interest—$50—and divide by the average value—$980. The result is the yield to maturity.

$$\frac{\$50 + \$6}{\$980} = 5.71\%$$

In purchasing a bond, suppose you had to pay a premium over the redemption value. In this event, the premium (the price paid minus the face amount) has to be divided by the number of years, and the resulting figure *subtracted* from the annual interest.

Convertible Preferreds

Preferred stock, like common stock, represents ownership in a company's net worth. It is junior, or subordinate, to all debts the company owes, but has a claim ahead of the common stock upon company assets and dividend payments. These facts are well known.

A special type of preferred stock is the convertible preferred. Like convertible bonds, convertible-preferred stocks combine the advantages of stock ownership with those of fixed-income securities. They are becoming increasingly popular.

A convertible preferred stock is one that gives the owner the right to convert it into a stated number of common shares. Suppose a company sold a new issue of convertible preferred which provided that each share could be converted to three shares of common stock at any time within the ensuing five years. Further suppose the preferred to be selling at $90 a share. The convertibility feature would increase in value as the common stock advanced toward $30 a share and would be eminently worthwhile once the stock crossed that level.

The price of convertible preferred usually reflects that of the company's common stock. If the company shows a good earnings record and the price of the common stock rises as a result, the convertible preferred is almost sure to rise, too. When the common falls, the convertible preferred is also likely to suffer.

Some convertible preferreds offer a "cumulative" feature, another plus. Should the company omit its dividend because of insufficient earnings, the amount due accumulates, becoming a claim of the stockholder against the corporation. It would be paid in the next year or whenever earnings were sufficient.

Like convertible bonds, preferred stock is often callable. A company will usually exercise its option to call and redeem an issue of preferred stock if it believes it can replace the issue with one carrying a lower dividend rate.

Convertible preferred stock is often issued in units of $100. The annual return is then expressed as a percentage of the face amount.

About 20 percent of all preferred issues traded on the New York Stock Exchange is of the convertible type. Here are some of them (prices are as of April 1970):

Corporation	Common Shares per 1 share of preferred	Common Price	Convertible Price
American Metal Climax 4	2.5	37½	95½
American Waterworks 1.25	1.3	9½	17
Beneficial Finance 4.30	1.4	49¼	76½
Federal Pacific Electric 1.26	.9	11¼	15½
FMC Corporation 2.25	1.2	23	36½
International Tel. & Tel. 4	3.4	49½	154
Kaiser Aluminum 4.75	1.6	37½	78
McCrory 4.50	2.5	20½	59
RCA 4	2.0	25½	67
Reynolds Metals 4.50	2.0	31½	82
Scovill Manufacturing 2.50	1.2	43½	56
Textron 2.08	1.1	23½	33½

So-called "straight" preferreds, those without any of the added benefits, have traditionally been regarded as conservative in nature. But the addition of the feature of convertibility adds excitement to the issue and makes it of special value.

Summing Up

Convertible bonds not only offer substantial protection against inflation, they give you the safety you expect from a bond plus the chance for capital gain just like common stock. But you have to be selective.

• Assure yourself that the issuing company will be able to redeem the securities and meet interest payments. Check the issue's rating in *Moody's* or *Standard & Poor's*.

• Deal with an established underwriter.

• Establish that the interest rate on the convertible is within 1 percent of the interest being paid on nonconvertible bonds issued by the corporation, and that the conversion price at issue is within 15 percent of the current stock price.

• Once you make a purchase, keep a close check on it, especially if the conversion rate is subject to change or if the issue is callable.

Warrants

A warrant is very similar to a convertible bond. It is a certificate that gives the holder the right to buy a specified number of shares of a stock at a certain price during a stated period of time, usually 10 years or so.

But warrants are more speculative than convertible bonds. Cynics call them "funny money."

Warrants won wide attraction in April 1970 when the American Telephone & Telegraph Company launched its massive rights offering, the biggest in corporate history. Its 1.57 billion in debentures carried warrants that entitled purchasers to buy company stock at $52 a share at any time between November 15, 1970, and May 15, 1975. The New York Stock Exchange promptly listed the warrants, breaking a tradition of more than fifty years. Formerly the Big Board had refused to list warrants with a life of more than ninety days.

Why does a company with the financial stature of AT & T issue warrants? They're simply an added inducement to buy the securities being offered. It's wiser to give away warrants, which cost the company nothing, than to pay a higher interest rate.

Warrants give you no direct equity in the company. You receive no dividends. You have no voting rights. What you do have is the opportunity for capital gain. You do, that is, so long as you have "leverage."

The degree of leverage is the first thing to look for in appraising a warrant. Ask yourself: "How much will the warrant move if the stock doubles in price?"

For instance, suppose you purchase a warrant for $1 that gives you the right to purchase stock at $5. The stock is trading at $5. Thus the warrant has no real value, only potential value.

Suppose the stock rises to $10. The warrant now has real value of $5—the market price ($10) minus the option price ($5). While the stock was doubling in price (from $5 to $10), the warrant increased five times in value. It's leverage factor was 5 to 1.

Consider a 5-to-1 rate extremely high, a rarity that is common to only the most speculative of issues. A leverage factor of 4 to 1 or 3 to 1 is high, too. But don't consider buying a warrant if the leverage factor is less than 2 to 1.

In addition to assuring yourself that you're getting plenty of leverage, look also for a stock that is volatile. Unless, by virtue of increased earnings or some special situation, the stock has the potential to rise in price, the leverage factor means nothing.

A third consideration is the life of the security. When is it due to expire? Occasionally a warrant runs to perpetuity; other times you have as long as twenty years to exercise your option. But usually the life of a warrant is much less, ranging down to a year.

You must assure yourself that you're getting sufficient time to allow the stock to move. It's wise to limit your warrant purchases to those with a life of at least five years.

Also be alert to the call provisions of the warrant. If you buy a warrant with a life of 20 years, then the issuing company has the right to redeem the security at a specified price— invariably a miniscule one—at its option. In essence, this is the right to cancel the warrant. Beware of callable warrants.

Summing Up

Warrants offer considerable upside appreciation, but there are downside risks as well. Cut the risk factor by following these guidelines:

- The leverage factor of the warrant, as compared to the price of the common stock, should be at least 2 to 1.
- The stock involved must have the potential to rise in price.
- The warrant must have a life of at least five years.
- Stay away from callable warrants.

Municipal Bonds

During the late 1960's and early 1970's, middle-income investors began to show an ever-increasing interest in municipal bonds. It's not difficult to understand why. The inflationary trend of the economy boosted millions of middle-income workers into the higher tax brackets, and the higher one's tax bracket the more attractive municipal bonds become, for, as is commonly known, municipal bonds are exempt from federal income taxes on their interest and from state taxes in the state where they are issued.

This rise in popularity has been accompanied by an upswing in the number of new municipal issues. In the years before World War II, new municipals were being issued at the rate of about $1 billion a year, and the total outstanding was less than $20. During 1968, more than $16 million in new municipals were offered for sale, a record. Basically, the increased volume is tied to the nation's ever-increasing demand for new public facilities—highways, schools, public housing and all the rest.

While municipals are usually purchased for the tax advantage they offer, they are highly regarded for their safety, too, ranking right behind U. S. government bonds. Merrill, Lynch, Pierce, Fenner and Smith, Inc., and other leading bond firms, point out that even in the severe depression of the 1930's, more than 98 percent of all municipals met their payment obligations in full. There is an active market in municipals in every part of the country, should you wish to sell before maturity.

Types of Municipals

Municipal bonds may or may not be concerned with municipalities. They are issued by states, cities, counties, toll roads, school districts and other types of local authorities to finance public facilities of various types.

When you purchase a municipal bond, the issuing authority promises to repay your money by a specified time and pay you a specific rate of interest. There are several basic types of municipals.

General Obligation Bonds. These are bonds backed by the "full faith and credit" of the issuing authority. In other words, the issuing body promises to use its unlimited taxing authority to assure that the interest on the bonds is paid in full when due and the full value of the bonds is returned to the holders at maturity. New York City, Philadelphia, Los Angeles, Chicago, Detroit, Boston and many other big cities have done much of their financing by means of general obligation bonds.

Limited Tax Bonds. This type of bond is backed only by a portion of the taxing power of the issuing authority, perhaps by a state's gasoline taxes or property revenues. The Michigan Limited Access Highway Dedicated Tax Bonds, for instance, are supported solely from a share of Michigan's gasoline taxes and motor vehicle fees.

Revenue Bonds. These bonds are secured by the revenues of a particular department of the issuing muncipality or state. The Los Angeles Department of Water and Power had issued bonds which are payable solely by the revenues derived from the city's power and water systems.

Revenue bonds can also be issued by a governmental "authority," which has been brought into being to create or operate a public facility. Toll-road and turnpike-authority bonds are well-known examples of these.

Housing Authority Bonds. The income from housing authority bonds goes to finance low-rent housing projects, and they are paid off not only by the rents charged but also by the federal government's Housing Assistance Administration. Housing authority bonds are often given an Aaa rating; this is because the Housing Act declares ". . . the full faith and credit of the United States is pledged to the payments of all amounts agreed . . . ."

Industrial Revenue Bonds. Industrial revenue bonds are issued by a municipality or authority. They are secured by lease payments made by tenants, usually industrial manufacturers, which occupy and use the facility financed by the issue. In 1967, for example, the City of Fort Madison, Iowa, issued industrial revenue bonds to finance construction of an industrial complex for Sinclair Petrochemical. The late 1960's saw a sharp upsurge in the volume of industrial revenue bonds.

Buying a Municipal

Purchasing a municipal bond is done in much the same way you buy common stock. The dealer calls and gives you a bid; you make a decision. Before you answer "yes" or "no," there are several factors to consider.

Who is the issuer? What type of bond is it? These are the first matters to consider. Suppose it's not a general obligation bond, the blue chip of the municipals, but a revenue bond. Then you should make an attempt to judge the bond on the basis of its own investment merits, on its profit and loss statement. Look at the ratio of net earnings to annual interest. The earnings, after deductions for operating expenses and bond repayment at maturity, should be twice the amount the authority requires to meet annual interest payments.

Don't be influenced by the legal opinion that accompanies the bond issue. Printed on the face of the bond, it attests that the bonds have been legally issued under existing laws. In other words, it is merely an opinion as to the issue's legality, not its quality.

When it comes to measuring quality, it's not wrong to accept the opinion of one of the advisory services, *Standard & Poor's* or *Moody's*. From the highest to the lowest, they rate municipals like this:

Standard & Poor's	AAA	AA	A	BBB	BB	B	CCC	CC	C
Moody's	Aaa	Aa	A	Baa	Ba	B	Caa	Ca	C

Generally speaking, it's not wise to invest in an issue that is rated below BBB or Baa. This doesn't hold true for the person who is extremely knowledgeable about the bond market and feels, because of his own research, that a low-rated issue is not a risky one.

Sometimes an issue is not rated, but this doesn't mean it is necessarily low in quality. *Standard & Poor's* rates municipals only under contract. In the case of *Moody's,* it might be that municipality has not supplied sufficient information to permit an evaluation.

It must be said that ratings are not an infallible guide to a bond's merit. All bonds above the BBB or Baa levels are of high quality, and to make several additional and minute assessments can be superfluous.

Another problem with ratings is that they affect the bond's price. The higher the rating, the easier it is to sell an issue and thus the issuing authority can charge more. In other words, the very bestowal of ratings tends to invert the relationship between true value and market value. It is significant that in the wide fluctuation of bond rates that occurred during the 1968-69 period, the broadest swings were in the AAA and Aaa groups. There were progressively smaller fluctuations on the next three groups. Ratings are very important, but don't rely on them exclusively.

Once you're satisfied as to the quality of an issue, then consider it from an investment standpoint. There are literally tens of thousands of municipal issues, and they vary widely in coupon rates, maturities and yields, but as long as you consider one factor at a time, keeping your basic investment goals in mind, it should not be difficult to reach a sound decision.

If you deal with a bond house, you are likely to receive a list of offerings, as shown below. These are all general obligations, incidentally.

Rating	Par Amount	Description	Coupon Rate	Maturity	Yield to Maturity	Approx. Price
Aaa	10,000	Rochester, N. Y.	2¾%	10/15/72	5.00%	99⅛
Aa	5,000	New York State	2.70%	3/1/94	6.50%	54⅛
Aa	10,000	Newington, Conn.	3.90%	2/1/84	6.25%	78⅝
A	5,000	Manchester, Conn.	2.70%	3/1/77	6.40%	80
Baa	25,000	New York City Housing Authority, Guaranteed	3¼%	11/1/83	6.85%	69
Baa	10,000	Philadelphia, Pa., School District	2⅜%	6/1/71	6.00%	96¼
Baa	5,000	East Brunswick, N. J.	3.80%	10/1/71	6.00%	97⅛
Ba	4,000	Chicago Transit Authority	4½%	7/1/72	6.70%	75⅛

Let's discuss this entry in depth:

Baa	25,000	New York City Housing Authority, Guaranteed	3¼%	11/1/83	6.85%	69

Par Amount: 25,000. Par amount, sometimes called par value, is the principal amount of the bond—in this case, $25,000. Even though the par amount is $25,000, most bond houses will sell the issue in multiples of $5,000.

Description: New York City Housing Authority. The interest and principal on this bond are the legal obligation of the authority. Moreover, since these are housing-authority bonds, they are guaranteed by the Housing Assistance Administration.

Coupon Rate: 3¼ percent. The coupon rate is the interest on $1,000 of face value. Use the figure to determine "current yield." In the case above, the coupon rate is 3¼ percent; the price of the issue is 69. Divide the coupon rate (32.50) by the sum invested

($690.). The resulting figure (4.71 percent) is the current yield. This is the vital figure to know if your goal is current income.

Maturity: 11/1/83. It is on this date that the last semiannual coupon falls due, and the bond itself becomes redeemable at 100 —or $1,000.

Yield to Maturity: 6.85 percent. This is the key figure. As explained above (page 164), yield to maturity is a combination of two things: the current yield, plus the difference between the selling price and the amount received at maturity, $310 in the above example. The yield to maturity, then, is the rate of return you receive on the sum invested.

Approximate Price: 69. The word "approximate" is standard in announcing a bond's price, for the exact price depends upon the number of days remaining in the life of the security on the day of the transaction. Usually the exact price differs from the approximate price by only a few cents.

Most municipal bonds are bearer bonds, which means you are presumed to own the security by virtue of your possession of it. Coupons are attached to bearer bonds, and every six months you clip one to collect your interest from the issuing authority.

In some cases, the bonds are registered, and your name is listed in the record of the issuing authority along with the bond itself. With registered bonds, your interest payments will be mailed to you like the dividends on common stock.

Many municipals are available in $1,000 units, although there is a growing tendency to make the minimum issue $5,000. In almost every case, a purchase of $5,000 or less represents an odd lot. But unlike odd lots in common stocks, the odd lots in municipals often sell at lower prices than the identical issue in blocks. The odd-lot buyer may actually receive a yield to maturity rate that is .05 to .10 percent better than the block buyer.

A municipal bond, like any other fixed income security, will rise and fall in value during the years it's in your possession. These fluctuations are tied to the changes in the prime-money rates. In the first months of 1970, prime-interest rates were at their highest levels in history. Yield rates on bonds were similarly high, while prices on bonds dipped. When yields began to move down, prices edged up.

The majority of bondholders are unconcerned with changes in market value. They look upon municipals as long-term investments and hold them to maturity.

But the secondary market is there, and it affords you the opportunity of selling the bond whenever you wish. This secondary market is not a formal marketplace as is the New York Stock Exchange, for example. It's an over-the-counter market, with dealers throughout the country negotiating by telephone and teletype.

Tax Exempt vs. Taxable Income

Is it worthwhile for you to invest in municipal bonds? This chart will help you to decide. It enables you to quickly compare tax-exempt yields (the column on the left) with taxable yields.

Joint Return

	$8,000 to $12,000	to $16,000	to $20,000	to $24,000	to $28,000	to $32,000

Single Return

Tax-Exempt Yields	$4,000 to $6,000	to $8,000	to $10,000	to $12,000	to $14,000	to $16,000
4.00	5.13	5.33	5.56	5.88	6.25	6.56
4.10	5.26	5.47	5.69	6.03	6.41	6.72
4.25	5.45	5.67	5.90	6.25	6.64	6.97
4.40	5.64	5.37	6.11	6.47	6.88	7.21
4.50	5.77	6.00	6.25	6.62	7.03	7.38
4.60	5.90	6.13	6.39	6.76	7.19	7.54
4.75	6.09	6.33	6.60	6.99	7.42	7.79
4.80	6.15	6.40	6.67	7.06	7.50	7.87
4.90	6.28	6.53	6.81	7.21	7.66	8.03
5.00	6.41	6.67	6.94	7.35	7.81	8.20
5.10	6.54	6.80	7.08	7.50	7.97	8.36
5.25	6.73	7.00	7.29	7.72	8.20	8.61
5.40	6.92	7.20	7.50	7.94	8.44	8.85
5.50	7.05	7.33	7.64	8.09	8.59	9.02
5.75	7.37	7.67	7.99	8.46	8.98	9.43
6.00	7.69	8.00	8.33	8.82	9.38	9.84

For example, a couple with a taxable income of $20,000 to $24,-000 would require a return of $7.94 in taxable interest to match a 5.4 percent yield on a municipal bond. (The table does not take state or local taxes into consideration.)

"The exemption which municipal bonds receive is based upon the doctrine of reciprocal immunity," as reaffirmed by the U.S. Supreme Court on several occasions over the past century. The doctrine enunciates the principal that the federal government may not tax the securities of the states and the states may not tax those of the federal government.

This exemption, be advised, applies to the income—the interest payments—received from the bonds. It does not apply to any gain you might realize on the principal amount when you redeem the bond. Suppose you pay $940 for a bond that brings $1,000 at maturity. When you sell, the appreciation—$60—is a long-term capital gain and taxable as such.

If, however, you pay $1,060 for a bond that matures at $1,000, you cannot credit yourself with a $60 tax loss when you sell. The Internal Revenue Service judges that you have no capital loss as long as you realize the promised yield to maturity. Of course, the premium you pay at the time of purchase—$60 in this case—is compensated for by a much higher-than-normal coupon rate.

As for the taxing policies of the various states, most do give preferential treatment to their own municipals. For instance, if you live in Los Angeles and purchase bonds issued by the State Highway Department of California or the Fresno Housing Authority, the bonds will not be subject to state income tax. But if you purchase bonds issued by a municipality or authority outside the state of California, the income on the bonds is taxable. This policy is also followed in New York, Pennsylvania, North Carolina and several other states.

The type of municipal you choose should be in keeping with your immediate financial goals. If your present earnings and those you anticipate in the immediate future are at high levels and you don't particularly need additional income, choose bonds with lower-than-average coupon rates, for these may be selling at sizeable discounts. Early in 1970, Massachusetts Housing Authority bonds, rated Aa, with a 2 1/4% coupon rate, were being offered at 55 1/4. They had a yield to maturity of 6.70 percent. I would not hesitate to suggest such an issue to someone looking for a reasonable non-taxable rate of return, but who was unconcerned about additional current income.

On the other hand, if you wish to add to your current income, buy bonds with a greater-than-average coupon rate. These are likely to be selling at close to 100, and you may even have to pay a premium.

Another point is important. While there is a ready market for municipals, some bonds are more liquid than others. In general, the shorter the maturity, the smaller the bid-asked spread, and the greater the liquidity. Keep this fact in mind if you're going into the municipal-bond market but feel there's a possibility you might need the invested capital later.

Even if you are in one of the higher-income brackets, do not look upon municipals as a substitute for the purchase of growth stocks or growth funds. Most investment experts regard municipals as supplemental investments, primarily useful in alleviating the burden of high taxes.

Tax-Exempt Funds

If the number and diversity of municipals bewilders you to such a degree you're unable to reach a buying decision, you may want to consider a mutual fund that offers the tax-exempt feature of bonds. Such funds are made up of a number different state and local bond issues, and usually they carry *Standard & Poor's* ratings of BBB to AA.

The principal underwriters of such funds are John Nuveen & Company (61 Broadway, New York, N. Y. 10006), Bache & Company (36 Wall Street, New York, N. Y. 10006) and Goodbody & Company (55 Broad Street, New York, N. Y. 10006). Write and request a prospectus.

Summing Up

Municipal bonds are a safe investment, one with a greater degree of stability than most common stocks. They give a reasonable rate of return and, because of the tax advantages they offer, have special appeal for persons in high-income categories. In purchasing municipals, follow these suggestions:

• In the case of revenue bonds, look at the profit and loss statement of the issuing authority. Earnings should be at least twice the amount required to meet annual interest payments.

• Check the opinion of *Standard & Poor's* or *Moody's* as to the bond's quality.

• If you are not seeking additional current income, choose a bond with a lower-than-average coupon rate.

7·Government Securities

The federal government, like a household or any business enterprise, often finds that its inflow of cash receipts does not equal its disbursements. To bridge the gap, the Treasury Department issues scores of money-market instruments—bills, bonds and notes with varying coupon rates, different maturities and an assortment of call provisions.

Many of these securities are available to the general public. But remember, when you purchase a government security, you become a lender; you have no equity. Nevertheless, some types are worth considering.

TREASURY BILLS

Treasury bills are short-term I.O.U.'s issued by the U.S. Treasury. Evaluate them as you would a savings account, on the basis of their yields, easy liquidity and safety.

Throughout most of 1969 and into 1970, "new" Treasury bills paid an interest rate of well over seven percent and sometimes above eight percent, and so-called "small" investors (any purchase of less than $200,000 is considered "small") flocked to buy them, putting a severe strain on Treasury market facilities. To reduce the bills' appeal to small investors, the Treasury raised the minimum bill denomination from $1,000 to $10,000 on March 2, 1970. This action served to decrease the number of people buying bills and market conditions stabilized somewhat, but it in no way affected the value of the bills. After all, the Treasury Department may be seeking a billion dollars or two in a single offering. The small investor has virtually no influence on a market of such enormous size.

Bills issued before March 2, 1970, in denominations of less than $10,000, can still be purchased privately on the securities market through a broker or commercial bank. This section, however, concerns only new Treasury bills, those bought directly from a Federal Reserve Bank or branch.

It's important to realize that Treasury bills do not pay a stated rate of interest. They are sold at a "discount" from face value, which means that your return on a given bill is the difference between the purchase price and the maturity value. This difference is called the discount. In the case of a bill with a $9,850 purchase price which pays $10,000 at maturity, the discount is $150.

Purchasing Treasury Bills

Treasury bills are issued regularly with maturities of three, six, nine and twelve months. They are available through Federal Reserve Banks or their branches.

New bills are sold at auction. To purchase a bill, you simply submit a bid, called a " tender." You can submit either a competitive tender or a noncompetitive tender, but if you submit a competitive tender you must naturally specify the amount you are willing to pay; you thereby run the risk of bidding so low you fail to buy the bill. Thus the normal practice for the small investor is to submit a noncompetitive tender, which does not specify a price. You then pay the average price of the competitive tenders submitted by the "large" investors—those whose bids are $200,000 or over—and accepted by the Treasury.

To some, dealing with a Federal Reserve Bank or branch in purchasing new Treasury bills may be a complicated piece of business. Admittedly, it does require some homework. You can avoid much of the involvement by dealing through a commercial bank or securities broker—that is, allowing one or the other to submit your tender for you.

If you make your purchase through a prime dealer, you will be assessed a service charge of at least $10 per transaction. The prime dealers include First National City Bank; Morgan Guaranty Bank; Bankers Trust Company; Chemical Bank; Merrill Lynch, Pierce, Fenner & Smith; and Salomon Brothers & Hutzler. If you make your purchase through any but a prime dealer, you will be charged an *additional* $10 to $15 per transaction. These charges can be so high as to offset any interest-rate advantage you gain by dealing in Treasury bills.

The better method is to buy the bill directly from your Federal Reserve Bank or branch, which acts as the Treasury's agent in bill auctions. The Federal Reserve never charges for this service. To determine your Federal Reserve Bank or branch, consult the map on Page 179 which shows the boundaries of the Federal Reserve Districts and their branch territories, and the accompanying list of banks and branches and the addresses for each. The method for submitting tenders varies slightly from district to district. Call or write your bank or branch and request information sheets and purchase forms.

But no matter where you live and what bank you deal with, certain basics apply. Auctions for new three-month and six-month bills are held every Monday. Tenders can be submitted in person or by mail. To make certain your tender is received in time for the auction, submit it on any business day of the previous week, advises a spokesman for the Federal Reserve Bank of New York.

Auctions for new nine-month and twelve-month bills are held monthly on a business day after the 20th day of the month. The Treasury announces the exact date a few days before the auction. To make certain your tender is received in time for the auction, submit it on the 18th, 19th, or 20th of the month, says the Federal Reserve Bank of New York. A tender received before the 18th of the month or after 1:30 P.M. on the auction date will be returned to you.

There are two methods of paying for the bill you purchase. The recommended method is to submit payment for the full face value of the bill—$10,000, for example—with your tender. The payment can be in currency, by certified check or by an official bank check, such as a cashier's or treasurer's check, made payable to the Federal Reserve Bank or branch. You can also pay for the bill using a previously purchased Treasury bill which is to mature on or before the issue date of the new bill.

LIST OF FEDERAL RESERVE ADDRESSES

BOSTON 30 Pearl St. (Boston, Mass. 02106)

NEW YORK 33 Liberty St. (Federal Reserve P.O. Station New York, N.Y. 10045)

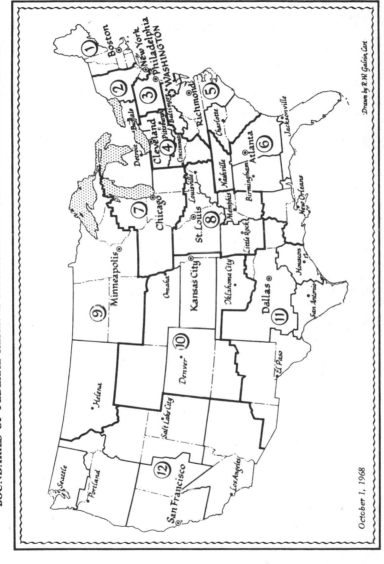

BOUNDARIES OF FEDERAL RESERVE DISTRICTS AND THEIR BRANCH TERRITORIES

October 1, 1968

Drawn by R. W. Galvin, Cart.

Boundaries of the Federal Reserve Districts and their branch territories in the continental United States. The states of Hawaii and Alaska are considered to be within the San Francisco Reserve District.

Buffalo Branch	P.O. Box 961 (Buffalo, N.Y. 14240)
PHILADELPHIA	925 Chestnut St. (Philadelphia, Pa. 19101)
CLEVELAND	1455 East Sixth St. (P.O. Box 6387, Cleveland, O. 44101)
Cinncinnati Branch	105 West Fourth St. (P.O. Box 999, Cincinnati O. 45201)
Pittsburgh Branch	717 Grant St. (P.O. Box 867, Pittsburgh, Pa. 15230)
RICHMOND	100 North Ninth St. (Richmond, Va. 23213)
Baltimore Branch	114-120 East Lexington St. (Baltimore, Md. 21203)
Charlotte Branch	401 South Tryon St. (Charlotte, N.C. 28201)
ATLANTA	104 Marietta St., N. W. (Atlanta, Ga. 30303)
Birmingham Branch	1801 Fifth Ave., North (P.O. Box 2574, Birmingham, Ala. 35202)
Jacksonville Branch	515 Julia St. (P.O. Box 929 Jacksonville, Fla. 32201)
Nashville Branch	301 Eighth Ave., N. (Nashville, Tenn. 37203)
New Orleans Branch	525 St. Charles Ave. (P.O. Box 61630, New Orleans, La. 70160)
CHICAGO	230 South LaSalle St. (P.O. Box 834, Chicago, Ill. 60690)
Detroit Branch	160 Fort St., W. (P.O. Box 1059, Detroit, Mich. 48231)
ST. LOUIS	411 Locust St. (P.O. Box 442, St. Louis, Mo. 63166)
Little Rock Branch	325 West Capitol Ave. (P.O. Box 1261, Little Rock, Ark. 72203)
Louisville Branch	410 South Fifth St. (P.O. Box 899, Louisville, Ky. 40201)
Memphis Branch	170 Jefferson St. (P.O. Box 407, Memphis, Tenn. 38101)
MINNEAPOLIS	73 South Fifth St. (Minneapolis, Minn 55440)
Helena Branch	400 North Park Ave. (Helena, Mont. 59601)
KANSAS CITY	925 Grand Ave. (Federal Reserve Station, Kansas City, Mo. 64198)
Denver Branch	1111 Seventeenth St. (Denver, Colo. 80217)
Oklahoma City Branch	226 Northwest Third St. (P.O. Box 25129, Oklahoma City, Okla. 73125)

Omaha Branch	102 South Seventeenth St. (Omaha, Neb. 68102)
DALLAS	400 South Akard St. (Station K, Dallas, Tex. 75222)
El Paso Branch	301 East Main St. (P.O. Box 100, El Paso, Tex. 79999)
Houston Branch	1701 San Jacinto St. (P.O. Box 2578, Houston, Tex. 77001)
San Antonio Branch	210 West Nueva St. (P.O. Box 1471, San Antonio, Tex. 78206)
SAN FRANCISCO	400 Sansome St. (San Francisco, Calif. 94120)
Los Angeles Branch	409 West Olympic Blvd. (P.O. Box 2077, Los Angeles, Calif. 90054)
Portland Branch	915 S. W. Stark St. (P.O. Box 3436, Portland, Ore. 97208)
Salt Lake City Branch	120 South State St. (P.O. Box 780, Salt Lake City, Ut. 84110)
Seattle Branch	1015 Second Ave. (P.O. Box 3567, Seattle, Wash. 98124)

Once the tender is submitted and payment made, a check for the difference between the purchase price and the face value of the bill —called a discount check—is mailed to you on the issue date. In the case of a $10,000 bill with a purchase price of $9,850, you will receive a check for $150.

The Federal Reserve Bank of New York offers a second but more involved method of paying for a bill. The purchaser submits a partial payment amounting to two percent of the face value of the bill—a payment of $200 on a $10,000 bill, for example, with the tender. This payment is made in currency, by certified check, or by an official bank check. The balance of the purchase price is paid on the bill's issue date, using one of the forms of payment mentioned above. If the purchaser fails to make the final payment on the issue date, the tender is canceled. The Treasury then has the option of returning or keeping the partial payment.

New three-month and six-month bills are issued on the Thursday following the weekly auction, while the new nine-month and twelve-month bills are issued on the last day of the month.

A word of warning here. Treasury bills are issued in bearer form only. This means they do not bear your name; they are not registered with the Treasury. They can therefore be sold or redeemed

Date_____

```
┌─────────────────────────────────────┐
│ FOR FEDERAL RESERVE USE ONLY         │
│                                      │
│ Series dated_____           │
│ Date issued_____           │
│ Maturity date_____           │
└─────────────────────────────────────┘
```

Securities Department
Federal Reserve Bank of New York
33 Liberty Street
New York, N.Y. 10045

Gentlemen:

This noncompetitive tender is submitted in the amount of $_____

for the next auction of 3-month Treasury bills. $10,000 or multiple

Payment for the full face amount of the bills is enclosed in the form of

☐ a certified personal check or a bank (cashier's) check payable
   to the Federal Reserve Bank of New York;

☐ cash;

☐ Treasury bills maturing on or before the issue date.

On issuance, the bills

☐ should be mailed to the bidder;

☐ will be picked up by the bidder between 11 a.m. and 3 p.m. on
   the business day following the issue date.

The check for the discount will be mailed to the bidder.

The bidder's name and complete address are

_____   _____
        Print or type   Bidder's signature

_____

**The Federal Reserve Bank of New York has prepared this tender-form for
use by those wishing to purchase Treasury bills.**

without your signature. So safeguard Treasury bills just as carefully
as you would currency or any valuable.

Once a bill is purchased, it can be picked up at the Federal
Reserve Bank or branch between 11 A.M. and 3 P.M. on the first
business day following the day of issue, or between 9 A.M. and 3
P.M. on any of the next five business days. You can also have the

bill mailed to you. It will be sent by registered mail and insured at the Treasury's expense.

You cannot leave the bill in the hands of the Reserve Bank. If it is not picked up within the time specified or accepted by mail, your tender will be canceled.

A typical noncompetitive tender form is printed on page 182.

Most Federal Reserve Banks or branches have available forms of this type. Or you can simply prepare a letter to your Reserve Bank or branch that contains the essential information:

* The full amount of the bill or bills you want.
* The maturity you want (three, six, nine or twelve months).
* The mailing address to which the discount check is to be sent.
* The delivery instructions for the bill or bills.
* The date.
* Your name and address.
* Your signature.

Treasury regulations require you to sign the tender form or letter, although you can have a friend, relative or financial institution submit the tender for you. Commercial banks are an exception. They are permitted to submit tenders in their own name to buy new bills for one of their customers.

Redeeming Bills

To redeem a Treasury bill, deliver or mail it, making certain to register and insure it, to the Issues and Redemption Section, Government Bond Division, or your Reserve Bank or branch. If you deliver or send in the bill a few days before the maturity date, you can pick up the check on the maturity date. Otherwise, the check will be mailed to you on the maturity date.

In lieu of payment, the bill can be "rolled over" for a new bill, that is, used in payment for a new bill. The procedure for rolling over a maturing bill is similar to that for buying a new bill. Simply submit your tender and the maturing bill to the auction. If you are due a difference between the purchase of the new bill and the face value of the maturing bill, it will be mailed to you on the new bill's issue date.

Keep alert to the fact that bills do not earn interest after maturity. It is wise to make arrangements to redeem bills and obtain payment at the earliest possible moment—that is, on the day of maturity—and then reinvest the money on that date.

Also be aware that a Treasury bill cannot be cashed at a Reserve Bank or branch, or even at the Treasury itself, before maturity. You can, however, sell the bill privately in the securities market through a commercial bank or securities broker. The amount you receive, of course, will be less than the face value of the bill.

The Wall Street Journal and some big-city daily newspapers publish reports on bill trading, giving bid, asked and yield prices for recent issues. Within a section titled, "U.S. and Agency Bonds," you will see a daily listing of this type:

TREASURY BILLS

March 31, 1970

Offering Date	Bid	Asked	Yield
April 2	6.90	5.62	5.70
April 9	6.76	5.62	5.71
April 16	6.48	5.62	6.29
April 22	6.52	6.18	6.29
April 23	6.50	6.04	6.15
April 30	6.46	5.99	6.10
May 7	6.38	6.01	6.13
May 14	6.38	6.01	6.14
May 21	6.38	6.01	6.15
May 31	6.41	6.02	6.17
June 4	6.31	6.15	6.30
June 11	6.31	6.15	6.31

The income you derive from Treasury bills is subject to Federal income taxes, but is exempt from state and local government income taxes. "Income" is defined as the difference between the purchase price and the maturity value of a given bill, or sale price received if the bill is sold before maturity.

The income is considered earned during the year the bills are redeemed or sold. Bills are not considered capital assets under the Internal Revenue code, and any financial gain or loss is to be considered ordinary gain or loss, even if the bill is held for more than six months.

Calculating the Rate of Return

You will not be notified by the Reserve Bank or branch as to the rate of return of any bill purchased. However, the results of bill auctions are reported in *The Wall Street Journal, The New York Times* and in the financial sections of some daily newspapers, and these reports announce the bill's price and also the equivalent annual rate expressed in percentage. Here is a typical report:

Result of Treasury's 9-Month and 12-Month Bill Offerings

RANGE OF ACCEPTED COMPETITIVE BIDS

| | 275-day Treasury Bills Maturing Dec. 31, 1970 | | 365-day Treasury Bills Maturing Mar. 31, 1971 | |
	Price	Approx. equiv. annual rate	Price	Approx. equiv. annual rate
High	95.427	5.986%	93.966	6.500%
Low	95.326	6.119%	93.694	6.220%
Average	95.340	6.100%	93.783	6.132%

Of course, once you know a bill's purchase price, you can figure out the rate of return. Divide the discount by the purchase price, and then divide the answer by a fraction which expresses the bill's maturity on an annual basis; the numerator is the number of months required for the bill to achieve maturity—three, six, nine or twelve months—while the denominator is twelve.

In the case of a $10,000 three-month bill purchased for $9,850, with the resulting discount of $150, the arithmetic would look like this:

$$\frac{\$150}{\$9,850} = .0152 \div \frac{3}{12} = .0608 = \frac{6.08 \text{ percent}}{\text{per year}}$$

If the bill has a maturity of six, nine, or twelve months, the fraction 3/12 becomes 6/12, 9/12, or 12/12. In the above example, the 6.08 percent per year is an approximate rate of return. The exact rate is calculated using a more complex formula.

Government Securities Fund

If you can't afford the $10,000 minimum required to purchase a Treasury bill, you can use an alternative method of investing in securities of this type—a mutual fund.

The Mutual Fund for Investing in U.S. Securities, Inc., was established in 1969 by Federated Investors of Pittsburgh to enable small investors to avail themselves of the investment benefits of Treasury bills and other securities. The minimum initial investment is $250 and subsequent investments are in multiples of $25. The fund invests exclusively in government securities and issues of government agencies.

The fund offers no sales charge, no redemption fee, quarterly dividends in cash or stock, and a systematic withdrawal plan on investments of $5,000 or more. The cost of the fund to the investor is the usual one-half of one percent management fee plus administrative expenses.

For a propectus, write: Mutual Fund for Investing in U.S. Government Securities, Inc., Federated Investors Building, 421 Seventh Ave., Pittsburgh, Pa. 15219.

Summing Up

Consider Treasury bills as an alternative to your savings account. They give liquidity and safety, and their interest rates are fairly attractive.

To purchase a Treasury bill, deal directly with a Federal Reserve Bank or branch, submitting a noncompetitive tender. Treat the bill with the care you give currency. Redeem the bill on the maturity date.

TREASURY NOTES AND BONDS

Besides the weekly and monthly sales of Treasury bills, the federal government also raises money through the periodic sale of notes and bonds. While bills mature in a year or less, notes are issued with a maturity of from one to seven years. Bonds may be issued with any maturity, but almost always it is of a long-term nature, from five to thirty years.

Another group of similar securities are federal-agency securities. They are listed along with Treasury issues in many newspapers and frequently confused with them. But agency bonds are those issued by the Federal Land Banks, Federal Intermediate Credit Banks, Banks for Cooperatives, Federal Home Loan Banks and the Federal National Mortgage Association ("Fannie Mae") to finance their own activities.

The public sale of federal-agency securities is handled through fiscal agents. The fiscal agent for the Federal Land Banks, the Federal Intermediate Credit Banks and the Banks for Cooperatives is Glenn G. Browne (1 Chase Manhattan Plaza, New York, N. Y. 10005). For the Federal Home Loan Banks, the fiscal agent is Alan

C. Knowles (25 Broadway, New York, N. Y. 10004), and for the Federal National Mortgage Association is John H. Claiborne, Jr. (20 Exchange Pl., New York, N. Y. 10005). For information about federal-agency securities, contact the fiscal agent, your local bank or securities broker.

Th Federal Land Bank issues securities in denominations of $1,-000 to $1,000,000 but with all other federal agencies the smallest denomination security is $5,000. Treasury bonds are issued in denominations of $500, $1,000, $5,000, $10,000, $100,000 and $1 million, while with Treasury notes the minimum denomination is $1,000.

By law, the U.S. Treasury may not issue bonds with an interest rate of more than 41 percent. Since this figure is not competitive with current market rates, the Treasury has not issued any new bonds since mid-1965.

Treasury notes and bonds are sold by subscription, however. The Treasury announces the maturity, interest rate and price, then invites investors to submit subscriptions. The Treasury reserves the right of allotment, which depends on the volume of subscriptions received.

Much of the Treasury's financing in recent years has been through exchange offerings. Investors must own a stated maturing security and be willing to exchange it in order to subscribe to the new security.

Treasury bonds and other government securities are traded in the over-the-counter market. Most of the transactions are handled eventually by one of a group of twenty or so "primary" dealers. They negotiate purchases, sales and exchanges of securities with each other and their customers, directly or through brokers. While in the case of Treasury bills, you can deal directly with a Federal Reserve Bank or branch, when you enter the market in government notes or bonds, you must go through your securities broker or a local commercial bank, thereby incurring the service charges involved. (The Federal Reserve Banks handle the subscriptions on all *new* Treasury offerings.)

As of April 1970, here is a list of some of the issues being offered:

Issue	Bid	Asked	Yield
May '70, 5⅝s	100.1	100.3	4.31
May '70, 6⅜s	100.2	100.4	4.44
Aug '70, 4s	99.5	99.9	6.23
Nov '70, 5s	98.31	99.3	6.65
Feb '71, 7¾s	100.22	100.26	6.74

Issue	Bid	Asked	Yield
Mar '71, 5s	98.9	98.17	6.70
Feb '72, 4s	94.16	94.24	7.12
Aug '73, 4s	89.26	90.2	7.42
Feb '74, 4⅛ s	88.26	89.2	7.46
Nov '74, 5¾ s	93.10	93.18	7.44
May '75, 6s	94.8	94.16	7.32
Feb '77, 8s	102.26	103.2	7.42
Nov. '80, 3½ s	72.6	72.22	7.23
May '85, 3¼ s	67.0	67.16	6.71
Feb '95, 3s	66.30	67.14	5.40
Nov '98, 3½ s	66.30	67.14	5.86

Notice that many of these issues were being sold at substantial discounts. But I find them unappealing, for it is generally true that the greater the discount, the longer the maturity. The long-term nature of investments of this type, combined with the economy's inflationary trend, represent a potential loss in purchasing power.

The Treasury will indeed pay the prescribed rate of interest and redeem the securities in full when they fall due. You can count on it. But this does not mean there is no risk involved. Take the case of a Baltimore woman whose husband died in 1953. On the advice of her lawyer, she put the $10,000 she received from the insurance company into government bonds, the best "no-risk" investment he could think of. She planned to redeem the bonds fifteen years later to finance the college education of a son and daughter. Well, the daughter never went to college. In 1968 the widow found to her dismay that the $10,000 was scarcely enough to pay for her son's education.

The safety factor of government bonds, like that of any other fixed-income, long-term investment is, at best, elusive. You are gambling—that the dollar's value will not be gutted by inflation.

For more information on Treasury bills, bonds and notes, obtain a copy of the *Handbook of Securities of the United States Government and Federal Agencies.* It's free from The First Boston Corporation (20 Exchange Pl., New York, N. Y. 10005).

The U.S. Treasury Department publishes a comprehensive if rather abstruse booklet on the subject, *General Regulations with Respect to United States Securities.* Also free, it is available from the Superintendent of Documents, Government Printing Office, Washington, D.C. 20042).

8 • Inflation-Proof Annuities

During the early 1950's, you might have glanced through any one of a number of national magazines and seen a full-page, full-color advertisement that depicted a beaming, gray-haired gentleman, and a headline that proclaimed, "How I Retired in 15 Years on $250 a Month." Then the advertisement went on to announce the virtues of a type of insurance that provided a guaranteed source of money after the policyholder had stopped working.

It sounded terrific. And in the early 1950's, $250 a month was pretty terrific.

But pity the poor people who signed up for the plan. Today many of them are trying to live on that same $250-a-month payment. It has to be an embittering experience.

This type of policy is known as an annuity, a contract wherein you promise to pay certain premiums, and when you reach a stated age you begin receiving installment payments. But like any retirement plan that is wired to a fixed-income schedule, the annuity is a prospective hazard. People who retired in the early to mid-1950's have experienced a cost-of-living increase of more than 35 percent. Those who retired in 1945 saw the cost of living jump 65 percent in the first fifteen years of their retirement. If the past is any indication, then people who are retiring today are likely to require a substantially greater amount of income ten or fifteen years hence than today's living costs suggest.

But now there is a plan available that makes it possible for you to receive not fixed, but ever-increasing monthly payments. "Possible" is an all-important word in that sentence. It means that there is a chance or a likelihood. There's no *guarantee* that the amount of the monthly payment will increase and there is even some risk that it will go down.

Under the terms of the plan, an insurance company takes your premiums and invests them in common stocks and preferred stocks. On the date your payments are to begin, the stock portfolio is likely to have gained in value, and you will then get fatter checks. If stock values drop, the checks are smaller.

As this brief rundown may have indicated, the variable annuity, as this type of policy is called, is not appropriate for every person. It is best suited for the individual who is in the upper-income brackets, probably above $25,000 a year, with a good-sized savings account, his home almost paid for and few financial obligations of any consequence.

But the man who is between the ages of 25 and 35 and burdened by the assorted financial obligations involved in raising a family is not a likely prospect for the variable annuity. He should be thinking in terms of other equity situations.

Whatever an individual's situation, the variable annuity should not be considered as one's only insurance policy. It never supplants —it merely supplements fixed insurance plans.

Building Value and Charges

The variable annuity can be clearly understood if you look upon it as involving two time periods: an accumulation period and a pay-out period. During the accumulation period, you make deposits on a regular basis, perhaps monthly.

Sales and administrative expenses are subtracted from your premiums. Then your *net* deposits, along with those of other policyholders with similar plans, are placed in a special account to be invested in equity-type securities. Investment income and capital gains realized are reinvested.

The pay-out period refers to the time during which you collect monthly payments. Since the fund from which these payments are made is invested in the special account, the amount of each month's check is different, varying with the swings of the stock market.

During the policy's accumulation period, you purchase "accumulation units." The price of one unit is based upon the total number of accumulation units outstanding divided into the total value of the assets held by the fund. For instance, if 200,000 accumulation units were outstanding and the assets of the fund totaled $2 million, each accumulation unit would be worth $10.

Your premiums go toward the purchase of accumulation units, which in turn are invested by the insuring company. What you own is a percentage of the fund, the amount determined by the ratio of the units you own to the total number of units outstanding.

The usual method of purchasing a variable annuity policy is for the buyer to set a retirement date and estimate how much money he wants to receive each month after that date. The company then figures the amount of premium required to make such a payment schedule possible. Usually the total annual premium is broken into monthly payments. Some companies allow policyholders to make payments in varying amounts instead of maintaining an unchanging payment schedule.

In the event you wish to discontinue paying premiums, you can either withdraw the full cash value or allow the money to remain on deposit with the company as a paid-up annuity. If you choose the last-named course, you can begin paying into the plan again at any time without any penalty.

Some companies allow you, upon retirement, to choose one of a number of options. You can elect payments for life, or you can elect payments for life with a specified number guaranteed. Then if you should die within the payment period, payments will continue to your designated beneficiary. Or you can elect to receive payments on a "joint and last survivor" basis. This means payments will be paid jointly to you and another person you designate. At the death of either, payments continue for life to the survivor.

There are tax advantages to the variable annuity. No income tax payments on investment gains can be assessed until retirement payments actually start. At that time, the policyholder pays tax on only that portion of his monthly payments attributable as investment gains.

To cover operating and sales expense and premium taxes, the insurance company usually deducts a small amount from each premium payment. In addition, the company is likely to make a period deduction of a certain percentage of the reserve for investment expenses and all other contingencies. All deductions and contingency items are specified in the contract, and the company cannot change the annuity table or the amount of the deductions.

The individual variable annuity has been subject to two different pricing policies, according to Arthur L. Blakeslee, executive vice-president of the Participating Annuity Life Insurance Company.

Year Contract Commencing	Accumulated Payments	Sales Expense	Minimum Death Benefit	Admin. & Other Expenses	Total Deductions	Accumulated Net Payments	Value on Sept. 30 of Following Year
Monthly Purchase Payment—$25.00							
Oct. 1954	$ 300.00	$ 142.50	$ 4.50	$ 21.90	$ 168.90	$ 131.10	$ 138.78
Oct. 1955	600.00	159.00	9.00	52.50	220.50	379.50	398.44
Oct. 1956	900.00	175.50	13.50	83.10	272.10	627.90	568.46
Oct. 1957	1,200.00	192.00	18.00	113.70	323.70	876.30	1,001.90
Oct. 1958	1,500.00	208.50	22.50	144.30	375.30	1,124.70	1,418.78
Oct. 1959	1,800.00	225.00	27.00	174.90	426.90	1,373.10	1,566.63
Oct. 1960	2,100.00	241.50	31.50	205.50	478.50	1,621.50	2,176.28
Oct. 1961	2,400.00	258.00	36.00	236.10	530.10	1,869.90	2,200.23
Oct. 1962	2,700.00	274.50	40.50	266.70	581.70	2,118.30	3,151.75
Oct. 1963	3,000.00	291.00	45.00	297.30	633.30	2,366.70	4,329.74
Oct. 1964	3,300.00	307.50	49.50	327.90	684.90	2,615.10	5,406.82
Oct. 1965	3,600.00	324.00	54.00	358.50	736.50	2,863.50	5,427.44
Oct. 1966	3,900.00	330.00	58.50	388.56	777.06	3,122.94	7,691.01
Oct. 1967	4,200.00	336.00	63.00	418.62	817.62	3,382.38	8,747.14
Oct. 1968	4,275.00*	337.50*	64.12*	425.76*	827.76*	3,447.24*	9,504.72*
Annual Purchase Payment—$300.00							
Oct. 1954	$ 300.00	$ 142.50	$ 4.50	$ 16.20	$ 163.20	$ 136.80	$ 168.29
Oct. 1955	600.00	159.00	9.00	36.00	204.00	396.00	459.68
Oct. 1956	900.00	175.50	13.50	55.80	244.80	655.20	636.16
Oct. 1957	1,200.00	192.00	18.00	75.60	285.60	914.40	1,095.18
Oct. 1958	1,500.00	208.50	22.50	95.40	326.40	1,173.60	1,576.83
Oct. 1959	1,800.00	225.00	27.00	115.20	367.20	1,432.80	1,721.24
Oct. 1960	2,100.00	241.50	31.50	135.00	408.00	1,692.00	2,410.30
Oct. 1961	2,400.00	258.00	36.00	154.80	448.80	1,951.20	2,422.41
Oct. 1962	2,700.00	274.50	40.50	174.60	489.60	2,210.40	3,503.72
Oct. 1963	3,000.00	291.00	45.00	194.40	530.40	2,469.60	4,824.53
Oct. 1964	3,300.00	307.50	49.50	214.20	571.20	2,728.80	6,017.94
Oct. 1965	3,600.00	324.00	54.00	234.00	612.00	2,988.00	6,041.61
Oct. 1966	3,900.00	330.00	58.50	252.78	641.28	3,258.72	8,599.75
Oct. 1967	4,200.00	336.00	63.00	271.56	670.56	3,529.44	9,754.34
Oct. 1968	4,500.00	342.00	67.50	290.34	699.84	3,800.16	10,810.18*

Monthly Purchase Payment—$100.00

Oct. 1954	$ 1,200.00	$ 570.00	$ 18.00	$ 53.40	$ 641.40	$ 558.60	$ 591.23
Oct. 1955	2,400.00	636.00	36.00	111.00	783.00	1,617.00	1,697.60
Oct. 1956	3,600.00	702.00	54.00	163.60	924.60	2,675.40	2,422.07
Oct. 1957	4,800.00	768.00	72.00	226.20	1,066.20	3,733.80	4,268.86
Oct. 1958	6,000.00	834.00	90.00	283.80	1,207.80	4,792.20	6,045.08
Oct. 1959	7,200.00	900.00	108.00	341.40	1,349.40	5,850.60	6,675.05
Oct. 1960	8,400.00	966.00	126.00	399.00	1,491.00	6,909.00	9,272.66
Oct. 1961	9,600.00	1,032.00	144.00	456.60	1,632.60	7,967.40	9,374.74
Oct. 1962	10,800.00	1,098.00	162.00	514.20	1,774.20	9,025.80	13,428.95
Oct. 1963	12,000.00	1,164.00	180.00	571.80	1,915.80	10,084.20	18,448.14
Oct. 1964	13,200.00	1,230.00	198.00	629.40	2,057.40	11,142.60	23,037.38
Oct. 1965	14,400.00	1,296.00	216.00	687.00	2,199.00	12,201.00	23,125.38
Oct. 1966	15,600.00	1,320.00	234.00	739.56	2,293.56	13,306.44	32,770.10
Oct. 1967	16,800.00	1,344.00	252.00	792.12	2,388.12	14,411.88	37,269.79
Oct. 1968	17,100.00*	1,350.00*	256.50*	805.26*	2,411.76*	14,688.24*	40,497.87*

Annual Purchase Payment—$1,200.00

Oct. 1954	$ 1,200.00	$ 570.00	$ 18.00	$ 47.70	$ 635.70	$ 564.30	$ 694.21
Oct. 1955	2,400.00	635.00	36.00	94.50	766.50	1,633.50	1,896.20
Oct. 1956	3,600.00	702.00	54.00	141.30	897.30	2,702.70	2,624.17
Oct. 1957	4,800.00	768.00	72.00	188.10	1,028.10	3,771.90	4,517.63
Oct. 1958	6,000.00	834.00	90.00	234.90	1,158.90	4,841.10	6,504.45
Oct. 1959	7,200.00	900.00	108.00	281.70	1,289.70	5,910.30	7,100.10
Oct. 1960	8,400.00	966.00	126.00	328.50	1,420.50	6,979.50	9,942.47
Oct. 1961	9,600.00	1,032.00	144.00	375.30	1,551.30	8,048.70	9,992.39
Oct. 1962	10,800.00	1,098.00	152.00	422.10	1,682.10	9,117.90	14,452.76
Oct. 1963	12,000.00	1,164.00	180.00	468.90	1,812.90	10,187.10	19,901.09
Oct. 1964	13,200.00	1,230.00	198.00	515.70	1,943.70	11,256.30	24,823.90
Oct. 1965	14,400.00	1,296.00	216.00	562.50	2,074.50	12,325.50	24,921.51
Oct. 1966	15,600.00	1,320.00	234.00	603.78	2,157.78	13,442.22	35,473.82
Oct. 1967	16,800.00	1,344.00	252.00	645.06	2,241.06	14,558.94	40,236.44
Oct. 1968	18,000.00	1,368.00	270.00	686.34	2,324.34	15,675.66	44,591.70*

*Through December 31, 1968.

Accumulated values from a variable annuity contract issued in October 1954. (*Participating Annuity Life Insurance Company*)

"In one type," says Mr. Blakeslee, "there is a level deduction from the purchase payment in the neighborhood of 8 percent to 10 percent. In the other, more closely related to the traditional policy approach of the life insurance industry, a deduction of approximately 30 percent to 50 percent is levied in the first year, dropping to 10 percent or lower until the tenth or twelfth year, with a substantial reduction thereafter." The deduction for investment expenses and contingencies has ranged from .5 percent to 1.5 percent per year of the assets of the reserve.

The table on pages 192–3, from the prospectus of the Participating Annuity Life Insurance Company, indicates the values which would have resulted in variable annuity contracts issued in October 1954. Four types of payment plans are tabulated—monthly-purchase payments of $25 and $100, and annual-purchase payments of $300 and $1,200.

The prospectus points out that the period covered in the table was one of generally rising common-stock prices. "The results shown in these tables should not be considered as a representation of the future," the prospectus states. "A program of the type illustrated does not assure a profit or protect against depreciation in declining markets."

Buying a Policy

It is not difficult to understand why insurance companies have been attracted to the variable insurance business. For the past two decades, the industry has watched in dismay as the public has veered away from life insurance as a means of savings. In 1945, the life insurance industry's share of the nation's saving dollar was 51 percent. In 1966, the figure was 16 percent.

It was the case of the public having found new uses for its savings dollars. Much of the money was put into mutual funds. Noninsured pension plans and accounts with savings and loan associations also offered sharp competition. The variable annuity policy, by offering an equity-based vehicle, is one of the methods the insurance industry devised to meet these challenges.

Variable annuity plans were introduced in the early 1950's, but their growth was sluggish for many years because of legal entanglements. Since these plans involve investment, companies that were formed especially to sell variable annuities encountered problems with state insurance laws and insurance commissioners. The laws were meant to protect the public's "guaranteed dollar values" and had to be revised to allow for the provision of variability.

Meanwhile, big companies were stymied, too. The Securities Exchange Commission claimed that a variable annuity is actually a mutual fund, and went into a Federal court to prove this contention. After several years of litigation, two main areas of variable annuity operation were established: the selling of plans to individuals, an area which was to be federally regulated, and the selling of group contracts, wherein employer contributions provide the benefits. This type was to be exempt from Federal regulation. At this time—1964—only three companies were engaged in selling variable annuity plans to individuals.

The following year the situation began to change. A group of Florida businessmen organized the National Life Insurance Company of Florida, and with it formed a subsidiary operation, the National Variable Annuity Company of Florida. They were then able to formulate an agreement acceptable to the SEC whereby the separate account of the subsidiary and its variable annuity contracts —not the company itself, a vital distinction—were to be subject to registration and Federal regulation.

During the late 1960's, well over a dozen major insurance companies began writing individual variable annuity contracts. Each followed the approach established by the National Life Insurance Company of Florida.

Today, there are three companies that specialize in the sale of individual variable annuity plans. They are:

• The Participating Life Insurance Company (7777 Leesburg Pike, Falls Church, Va. 22043). Formed in 1954, this was the first commercial insurance company to offer individual variable annuities to the general public. The company was acquired by Aetna Life Insurance Company in 1967.

• The National Variable Annuity Company of Florida (2255 Phyllis St., Jacksonville, Fla. 32204).

These companies also write variable annuity policies:

THE NORTHWESTERN MUTUAL   Self-employed or small corporate
LIFE INSURANCE COMPANY   plans only
720 East Wisconsin Ave.
Milwaukee, Wis. 53202

OCCIDENTAL LIFE INSURANCE   Group contracts only
COMPANY OF CALIFORNIA
Hill & Olive at 12th St.
Los Angeles, Calif. 90054

THE PAUL REVERE LIFE   Issued by Variable Annuity Life Insur-
INSURANCE COMPANY   ance Company, a wholly owned sub-
18 Chestnut St.   sidiary
Worcester, Mass. 01608

PIEDMONT NATIONAL LIFE
INSURANCE COMPANY
1197 Peachtree St., N.E.
Atlanta, Ga. 30309

THE PRUDENTIAL INSURANCE
COMPANY OF AMERICA
Prudential Plaza
Newark, N. J. 07101

STANDARD LIFE INSURANCE
OF INDIANA
300 East Fall Creek Blvd.
Indianapolis, Ind.

STATE MUTUAL LIFE ASSUR-
ANCE COMPANY OF AMERICA
440 Lincoln St.
Worcester, Mass.

THE TRAVELERS LIFE INSUR-
ANCE COMPANY
The Tower Square
Hartford, Conn. 06115

WASHINGTON NATIONAL LIFE
INSURANCE COMPANY
2310 Cass Avenue
Detroit, Mich. 48201

CONFEDERATION LIFE ASSOCI-   In Canada only; group contracts only
ATION
321 Bloor Street, E.
Toronto, Canada

CONNECTICUT GENERAL &　　Group contracts only
LIFE INSURANCE COMPANY
Hartford, Conn.

CONTINENTAL ASSURANCE　　　Group contracts only
COMPANY
310 S. Michigan Ave.
Chicago, Ill. 60604

THE EQUITABLE LIFE ASSUR-　Group contracts only
ANCE COMPANY OF THE
UNITED STATES
1285 Avenue of the Americas
New York, N. Y. 10019

JOHN HANCOCK MUTUAL LIFE
INSURANCE COMPANY
200 Berkeley St.
Boston, Mass. 02117

THE LINCOLN NATIONAL LIFE　　Group contracts only
INSURANCE COMPANY
1301-27 South Harrison St.
Fort Wayne, Ind. 46801

METROPOLITAN LIFE INSUR-
ANCE COMPANY
1 Madison Ave.
New York, N. Y. 10010

THE MINNESOTA MUTUAL LIFE　Group contracts only
INSURANCE COMPANY
Victory Square
St. Paul, Minn. 55101

THE MUTUAL LIFE INSURANCE
COMPANY OF NEW YORK
1740 Broadway
New York, N. Y. 10019

NATIONWIDE LIFE INSURANCE　Group contracts only
COMPANY
246 North High Street
Columbus, Ohio

NEW ENGLAND MUTUAL LIFE   Group contracts only
INSURANCE COMPANY
501 Boylston St.
Boston, Mass.
Group contracts only

If you write companies and request information, you are likely to receive a prospectus and a descriptive brochure. Some companies may have an agent contact you. Or you can simply consult the "Yellow Pages" to see if any of the above-named companies are listed.

If you correspond with a company, you may be solicited to buy a policy by mail. Be wary of this. The company may not be licensed to sell variable annuities in your state, and in dealing with the firm you will not have the full protection of your state's insurance commission.

Dollar-Cost Averaging

As I mentioned in the opening paragraphs of this chapter, when you purchase a variable annuity policy, you build up what insurance companies call "accumulation units." These represent a portion of ownership in the company's stock portfolio. The value of a unit rises and falls with the fluctuations of the stock market. To figure the value of a unit on a given day, the company divides the total number of units outstanding into the total value of stock in its portfolio.

Suppose you pay $100 a month as a premium. Let's say that in January, an individual unit is valued at $20. Your $100 premium payment would result in five units being credited to your account. But suppose the market is heading downward. In February, the unit's value is $19.50. Then your $100 would purchase 5.1 units.

What you're doing is dollar-cost averaging. When the market is down, you buy more units than when the market is rising (providing, of course, the stocks in the company's portfolio are representative of market performance as a whole). Moreover, your average cost per unit will be less than the average price per unit. This table demonstrates:

Month	Premium	Value of One Unit	Number of Units Purchased
January	$ 100	$ 20.00	5.0
February	$ 100	$ 19.50	5.1
March	$ 100	$ 19.80	5.1

April	$ 100	$ 22.00	4.5
May	$ 100	$ 23.50	4.3
June	$ 100	$ 24.10	4.1
July	$ 100	$ 25.00	4.0
August	$ 100	$ 25.50	3.9
September	$ 100	$ 27.70	3.7
October	$ 100	$ 31.00	3.2
November	$ 100	$ 32.50	3.1
December	$ 100	$ 34.00	2.9
	$1200	$304 .60	48.9

According to these figures, the average price per unit ($304.60 divided by 12, the number of payments) is $25.38. But the average cost per unit ($1200 divided by 48.9) is $24.54.

The Variable Annuity vs. the Mutual Fund

At first glance, the variable annuity seems to have many similarities to the mutual fund. The most obvious is that in both cases the equity that accrues is related to a stock portfolio. But there are several differences. The most important concerns taxes. Under the variable-annuity concept, the taxes on the gains achieved are deferred until the pay-out period, at which time the policyholder is very likely to be in a much lower tax bracket. But mutual-fund gains and dividends are taxed currently, that is, during the share owner's high income years, an obvious disadvantage. This chart points up other differences:

	Mutual Fund	Variable Annuity
Does the contract provide loan provisions?	No	Yes
Can the value be determined by newspaper listings?	Yes	No
Does the contract outline state deductions for expenses?	No	Yes
Are there minimum cash-value guarantees?	No	Yes
Can the contract provide for waiver of premium in the event of disability?	Yes	No
Does the contract offer a guaranteed minimum death benefit in the event of death before retirement, that is, does it guarantee that the beneficiary will receive an amount not less than the policyholder has paid in?	Yes	Yes
Upon the death of the policyholder can funds be subject to the claims of creditors of the deceased or the beneficiary?	Yes	No
Are there minimum cash-value guarantees?	No	Yes

Summing Up

The variable annuity, a retirement-income plan which yields a continually fluctuating monthly payment geared to the value of a stock portfolio, can offer positive protection against inflation. When buying a policy:

• Deal with an established, reliable firm.

• Choose a plan that best suits your needs; that is, one that provides payments for life or a guaranteed number of payments, or a "joint and last survivor plan." Ask your agent about the various options.

• In general, variable annuity plans are best suited for the retirement-oriented individual with a minimum of financial obligations.

• The variable annuity should supplement an individual's fixed insurance policies, not replace them.

9 · Real Estate Investing

Real estate may not be the perfect inflation hedge, but it rates very high. Raw land, apartments, commercial properties and vacation homes protect against the gradual erosion of the buying power of the dollar as well as or better than stocks or funds, stamps or coins or almost anything else.

Everyone knows that real estate appreciates in value during periods of inflation. And there are other plus factors. Income property often yields an extremely high return on invested capital, as much as 10 or 15 percent. There are tax advantages. You can usually depreciate income property at the rate of three to five percent a year. And, of course, there are opportunities for capital gains.

Real estate also has appeal to the investor who likes to be in full control. He is the captain of the ship, a feeling you hardly get in owning a couple of hundred shares of General Motors. It's no wonder that real estate is second only to life insurance in terms of the number of investors.

But real estate investment is not precisely perfection. There are drawbacks. For one thing, when you buy real estate you require a greater amount of capital than in other forms of investment. Second, the real estate market does not always hum. Selling a piece of property can be slow and arduous. You need time and patience—besides capital—to be successful in real estate, and almost always your profits are long-range.

Owning Raw Land

As the country's population increases, the available supply of raw land steadily decreases. A friend of mine owned several acres of New Jersey swampland, property that seemed of value only to mosquitoes. But the county paid him a handsome sum for the land because it was needed for dumping grounds. Gullies and gulches, quarries and abandoned strip mines—even the most forlorn property is going to be needed eventually to fill the growing demands of commerce and industry.

The greatest advantage in investing in raw land is the leverage factor. Whereas you need a minimum of 60 percent down to by listed stocks, you can often purchase raw land for only 20 to 25 percent of the selling price.

But there are pitfalls. Be certain you're aware of them.

One glaring shortcoming is that land investment can be awfully long-term. You can indeed realize a one-thousand percent return on your investment, but you may have to wait 20 to 25 years for your money.

And during the years your money is invested, it brings no income. Quite the opposite, in fact. You're almost certain to pay property taxes to the local municipality, and if the land happens to be in a developed area, these can be substantial.

Real estate brokers will tell you that money put into land is as safe as cash in the bank. Well, it's not. Raw land *is* more liquid than that of any other form of real estate. You can almost always find a buyer. The catch is that you may not get the price you're asking.

Huge fortunes have been made in land speculation. But if you're a part-time investor, with a job or business to occupy you, leave speculation to the speculators. They operate on a grandiose scale. In the early and mid-1950's, when Suffolk County, Long Island, was in the throes of a land boom, a speculator would offer to buy a large farm for more than the land was worth. But he would give the awestruck farmer perhaps one percent of the named purchase price for a one-year option. Or he might offer a small down payment, and no sizeable payments for at least a year. Using such tactics, speculators were able to realize fantastic profits, not only in Suffolk County but in many of the country's suburban areas.

But very few people can operate in this fashion. There is money to be made in real estate, but you cannot dabble in the market, at least on a large scale. Buy convertible bonds or warrants, if you want excitement.

Let's suppose you're interested in purchasing a small piece of land, an acre or so. "Buy on the fringe and wait," was John Jacob Astor's counsel. But it's advice that's as outdated as a buggy whip. There are very few investment opportunities in raw land on the outskirts of metropolitan areas nowadays. You must go beyond, to the fringe of the fringe.

Take New York City, for example. The principal fringe or suburban counties are Westchester, Rockland, Fairfield and Nassau. But looking for growth real estate investments in these areas is like shopping for bargains at Tiffany's. There aren't any.

To find investment property today, the New Yorker must head west toward Binghamton or north toward Albany. There are still opportunities in Orange County, but they won't remain for very long. Even in the Western sections of the county, prices have been escalating at a rapid clip in the past two years. In Monroe, for example, building lots are at $5,000 an acre and heading skyward. Bulk acreage is about $3,500 an acre.

You have to go all the way to Port Jervis on the New York, Pennsylvania and New Jersey border to find land with any worthwhile leverage factor. Here it's possible to purchase lakefront property at $1,000 an acre. But hurry.

When you go north from the City, you must go far. In Putnam County, which is north of Westchester County, there is land available at reasonable prices—up to $1,500 an acre—but is heavily wooded and far from the glorious Hudson River views.

Dutchess County, farther up the Hudson, offers little that is better. You must keep going until you reach Columbia County, a three-hour drive from New York City, before you find anything really attractive. Here real estate brokers list land at $500 to $1,000 an acre. It sounds like something of a bargain, but in the mid-1950's the same land was being offered at one-fifth the price.

An investor seeking land in Connecticut should search the northwest corner of the state, away from the coastal areas. In Litchfield County, near the towns of Torrington, Salisbury and Winsted, land is available at around $1,000 an acre. In New Jersey, land along the coast has been the traditional choice of both speculators and investors—and still is.

As far as Pennsylvania is concerned, the best buys are the inland farms of the woods of Monroe and Pike counties. Farmland in bulk, up to 100 acres, is priced at $500 to $1,000 an acre. But it won't be for long. The Tocks Island Dam across the Delaware, to be completed later this decade, is going to back up the river and form a 40-mile-long lake, creating the largest national park in the East. In terms of recreation, it's Pike and Monroe counties that are going to reap the greatest benefits.

It's the same no matter where you live, if you're a city dweller. You have to travel to find the opportunities.

There are virtually no growth situations in the city of Los Angeles, but the southern California desert is another story. A Bostonian would do well to look far north of his city, investigating lake frontage in northern New Hampshire.

If you're seeking information about the availability of real estate in an area distant from your home, one of two national realty companies can be helpful to you in your research. Each of these firms will send you a 200-plus-page catalog that lists thousands of offerings in every section of the country, everything from retirement homes to recreational properties, from ranch and lake frontage to small or large farms, plus a wide selection of business property, including apartments, motels, hotels, trailer camps and speciality stores of every type. And through their local-affiliated real estate offices, each of these firms will send you additional and detailed listings for the area that interests you, if you request them.

The largest of these two firms is Strout Realty. Requests for its catalog should be addressed to the office nearest you:

Summit, N.J. (311 Springfield Ave.)

Springfield, Mo. (Box 2757, 1711 North Glenstone)

Pasadena, Calif. (521 East Green St.)

The second of the national real estate companies is the United Farm Agency. Like the Strout firm, United has offices in virtually all major cities. Its national headquarters is located at 612 West 4th St., Kansas City, Mo. 64112.

One word of caution concerning land investment. Don't be led astray by mail-order advertisements for land or the salesman who relies exclusively on the telephone to make his pitch. In recent years thousands of unwary investors in every part of the United States have been hoodwinked into buying worthless desert acreage in Arizona and New Mexico, and vast tracts of Canadian forest wilderness and Florida swampland have been bought up by unscrupulous speculators with the idea of enticing the naive to buy small patches.

The National Better Business Bureau advises prospective buyers to personally examine any property in which they are interested. "Buying property sight unseen," says the NBBB, "opens the door for exaggerated descriptions, misrepresentations and deceptive concealment of essential facts on the part of promoters."

The NBBB also gives this warning: "Know with whom you are dealing." Be sure your broker is liscensed and a member of the local real estate board. If you have any doubts as to his integrity, check with the local Better Business Bureau or the real estate board in your area.

The Real Estate Syndicate

What often prevents a small investor from purchasing raw land is the fact that he is small. Many brokers say that a minimum of $10,000 is necessary if you want to be serious about land investment. For this reason investors of modest resources often group together to buy property. Family members, friends or business associates form syndicates or partnerships to purchase land in large parcels.

Lawyers often combine to do this. A group of ten or so will each put up $5,000, giving them a total of $50,000 as a down payment. With this type of cash, a quarter-of-a-million dollar package is possible. Besides the investment opportunity, a syndicate pays no income tax itself; each member pays his share on a pro-rated basis. A syndicate is not like a corporation, which is subject to a federal corporation tax on its profits.

One person is appointed to manage the syndicate investment. Sometimes the manager is given a free share for his work in setting up and supervising the deal. Sometimes it is ten percent of the entire package. The manager may also buy into the syndicate to give evidence of his good faith.

Often a syndicate will have as its goal finding properties that are not currently profitable, will buy them at rock-bottom prices and then upgrade them or convert them to a new and profitable use. For example, in New York City, in recent years, syndicates have been purchasing old and sometimes run-down hotels and converting them to apartment houses, a changeover that can lead to a substantial increase in rents with a concurrent reduction in operating costs.

The individual investor's lack of liquidity is probably the foremost disadvantage of the syndicate. There is seldom an active market for syndicate membership, and withdrawing from the syndicate and disposing of one's share can be a long and involved process.

Lack of diversification is often a second drawback. Usually a syndicate invests on only one property or in a limited number of properties of the same type. Other types of real investment (described below) are not so narrow in scope.

Owning Rental Property

Owning and operating a small apartment house—let's say four to eight units—is a tried and proven method of producing steady income. It can be an especially advantageous investment during inflationary times—if you follow the counsel set down in this section. You want a well-located building at a favorable price that assures you a good return. That much is basic. But in seeking rental property today, one other consideration should be uppermost in your mind: Put down as little cash as you possibly can.

Don't be afraid to borrow. Not today. As long as the terms are favorable, get as large a mortgage as you can. The thinking behind this policy is that you'll be paying back with inflated dollars.

Forget owning a new building. A mortgage at 1970 rates is about as desirable as a leaky roof. More about mortgages later.

There are buys in older buildings, but you have to search for them. It may take several months to find just what you're seeking. Of course, you'll want to keep in contact with brokers in your area for news of offerings, but this should be only a first step. Watch your local newspaper for news of public auctions, bank foreclosures and divorce settlements—anything that could trigger a change in property ownership.

A friend of mine who owns and operates several apartment buildings in Hudson County, New Jersey, reads newspaper death notices. From friends or relatives of the deceased, he learns the name of the attorney handling the estate, and then makes an offer for the real estate holdings. Being first in such cases is often an immense advantage, and another is that he often avoids paying a broker's commission.

Another ploy is to follow Federal Housing Administration and Veterans Administration foreclosure sales. These properties, like conventional bank foreclosures, are sometimes offered at near 100 percent financing. In the case of FHA foreclosures, the properties are sold either at an auction or at a stated price, with a drawing held to determine the buyer. VA properties are sold at auction only.

The general policy of the FHA is to sell property in "livable" condition. This implies that the purchaser can expect to occupy the dwelling without making extensive repairs.

The FHA markets acquired properties on an "open" basis, that is, its offers to purchase are submitted through licensed local real estate brokers. In the event a purchaser is unable to secure the services of a qualified broker, he may submit his offer to the FHA himself. There is no difference in the sales price or terms in such cases. See page 208.

The FHA lists three methods for financing the purchase of FHA-acquired property:

• The purchaser pays the entire amount in cash.

• The purchaser obtains a mortgage loan from a private lender and uses the mortgage proceeds to make the purchase.

• If private financing cannot be obtained, the FHA will assist purchasers by furnishing brokers with a list of mortgagees who will finance acquired property at terms the FHA deems reasonable.

Local lawyers, your friends and your own "real estate wanted" advertisements will also serve in your quest for an attractive purchase. Location is always a critical factor. Don't compromise this point by the slightest degree. Check the building at different times of the day and on different days of the week. A street presents one side of its character on a Sunday morning, but often displays entirely different features late on a weekday afternoon.

In general, seek an apartment with modest rentals. It's at the lower end of the scale that demand is the greatest. And an apartment with high rents implies you'll be repurchasing air-conditioners, electric dishwashers and other expensive appliances.

Once you find a piece of property that seems attractive, appraise it carefully from a financial standpoint. What you want to do is determine the building's present value based on future estimated net income. In today's market, a capitalization rate of 12 percent is considered the standard rate for most older buildings. In other words, an income property that yields $12,000 annual net income is fairly priced at $100,000.

Or you can relate the selling price to gross income. The rule is that an older building, well located and in good condition, should sell at about six times gross income. For a newer building the figure is seven percent or even higher.

Get a perfect understanding of what your income and expenses are going to be. Prepare a chart similar to the one on page 209.

Don't take the seller's figures. Talk with the tenants yourself. Obtain copies of receipted bills for all expense items.

Give careful attention to both the vacancy rate and the management expenses. As a matter of policy bank appraisers deduct both

FHA CASE NUMBER	SALES PRICE	PROPERTY ADDRESS	TYPE CONST	BED RMS	BATH	% OF BSMNT	GAR C/P
		QUEENS COUNTY					
		Jamaica					
373-032842-203	10,000	150-15 Shore Avenue, Jamaica, N.Y.	Fr Semi-Det	5	1-1	100	0
373-065343-203	15,000	150-25 Shore Ave.,So.Jamaica, N.Y.	Fr Det	6	1-1-1	100	0
37-080392-203	4,000	127-31 140th St.,Jamaica,N.Y.	VACANT LAND		Approx 28' x 100'		
		So.Ozone Pk					
37-096108-203	1,200	155-33 115th Ave.,So.Ozone Pk., N.Y.	VACANT LAND		Approx. 20' x 100'		
37-399038-203	2,500	131-21 140th St.,So.Ozone Pk.,N.Y.	VACANT LAND		Approx 20' x 155'		
		NASSAU COUNTY					
		Long Beach					
37-611742-203	2,000	117 W. Fulton St., Long Beach, N.Y.	VACANT LAND		Approx. 30' x 100'		
		SUFFOLK COUNTY					
		Amityville					
37-142429-203	2,200	33 Emerald La.,No.Amityville, N.Y.	VACANT LAND		Approx. 60' x 100'		
		KINGS COUNTY					
		VACANT LAND					
373-058250-203	2,500	437 Cleveland Street,Brooklyn, N.Y.	VACANT LAND		Approx. 25' x 98'		
373-043051-203	8,000	867 Dumont Avenue, Brooklyn, N.Y.	Vacant Land		Approx. 50' x 100'		
373-039321-203	3,500	245 Montauk Ave., Brooklyn,N.Y.	VACANT LAND		Approx. 20' x 100'		
373-052824-203	2,500	303 Schenck Avenue, Brooklyn,N.Y.	VACANT LAND		Approx 34.5 x 50		
		Bedford-Stuyvesant					
373-006024-203	3,000	724 Monroe St.,Brooklyn,N.Y.	VACANT LAND		Approx. 22' x 100'		
		BRONX COUNTY					
373-091325-203	7,500	621 Casanova St., Bronx, N.Y.	Mas.Semi-Det	5	1-1	100	0

Buyers Income and Expense Form

Address _____

Legal Description _____

Assessed Valuation:
      Amount _____
      Date _____
      Tax Rate _____

Mortgages:
      1st: $_____ at _____%
      2nd: $_____ at _____%
      3rd: $_____ at _____%

Rental Income

Apartment Number	Tenant	Number of Rooms	Lease Information (security deposit, term, etc.)	Rent
1				
2				
3				
4				
5				
6				
7				
8				

                           Total: ____

     Less ____% for vacancies: ____

  Less____% for uncollected rents: ____

      GROSS ANNUAL INCOME: ____

Annual Expenses

Fixed Expenses:
    Real Estate Tax _____
    Personal Property Tax _____
    Insurance _____
    Other _____

Operating Expenses:
    Electric _____
    Water _____
    Gas _____
    Oil _____
    Janitor _____
    Supplies _____
    Grounds Maintenance ____
    Miscellaneous _____
           Total:_____

TOTAL EXPENSES:_____

vacancy and management expenses from the gross income to determine the "real" gross income. You should do this, too. The vacancy expense is likely to be five to ten percent of the gross income. The management expense will be about five percent of the amount collected.

Be sure to allow for normal increases in all your expenses (and rental income, too). Tax-rate increases are almost a certainty.

Find out what other and similar apartment buildings in the area are selling for. The property you are planning to buy should not be selling at a higher gross income to price ratio than the other properties. In addition, the rents you are planning to charge should be in line with other rental properties in the area.

Check the building's structure carefully or have it inspected by an expert. How long can you expect the heating system to last? Does the roof leak? What about the cellar? A wet cellar is a curse.

Estimate the remaining economic life of the building. Most real estate experts figure an apartment dwelling to have an income producing life of 50 to 75 years. Check to see that the building meets local codes and zoning ordinances.

Buying a rental property is not like purchasing a stock or a mutual fund. There are many more points to be considered and the amount of capital involved is never small. Successful investors take their time, sometimes searching a year or more. A poor real estate investment can cause you years of financial pain, but a wise one is pure gold.

The mortgage can be your key to success. You must seek to use as much of the bank's money as you possibly can. "I'd take the money out of there in wheelbarrows, if they'd let me," a colleague of mine said recently. "With the economy the way it is, I figure I'll be paying them back with 75-cent or 60-cent dollars."

It is fairly standard practice for banks across the country to lend as much as 70 percent of the sale price on a modern brick apartment building, and somewhat less on older or wood-frame structures. But the chance of getting a *new* mortgage at reasonable terms has gone the way of the 5-cent candy bar. You will have to plan to assume the existing financing.

There are some exceptions. The Federal Housing Administration and the Veterans Administration guarantee and back mortgage loans, and in so doing provide small investors with some remarkable opportunities. Both the FHA and the VA stipulate that the property cannot be larger than four dwelling units, however (although the VA allows one extra unit above four units for each veteran when two or more veterans make a joint purchase). Also, both of these agencies expect the owner to occupy the dwelling. The interest rate on FHA mortgages is 8 1/2 percent while the down payment ranges up to ten percent of the purchase price.

Once you're prepared to enter into a contract to purchase property, get legal counsel. Do not sign any agreement or document—not even a binder—without your lawyer's approval. Remember, the broker is an agent for the seller. His advice is hardly objective.

If you feel you are in a situation in which you must submit a genuine offer, do so with the utmost caution. Make out your deposit check to the broker, not the seller, and with the proviso that the broker is going to hold the check in escrow until the purchase and sale agreements have been drawn to the mutual satisfaction of you and the seller.

On the reverse side of the check, write the following: "To be used only as a deposit on an offer to purchase property at (address)." List the total price you are willing to pay for the property, the cash amount you are going to pay and the amounts of the mortgages involved. Then write out this statement: "Subject to the verification of figures and the signing of purchase and sale agreement wholly acceptable to me."

This is the starting point. Never go beyond this stage without a skilled lawyer.

Real Estate Investment Trusts

If you're sold on real estate as an investment but lack the required capital to make a purchase of significant size, or the time to research property, there is an alternative you might wish to consider. It's the real estate investment trust, often called REIT.

A real estate investment trust is an incorporated association owning real property or mortgages. REIT shares are traded in the over-the-counter market, on local exchanges and, in a few cases, on the two major exchanges. There were approximately 60 trusts in operation in mid-1968, and by early 1970 the number had increased to over 100. The proliferation ended with the market break which saw some REIT stocks lead the market averages on the downside.

These firms operate under the provisions set down in the Real Estate Investment Trust Act of 1960, which was passed by Congress with the very intent of providing the small investor with the opportunity to enter the real estate market with none of the usual involvements.

The legislation provides that a trust cannot manage its own properties; all property management must be in independent hands. The trust is merely a "passive" investor. The Act also stipulates that at least 75 percent of a trust's gross income be derived from real estate or mortgage-loan investments, and at least 75 percent of its assets must be in real estate (including mortgages), cash and government securities. Further, the legislation requires that at least 90 percent of a trust's net income be distributed to shareholders each year.

Trusts that conform to these regulations are granted valuable tax exemptions. Indeed, the trust can pass full income and capital gains on to stockholders. They are not first whittled down by federal taxes. Of course, the individual shareholders must declare profits as ordinary income or capital gains, as the case may be.

There are two principal types of trusts: equity trusts, which derive their income primarily from rent, and mortgage trusts, whose income comes from interest on loans granted for real estate development and insurance. (A third type combines investment with both the equity and mortgage features.)

Equity trusts put their money into higher-quality real estate—office buildings, apartment houses and commercial property such as shopping centers and housing developments. Among the larger and best-known of the equity trusts are U.S. Realty Investments, Bradley Real Estate Trust, Greenfield Real Estate Investment Trust and Pennsylvania Real Estate Investment Trust.

To many investors the great attraction of equity trusts is the tax advantages they are able to realize through depreciation allowances. These are meant to compensate owners for the aging of properties, and they apply even though the equity may be increasing in value.

Suppose that a trust owns an apartment building that cost a million dollars and brings in $140,000 in rent annually. The building's operating expenses (taxes, insurance, heat, water, etc.) amount to $45,000 for the year, and the mortgage payment is $12,000 ($3,000 in principal and $9,000 in interest). This means that there is $83,000 in cash ($140,000 rental income minus the $57,000 in expenses) available for the shareholders.

But because of the depreciation privilege the actual return is much better than these figures imply. Under the provisions of the tax law, the trust can add the $45,000 in expenses plus the $9,000 paid in interest to the building's annual depreciation figure, which is likely to be about $50,000. Thus total expenses would amount to

$104,000 ($45,000 plus $9,000 plus $50,000). Subtracting the $104,000 from the $140,000 would give a figure of $36,000. And this is the amount on which the trust pays tax, not the $83,000 actually received.

Mortgage trusts, on the other hand, reap no such depreciation privilege. Since their investment funds go into long-term mortgages and short-term construction loans, the income they derive is taxable as ordinary income.

Mortgage trusts derive their profits from the "spread" that occurs between the cost of money borrowed and the price they receive for money loaned. The difference can be substantial. Late in 1969, mortgage trusts were making construction loans at interest rates as high as 14 percent. The prime interest rate at the time was 8 1/2 to 9 1/2 percent.

The mortgage trusts went through a period of sharp growth during the late 1960's. The tight money situation forced banks out of high-risk construction and development-loan fields and the mortgage trusts moved in to fill the vacuum. The prices of mortgage-trust stocks zoomed upward as a result, but they slid back during the general market slump.

Most analysts believe that mortgage trusts have shouldered their way into the construction and development-loan field to stay, and indeed that they will remain a significant factor whether the money situation is loose or tight. The older, better-known mortgage trusts include: First Mortgage Investors, Continental Mortgage Investors and the B.F. Saul Real Estate Investment Trust.

When considering investment in a real estate investment trust, first decide whether you want an equity trust or a mortgage trust. I am more bullish about the equity type. It is a real estate; it is a stock—a unique double-pronged hedge against inflation. I don't believe that mortgage trusts are quite so attractive. During inflationary times, it's much better to be a borrower than a lender, although the terms involved are critical, of course. Besides, during the late 1960's and early 1970's, some of the newer mortgage trusts encountered difficulty in obtaining money at prices low enough to assure even a reasonable profit.

Your broker is likely to be of only limited help to you in your appraisal of the various real estate trusts. After all, these stocks represent a fairly new field. Analyze them much as you would mutual funds. Look for astute management and experience in real estate investment, be it equity investment or mortgage lending. Compare earnings records and stock prices with the market performance in general. You are likely to find that the older and established trusts present the most attractive buys.

Land Developers

One of the fastest-growing segments of the building industry is the sale of vacation dwellings and retirement homes. During the period from 1966 through 1969, the field jumped in volume by 67 percent. How does one take advantage of this booming industry? The simplest method is by purchasing stock in a land-development company.

Most such firms are independent operations, and some, like General Development, Horizon Corporation and Frank Mackle's Deltona Corporation, are extremely well-known. In recent years brokerage firms and some blue-chip corporations have entered the field. Eastman Dillon, Lazard Freres and Merrill Lynch have established real estate operations, and such corporations as ITT, Gulf Oil, Chrysler and Westinghouse Electric now have real estate subsidiaries, too.

The principal independent operators are listed below. In appraising their stocks, carefully scrutinize all financial information. The industry in general has been criticized for its accounting practices, particularly its inclination to record the full sale price of a homesite at the time the purchaser makes his first monthly payment, when actually the total amount may not be received for another five to ten years. The failure to thoroughly investigate customer credit standings has been another criticism.

It's not always easy to compare one company in the field with any other. Very few are exactly alike. The Deltona Corporation builds and develops with the emphasis on the former. But Land Consultants of America does no building. Some companies concentrate on luxury residences. Others specialize in the development of vast retirement communities.

The firms also vary as to where they operate. For example, Horizon Corporation's holdings are concentrated in Arizona, Texas and New Mexico. The company buys up hugh tracts of land for future resale in the form of small lots or commercial and industrial property.

Leisure Living Communities, Inc., has focused its activities on the State of Maine, developing and selling vacation homesites in the southern part of the state. Leisure Technology Corporation is another firm that is active in the East. It has developed a complete retirement community with garden apartments and community buildings in Lakewood, New Jersey, and is moving ahead on similar projects in Burlington County, New Jersey, and Suffolk County, New York.

Florida has always been much favored by land developers and the recent past is no exception. There is the Deltona operation, the state's biggest developer, General Development, another giant, and Punta Gorda Isles, a corporation with about 95 percent of its home-sites located on Florida's waterways.

In general, land development firms have shown excellent earning records over the past few years. The stock prices of some companies have hit new levels during 1969, but all fell sharply in the 1969-70 market slide.

The major land developers include:

Company Name	Where Traded
Amrep Corporation	ASE
Canaveral International	ASE
Cavanagh Leasing	OTC
Deltona Corporation	ASE
General Development	NYSE
Horizon Corporation	OTC
Land Consultants of America	OTC
Leisure Living Communities	OTC
Leisure Technology	ASE
Major Realty Corporation	OTC
Presley Development	OTC
Punta Gorda Isles	OTC
Viking General	OTC

Property Research Corporation must also be mentioned in any discussion of land development. A 13-year-old real estate investment management firm, headquartered in Los Angeles, with offices in Atlanta, San Diego and San Francisco, PRC selects, acquires and manages real estate property investments on behalf of its investor clients. These investments—the minimum amount is $10,000— include predeveloped land, large apartment complexes, industrial parks and recreational communities.

The largest firm of its type, PRC has a technical and management staff of 170. Property under PRC management is valued at an estimated $200 million.

Each investor participates in a program best suited to his financial needs. For example, an individual whose primary interest is tax-sheltered income might be offered an apartment investment, while an investor who is seeking capital appreciation would be presented unimproved land.

The company describes its services as being somewhat like those of an investment banker. "We research real estate opportunities, select the best and then arrange for the investment," says a company spokesman. "We also manage the investment and after it has matured we assist the client in divesting."

For more information, write Property Research Corporation, 200 East 42nd St., New York, N. Y. 10017.

Summing Up

Real estate investment can be an effective inflation hedge, but be wary of certain drawbacks:

• In the case of raw land, you tie up your capital with no year-to-year return.

• Your investment may lack liquidity.

When seeking a rental property, keep alert to FHA and VA foreclosures. Contact local real estate agents and lawyers. Follow these guidelines:

• Never buy in a declining neighborhood.

• In appraising the investment, prepare a detailed income and expense form. Use your own—not the seller's—figures.

• Getting favorable mortgage terms is a must.

• Never sign any document without legal counsel.

As an alternative to direct investment in raw land or income property, consider the purchase of stock in a real estate investment trust or a land-development company.